# VOTED OUT

## QUALITATIVE STUDIES IN PSYCHOLOGY

This series showcases the power and possibility of qualitative work in psychology. Books feature detailed and vivid accounts of qualitative psychology research using a variety of methods, including participant observation and field work, discursive and textual analyses, and critical cultural history. They probe vital issues of theory, implementation, representation, and ethics that qualitative workers confront. The series mission is to enlarge and refine the repertoire of qualitative approaches to psychology.

GENERAL EDITORS
Michelle Fine and Jeanne Marecek

Everyday Courage:
The Lives and Stories of Urban Teenagers
by Niobe Way

Negotiating Consent in Psychotherapy
by Patrick O'Neill

Voted Out:
The Psychological Consequences of Anti-Gay Politics
by Glenda M. Russell

# VOTED OUT

The Psychological Consequences of
Anti-Gay Politics

## GLENDA M. RUSSELL

 **New York University Press**
New York and London

NEW YORK UNIVERSITY PRESS
New York and London

Library of Congress Cataloging-in-Publication Data
Russell, Glenda Marie.
Voted out : the psychological consequences of anti-gay politics /
Glenda M. Russell.
p.   cm.
Includes bibliographical references and index.
ISBN 0-8147-7544-6 (pbk. : alk. paper) —
ISBN 0-8147-7543-8 (cloth : alk. paper)
1. Homophobia—Colorado.  2. Gays—Colorado—Attitudes.
3. Bisexuals—Colorado—Attitudes.   I. Title.  II. Series.
HQ76.3.U52 C67  2000
305.9'0664'09788—dc21          00-009267

New York University Press books are printed on acid-free paper,
and their binding materials are chosen for strength and durability.

Manufactured in the United States of America

10  9  8  7  6  5  4  3  2  1

**To Shana and Karen**

# Contents

■ ■ ■ ■

# Preface and Acknowledgments

The day after the election, I was definitely depressed. I felt as if I'd awakened to Nazi Germany. In the next few weeks, I experienced some fear but eventually I did begin to feel a sense of empowerment. I decided as others have, that the best way to fight Amendment 2 is to be more open and to come out to more people—and I have.

At first I was appalled, in shock. Then I became extremely angry. I used to just accept that I had to hide my life—that's the way it is. I can no longer do that. It is not OK to make people live in closets. . . . I want more now than I ever dared hope for before Amendment 2.

On November 3, 1992, voters in Colorado passed Amendment 2, which effectively legalized discrimination against lesbians, gay men, and bisexuals (LGBs) in the state. The above two statements reflect two individuals' experiences of the amendment and capture one of the paradoxes that emerged from the election: LGBs reacted to Amendment 2 with deep distress and anger but they also used the election as a catalyst for personal empowerment and political activism. In 1996, the U.S. Supreme Court opinion on Amendment 2 argued that, by endorsing the amendment, Colorado voters had attempted to fence gay men, bisexuals, and lesbians out of the political process. However, LGBs refused to be fenced out; instead, they came out of the closet. That was only one of many paradoxical consequences of Amendment 2.

This book has two purposes: to convey the results of a research project exploring the psychological effects of Amendment 2 on LGBs—the content—and to describe the research project from which those results were obtained—the process. The two aims are of equal importance. In describing the research results, we will examine how nearly five hundred bisexuals, lesbians, and gay men characterized their reactions to this anti-gay initiative. Their descriptions cover a broad range of issues, both personal and political in nature. They convey a great deal of raw emotionality expressed in the heated aftermath of an election that felt hurtful and hateful to many. The book relies extensively on the actual data—on the statements from LGBs—to illuminate the findings. The paradoxical nature of the results are highlighted; as hurtful as Amendment 2 was, it also galvanized individual LGBs and the LGB community. This was not what its proponents might have expected or hoped for.

The book's second aim, to elucidate the processes by which the research was conducted, will attend to each phase of the research endeavor. The description shows how the data collection was conceptualized and carried out and how the qualitative data were analyzed, and concludes with considerations about making the research findings available to others, not only to professional audiences but also to the LGB community where the research originated. A distinctive feature of the data analysis for this project was the use of a five-member team to code and conduct an interpretive analysis of the qualitative data. The text explains the philosophy behind this approach and offers a detailed account of the team's processes. The latter is rendered using the descriptions of all five members of the coding team.

While I have written this book with equal attention to its twin aims, I realize that some readers might be primarily interested in one or the other. Accordingly, although content and process considerations are to some degree interwoven throughout the text, the book can be read to fit each reader's unique interest by focusing on particular chapters. Readers primarily interested in learning about the research process should consult chapters 1, 2, 3, 7, 10, and 11. Those who wish to focus their attention on the specific consequences of Amendment 2 and its applications to bisexuals, gay men, and lesbians will want to pay particular attention to chapters 1, 4, 5, 6, 8, 9, and 11. Both the process and the content of this project, it is hoped, will be of interest to many readers.

I am grateful to many people for their contributions to both stories in this book. Sue Larson and Karen Raforth helped to ensure that respondents from throughout Colorado would be represented in this research. Sue had contacts, born of her grassroots political organizing, across the state; these people, in turn, distributed research surveys in small towns and mountain communities. I am grateful for their efforts on behalf of a stranger.

I am similarly grateful to the hundreds of lesbians, gay men, and bisexuals who took the time to respond to my research survey, and especially to the 496 who entrusted me with their tender and outraged feelings and their wonderful insights.

For financial support at various points in the research process, I gratefully acknowledge the Society for the Psychological Study of Social Problems' (SPSSI) Grants-in-Aid program as well as two friends, Robin Lopez and Elyse Morgan.

I have been privileged to have had the support of a number of individuals as I worked on issues related to internalized oppression. Several of them consult and conduct workshops through VISIONS, an antiracism and antioppression training group based in Cambridge, Massachusetts: Wekesa Madzimoyo, Sarah Stearns, Angela Giudice, Valerie Batts, and Hilda Baldoquin. I also acknowledge Jim Marquardt, Karen Raforth, Deborah Flick, Ellen Greenhouse, Janis Bohan, Jim Davis-Rosenthal, and my clients for helping to extend my thinking in this area.

Fulfilling my goal of returning research to the community required the cooperation of many people. I am grateful to everyone who participated in the efforts to make use of this research. I am especially thankful to the following: from the city of Boulder, Leslie Durgin, Susan Purdy, Linda Hill-Blakley, the late Kelvin McNeill, Valuing Diversity, and the Boulder Police Department; Karen Bensen and others at the Gay, Lesbian, Bisexual, and Transgendered Student Services at the Auraria Campus in Denver and Counseling Services at Metropolitan State College in Denver; Jan Johnson, Karen Raforth (then), Joanna Dueñas (then), and Joanne Arnold from the University of Colorado, Boulder; Barbara Jabaily from KBDI;

Vicki Burrichter, James Herringer, the singers, and support staff of Harmony: A Colorado Chorale; Bob McDowell; Judith Dowling; Carl Nash, Dave Fleischer, Jeanne Marecek and Michelle Fine; Tim Bartlett, Despina Papazoglou Gimbel, and Jennifer Hammer.

A wonderful mother-daughter team has assisted me at every stage of this project, from preparing the research instrument to preparing the manuscript for this book. Thanks to Eloise Pearson and Chris Stilson.

Janis Bohan has read my words and offered suggestions for improving them. Janis's presence has helped me reach higher than I would have were it not for the knowledge that she would catch me if I fell.

The members of the team who analyzed the data for this project are colleagues and friends with whom I shared a magical journey. With loving respect, I salute Sylvie Naar, Sean Riley, Rob Perl, and Lou Bardach.

Many other friends have supported and sustained me as I undertook this project. I am grateful to them all, and especially to Shana Burch, Karen Raforth, and Janis Bohan.

1

■ ■　■　　■　　■　　　■　　　　■　　　　　■

# Studying Anti-Gay Politics

*The Case of Amendment 2*

## The Context of Anti-Gay Politics

In the past two decades, American voters have decided on more than sixty state and local ballot measures related to the rights of lesbians, gay men, and bisexuals (Smith 1997). These initiatives, associated with a nationwide campaign to undermine the progress of the gay rights movement (Eastland 1996b), have stirred significant public attention. Conflicts over equal rights for LGBs have typically gone beyond the specific content of such initiatives and have become symbolic representations of fundamental schisms in Americans' attitudes toward a number of issues, including tolerance, minority rights, sexuality, and other basic values (Gibson and Tedin 1988; Haider-Markel and Meier 1996; Pitman 1997).

At the most obvious level, anti-gay initiatives have been mechanisms for denying LGBs protection against discrimination (Colorado for Family Values 1992a, 1992b; O'Rourke and Dellinger 1997). At another level, the initiatives have been "clearly aimed at controlling the public image of homosexuality and sexual identity" (Levin 1997:45). Initiative proponents have acted "to construct gay men and lesbians as 'other' and thereby to distance them through discourse and law" (Eastland 1996b:60). The initiative process has generated considerable hostility as well as stress and public stigmatization for LGBs (Donovan and Bowler 1997).

It is within this context that Colorado's Amendment 2 was passed on November 3, 1992, with 53.4 percent of voters endorsing the initiative ('92 Election Results 1992). A deceptively brief ballot item, the full text of Amendment 2 read:

> Neither the State of Colorado, through any of its branches or departments, nor any of its agencies, political subdivisions, municipalities or school districts, shall enact, adopt or enforce any statute, regulation, ordinance or policy whereby homosexual, lesbian, or bisexual orientation, conduct, practices, or relationships shall constitute or otherwise be the basis of, or entitle any person or class of persons to have or claim any minority status, quota preferences, protected status or claim of discrimination. This section of the Constitution shall be in all respects self-executing. (Ballot Wording 1992:3A)

## The Amendment 2 Campaign: Psychological Implications for LGBs

This brief amendment had engendered profound psychological consequences for lesbians, bisexuals, and gay men. In considering the psychological implications of Amendment 2 for LGBs it is useful to distinguish between the campaign and the actual election. Amendment 2 was placed on the ballot after Colorado for Family Values (CFV), the sponsoring organization, collected more than 60,000 signatures from registered voters in the state (O'Rourke and Dellinger 1997). From the time that CFV made its intentions known, the issue of equal rights for lesbians, bisexuals, and gay men was the subject of considerable debate. The debate intensified once CFV had an adequate number of signatures to qualify for the ballot, and it grew especially heated in the summer and fall months prior to the election (Cornett 1992; Gavin 1992; Lowe 1992).

The campaign for the passage of Amendment 2 mirrored other public debates and elections regarding equal rights for LGBs.[1] As in elections elsewhere, Colorado for Family Values' formal campaign strategy took full advantage both of the public's limited knowledge of LGBs (Gavin 1992; Smith 1993; Whillock 1995) and of abundant levels of preexisting homophobia and heterosexism (e.g., Blumenfeld and Raymond 1993; Herek 1992a, 1995, 1996; Kite 1994; Schneider and Lewis 1984). The CFV campaign portrayed homosexuality as a behavior disconnected from relational or identity considerations (Colorado for Family Values 1992a); emphasized the purported central role of sex among LGBs, with extensive and explicit descriptions of sexual behavior (Family Research Institute 1992); and inaccurately linked homosexuality and pedophilia (Colorado for Family Values 1992a, 1992b).

CFV conducted television and radio advertising, and "The Gay Agenda" (1995), a provocative anti-gay video that has been used in campaigns elsewhere (Colker 1993; Flanders 1995; Moritz 1995; Spears 1992), was distributed widely. One of CFV's proposed television ads carried excerpts from "The Gay Agenda"; its content was so objectionable that some television stations refused to carry it. Other CFV advertising was carried by television stations without restriction.

CFV's campaign materials relied heavily on questionable "research" data from Paul Cameron and the Family Research Institute, Inc. Cameron had previously come under significant criticism from a variety of quarters, including professional organizations, for his use of distorted data and misinformation about LGBs (Anti-Gay Adviser 1985; Booth 1992a; Fettner 1985; Harkavy 1996; Herek 1998; Walter 1985).

While the tone of CFV's materials may have appeared at first glance to have been reasoned and informational, the cumulative picture of gays and lesbians they promulgated was one of strange, sex-obsessed creatures whose secret agenda was to erode the nuclear family and prey upon innocent children, meanwhile seizing "special rights" that they did not deserve (Douglass 1997; Pharr 1992, 1993). Furthermore, much of CFV's campaign materials not only attacked the self-worth of LGBs, but undermined their standing within the larger community as well (Pharr 1993). While a degree of restraint characterized some campaign materials, others were riddled with misinformation and innuendo. Some live debates were occasions for name-calling and personal attacks.

In the course of the campaign for the passage of Amendment 2, LGBs were discussed and debated in public (and in many private) arenas virtually continuously. Gays, lesbians, and bisexuals were subjected to constant scrutiny, anger and vitriol, unfair accusations, and blatant distortions about their lives. Many could not be sure if their friends, family members, or colleagues would vote for Amendment 2. Many expressed increasing fears that they would be the targets of discrimination or violence (Spring 1992a, 1992b).

Not all LGBs were directly confronted with person-to-person instances of verbal harassment. Some were not open about their sexual orientation; others took no visible role or no role at all in the campaign against Amendment 2. Nonetheless, any lesbian, gay, or bisexual Coloradan who read newspapers, listened to radio, watched television, or engaged in regular commerce with their communities at large had ample opportunity to be exposed to the anti-gay rhetoric of the campaign as well as to informal debates about the merits (or lack thereof) of gays and lesbians.

## The Election Outcome: Psychological Implications for LGBs

The passage of Amendment 2 did much more than deny LGBs any legal remedy in the face of discrimination based on sexual orientation. It also confirmed to this segment of the population that the campaign materials distributed by CFV had struck a credible chord with the majority of voters in the state. Certainly, many LGBs were concerned that the passage of Amendment 2 would make them vulnerable to discrimination in employment, housing, or public accommodations. In truth, however, at the time of the election, laws prohibiting such discrimination had been enacted in only three Colorado municipalities and, by an executive order of the governor, for state employees. The passage of Amendment 2, therefore, did not substantively change the legal status of a large number of LGBs in the state. For many LGBs the psychological message of the amendment seemed to be as important as its legal consequences—and even more important for others.

## Understanding the Impact of Amendment 2

Any effort to anticipate the specific psychological effects of the Amendment 2 campaign on LGBs in Colorado was impeded by its lack of precedent. Amendment 2 was the first statewide ballot issue with this particular focus.[2] Constructing a framework for understanding the amendment's psychological effects on LGBs therefore had to rely on ideas and data drawn from related areas.

*Conceptual liquidation.* Eastland (1996a), in her analysis of anti-LGB campaigns in Oregon, echoes the observation made by many on both sides of the issue: the struggle over the rights of LGB people represents a culture war (see, e.g., Berlet 1995; Bull and Gallagher 1996; Shaw 1997). She writes, "Wars of 'meaning' and 'identity' can be every bit as violent as wars of might" (Eastland 1996a:3). Casualties are typical in wars of might; less is known about the wounds resulting from culture wars.

Eastland (1996b) borrows Berger and Luckmann's (1966) notion of conceptual liquidation as a framework for understanding anti-LGB campaigns. According to Eastland, a group is conceptually liquidated—or demolished in a culture's thoughts—when its members are seen as less than human, as massively confused about the right order of things, and as lost in a hopeless cognitive and spiritual morass. Eastland goes on to enumerate four steps in the process of the conceptual liquidation of LGBs by anti-gay campaigns. The first step involves portraying LGB people as a threat. Step two focuses on equating LGB orientations with pathology. The third step is the construction of an explanation for their orientations: "This is accomplished through the creation of a homosexual agenda, which has as two of its purposes (a) the seduction of children into the homosexual lifestyle, and (b) the right to display extreme sexual practices publicly, including sadomasochism and pedophilia" (Eastland 1996b:69). Eastland's final step is the social construction of a cure for the presumed pathology of LGB orientations.

Eastland contends that the most devastating effect on LGBs of this conceptual liquidation process is emotional in nature, and takes the form of "stress-related disease" not only among LGBs but among their heterosexual supporters as well. She offers a number of "war stories" as evidence of the negative effects of the conceptual liquidation process on LGBs (Eastland 1996b:74).

*Ethnoviolence.* Ehrlich's framework of ethnoviolence serves as another potential avenue to understanding the effects of the Amendment 2 campaign. He uses the term "ethnoviolence" to refer to "an act or attempted act in which the actor is motivated to do psychological or physical harm to another, where the 'other' is perceived as a group representative or is identified with a group, and where the motivation for the act is group prejudice" (Ehrlich 1992:107). In Colorado, Amendment 2 and the rhetoric that went with it were directed toward a single group of people based solely and specifically on their sexual orientation. From the beginning, CFV's language about Amendment 2 implicitly singled LGBs out as a target. Legal remedy for discrimination based on sexual orientation was prohibited only when lesbians, gay men, and bisexuals were the targets of discrimination; heterosexuals who were the targets of discrimination continued to have legal recourse.

Ehrlich has proposed that ethnoviolence has a greater impact on its victims than do other types of victimization.

> The substantive character of ethnoviolence victims' responses is quite serious, ranging across the standard psychophysiological indicators of increased stress. These include higher levels of depression and withdrawal, increased sleep difficulties, anxiety, and loss of confidence. Further, an extraordinary percentage of victims report serious interpersonal difficulties with friends and significant others. (Ehrlich 1992:110)

Lesbians, gay men, and bisexuals in Colorado were not necessarily the individual targets of ethnoviolence in the strictest sense of that word. However, collectively LGBs were targeted both by the intent underlying CFV's campaign and by the rhetoric associated with the campaign. The effects of such targeting of a group of people might be expected to bear some resemblance to the kinds of effects that occur in cases of ethnoviolent victimization (see also Ehrlich, Larcom, and Purvis 1995).

*Harassment and violence.* Another potentially useful framework for discussing the psychological effects of Amendment 2 is the literature on verbal harassment. Garnets, Herek, and Levy (1992) have enumerated many of the effects of verbal harassment on gays and lesbians. They note that such harassment both conveys raw hatred and prejudice and reminds gays and lesbians of their inferior status in society. They further point out that "verbal abuse constitutes a symbolic form of violence and a routine reminder of the ever-present threat of physical assault" (1992:215). Garnets, Herek, and Levy go on to assert that verbal harassment reinforces lesbian and gay people's sense of being outsiders. Harassment of this type challenges one's sense of security. They note that verbal harassment affects gay people's sense of self but often does so without their understanding why they are feeling less valued or worthwhile. Finally, because it carries an implicit threat of physical violence, verbal harassment tends to restrict the everyday behavior of gays, bisexuals, and lesbians.

*Effects of victimization.* A final framework which promises to aid the understanding of Amendment 2's effects is drawn from the research on the cognitive substrates of trauma. Janoff-Bulman (1992) has examined the literature on the different effects of victimizations attributable to natural or random occurrences in contrast to the effects of intentional, human-induced victimizations. She concludes that "survivors of human-induced victimizations are most apt to hold more negative assumptions about themselves and the benevolence of the world" (1992:77). Janoff-Bulman goes on to say that survivors of intentional, human-induced victimization are forced to question the trustworthiness of people. In addition, they "experience humiliation and powerlessness and question their own role in the victimization" (1992:78).

Gays, bisexuals, and lesbians in Colorado were exposed to an anti-LGB campaign that involved extensive planning and execution and considerable outlays of money. In no way could the campaign be construed as a random or natural event. Moreover, given that Amendment 2 passed by a margin of 53.4 percent ('92 Election Results 1992), LGBs knew that a majority of their fellow Coloradans (at least a majority of those who voted) saw fit to deny them equal rights in the face of discrimination. Many LGBs knew that some votes for Amendment 2 had been cast by members of their own families, employers and employees, neighbors and friends. As a result, many felt betrayed (Booth 1992b).

Many LGBs also experienced significant fear in the aftermath of the election (Booth 1992b; Spring 1992b). There were reports of increases in hate crimes against LGBs in the Denver metropolitan area after the election (Robbins 1993; Spring 1992b; Stepanek 1992). Because a community-based antiviolence project received a greater number of calls than did police departments, there was some confusion as to the actual level of increase. This confusion resulted from several factors, including the differential willingness of victimized LGBs to make reports to the community-based project rather than to police departments, and uneven education about and motivation for documenting bias crimes among police personnel (Frank 1993). Certainly, the politicization of the question of whether hate crimes had increased following the passage of Amendment 2 (Booth 1993b) did not add clarity to the issue.

To some degree, knowing the actual level of hate crimes may not be as important as the perception of a changed environment. Lesbian, bisexual, and gay Coloradans reported a sense of intensified anti-gay sentiment (Spring 1992a). That sentiment had obviously begun during the acrimony of the campaign. At least some gays, lesbians, and bisexuals feared that Amendment 2, once passed, would offer a kind of cultural permission for violence against them. This perception was not unique to people who resided in Colorado. John Gonsiorek, a psychologist who visited Denver in January 1993 to testify on behalf of plaintiffs seeking an injunction against Amendment 2, observed: "The hatred in Colorado is palpable; one could feel it in the courtroom, read it in the newspapers, see and hear it on the media. No different, really, from the garden variety of hatred of lesbian, gay, and bisexual citizens extant just about everywhere; just unabashed, unleashed, unrepentant" (Gonsiorek 1993:2).

March (1993:37) has pointed out that "perceived life threat, potential for physical violence, fear and helplessness" are part of what constitutes a stressor. Kilpatrick and Resnick (1993:129), in similar vein, have inferred from their review that "subjective factors such as the perception of serious life threat are very important to our understanding of psychological distress produced by events, perhaps as important as objective indices of threat including extent of injury sustained."

## The Study

I began to frame my understanding of Amendment 2 by using what I knew about the theory and research both on trauma in general and on traumatic reactions to oppression more specifically. In the context of my clinical practice and my personal life, I had had a number of conversations with lesbians, gay men, and bisexuals about their reactions to Amendment 2. In addition, the news reports occasionally alluded to LGBs' emotional responses to the election; these reports emphasized fear, demoralization, and a sense of betrayal and personal injury (Booth 1992b; Johnson 1992; Moses-Zirkes 1993; Nash 1992; Spring 1992a). The passage of Amendment 2 was implicated in press reports of the suicide of one gay man (Gibney 1992). One news article reported that clinicians who worked with

LGB clients had remarked on the degree of distress caused by the campaign and the election (Booth 1992b). Surprisingly, the reports also sometimes referred to a sense of empowerment among LGBs. This apparent paradox hinted at the complexity of people's responses to these events.

With reports and anecdotes such as these as background, I set out to systematically study the psychological effects of Amendment 2 on LGBs in Colorado. I had had experience with and a strong appreciation for qualitative methodologies and was interested in sampling a large number of LGBs from around the state and doing so quickly. I therefore opted to conduct a survey of LGBs.

## Participants

Participants in this study included 663 self-identified lesbians, gay men, and bisexual individuals who resided in Colorado at the time of the data collection, which took place from 89 to 293 days following the election, from January 31, 1993 to September 2, 1993. The participants constitute a convenience sample.

I recruited participants for the study by a letter of introduction that accompanied the questionnaire. A total of 2,682 questionnaires were distributed throughout the state through a variety of avenues. I sent questionnaires to social and political organizations; I gave them out at community events, including a dance to raise funds for a political group and a conference on psychotherapy with gays, lesbians, and bisexuals. Questionnaires were mailed as an insert in a newspaper for LGBs; others were distributed by asking friends and acquaintances if they would take a few for people they knew. Finally, questionnaires were sent to individuals in numerous locales around the state. These individuals had been identified by Sue Larson, one of the field organizers for the campaign to defeat Amendment 2. In turn, these people were asked to hand out questionnaires to their friends and acquaintances. Particular efforts were made to distribute questionnaires to rural areas and to gays, bisexuals, and lesbians of color.

## The Survey

The survey was eight pages long. Each survey included a letter of explanation and a stamped, self-addressed envelope. The letter informed participants how to respond to the questionnaire and assured them that the data would be anonymous. It went on to explain that the results would be used to help LGBs deal with the effects of Amendment 2. Because clinical observations had strongly suggested that Amendment 2 had had very negative effects, the letter cautioned that completing the survey could evoke feelings related to the amendment. It also told participants how to request a brief discussion of the survey or locate resources for additional help.

*Demographic items.* The first page of the actual questionnaire solicited standard demographic information. It also asked respondents to indicate their degree of involvement in the campaign to defeat Amendment 2. A final item on the first page was a series of descriptors indicating how open the respondent was about his or her sexual orientation with respect to friends, place of work, and family of origin during three separate time frames: before the campaign, during the campaign, and after the election.

*Diagnostic categories.* The bulk of the survey consisted of symptoms representing three separate diagnoses drawn from DSM-III-R (American Psychiatric Association 1987): major depressive episode, post-traumatic stress disorder (PTSD), and generalized anxiety disorder. I chose these three diagnoses because of their tendency to occur together, as indicated by earlier studies (McFarlane 1986; Sanderson, DiNardo, Rapee, and Barlow 1990; Solomon et al. 1991), and because my clinical observations had suggested their presence among lesbians, gays, and bisexuals in the aftermath of Amendment 2. A complete explanation of the diagnostic scales in the survey, along with reliability computations for each scale, are available in Appendix A.

In addition to the items describing symptoms for each of the three diagnoses, several other items were included in the survey. All based on clinical observations, they included levels of outness before and after the election (see Appendix B) and positive as well as negative emotional experiences related to Amendment 2. Respondents were asked to indicate the degree to which these statements were true, based on a 10-point Likert scale, for each of the three time frames (Table IV, Appendix C). The final item at the end of the survey was an open-ended question that invited respondents to say anything they wished about their response to any aspect of Amendment 2.

## Sample Characteristics

Six hundred and sixty-three people returned completed surveys, for a return rate of 24.7%. Of the respondents, 418 (63%) were female, 242 (36.5%) were male, and the remaining .5% of the sample did not indicate sex.

In terms of race, 573 respondents, representing 86.4% of the sample, were white. Responses were received from 79 gays, lesbians, and bisexuals of color; they represented 12.1% of the sample. Included in this figure were individuals who self-identified as African Americans (1.1% of the total sample), Chicanos (.2%), Hispanics (2.4%), Asian Americans (.3%) and a variety of biracial descriptions (8.1%). The proportion of LGBs of color in the sample was quite close to the proportion of people of color in the state as a whole (U.S. Department of Commerce 1992). Data on race were missing for 1.8% of the sample.

The ages of respondents ranged from 16 to 72 years with a mean of 35.6 years. Participants indicated residence in seventy different cities and towns spread throughout most of the state. Slightly more than one-half (52%) of the respondents resided in the Denver metropolitan area.

Participants were asked to indicate their highest level of educational attainment. Only ten people in the sample (1.5%) had not graduated from high school. Another 14 (2.1%) were high school graduates. A total of 256 respondents (38.6%) had at least some college education. Some postgraduate education had been pursued by 144 respondents (21.7%) and 235 additional respondents (35.4%) held postgraduate degrees.

With respect to employment, respondents represented the following categories: 68 students (10.3%); 33 sales or marketing (5%); 322 professional or technical (48.6%); 38 clerical or service workers (5.7%); 41 upper management and executives (6.2%); 28 tradespersons and laborers (4.2%); 8 retired (1.2%); 38 middle management (5.6%); and 74 other or multiple categories (11.2%).

## Results of Quantitative Analyses

The results of quantitative analyses of the survey data were consistent with my expectations. Participants reported significant increases in symptoms associated with generalized anxiety, depression, and post-traumatic stress disorder from the time the campaign began to after the passage of Amendment 2. Ten of the sample of 663 LGBs reported diagnosable cases of one of these three syndromes before the campaign began. That number increased more than tenfold to 106 diagnosable cases after the election (see Appendix C).

In addition, LGBs in the sample reported changes on a variety of other negative dimensions between the two time periods. These included relationship difficulties, fear of physical and verbal assault, fear of discrimination, and weariness with being the object of discussion and debate. Changes along a half-dozen positive dimensions were reported as well. Between the beginning of the campaign and its aftermath, these LGBs perceived that their heterosexual family members and their heterosexual friends and colleagues had a better understanding of what homophobia was. They also reported an increase in a sense of community with other LGBs, in comfort levels with being LGBs, in comfort levels working on LGB civil rights causes, and a sense of empowerment by virtue of working with other LGBs (Table IV, Appendix C).

These results are described in greater detail in Appendix C. As a whole, they offer a strikingly mixed picture of the psychological effects of Amendment 2 on LGBs in Colorado. We see clear indications of powerfully negative effects, including self-reported growth in symptoms of the kind that arouse concern on the part of people who experience them and that sometimes interfere with their optimal functioning. We also see reports of increases in various fears and frustrations that might make LGBs cautious and suspicious, using energy that otherwise could be spent in more creative endeavors.

As reported above, on the other hand, some LGBs simultaneously reported feeling stronger in their sense of identity as LGBs, more empowered and comfortable working on behalf of their own civil rights, and more confident that at least some heterosexuals in their lives appreciated the burden of the homophobia they confronted. This mix of negative and positive results was both provocative and elusive. The quantitative findings were consistent with the mix of reactions to Amendment 2 that I had seen and read about. They were also consistent with a small but developing body of literature on the positive effects that traumatizing situations and oppressive circumstances have on some people (e.g., Burt and Katz 1987; Coleman 1986; Crocker and Major 1989; Garnets, Herek, and Levy 1992; Janoff-Bulman 1992; Joseph, Williams, and Yule 1993; Lyons 1991). The interpretation of the results of the quantitative analysis, however, was limited by a number of factors.

## The Question of Epistemology

*Positivist approaches.* Survey research is grounded in positivist epistemology,[3] which makes a number of basic assumptions: "that there exists a real world whose existence and nature are independent of its being observed; that it is possible to know this reality through the careful implementation of methodologies that are founded on the certainty of objective, value-neutral observation; and that such careful application of methods allows us to 'discover' and 'describe' that reality" (Bohan and Russell 1999a:14).[4] It is assumed that once this free-standing reality has been carefully and accurately measured, generalizations to other locales can be made, albeit with some degree of caution (Campbell and Stanley 1963; Gergen 1973).

Quantitative data are typically taken as objective descriptors of some external reality. In studying the psychological consequences of Amendment 2, the questionnaire was designed to describe numerically LGBs' reactions to the campaign and election. Implicit in that attempt is the idea that symptoms of anxiety, depression, and PTSD are actual phenomena that people experience and express rather than descriptive or heuristic constructs that mental health professionals have developed as a means of communicating putative information about (usually other) people's experiences and functioning. The goal of amassing numerical information of this sort is to find general patterns; individual variations are not of significant interest. Indeed, individual reactions that vary greatly from the typical data patterns are referred to as "outliers" and are frequently treated in distinctive ways or even dropped altogether from analyses.

Beyond these general considerations about positivism, this study presents some specific challenges to positivist assumptions. First, in order to make generalizations from a sample, it is necessary that the sample be representative of the population of interest. In other words, to generalize from this sample of Colorado LGBs to all LGBs in Colorado, it is necessary that all LGBs in the state have had an equal chance of being included in the study. This assumption is not warranted, given the fact that LGBs are widely dispersed and some never have contact with the people and situations through which the survey was distributed.[5]

The positivist approach is further compromised by the fact that the LGB respondents in this study were required to make retrospective, numerical assessments of symptoms.[6] Within a framework that assumes that such symptoms are verifiably "real" phenomena, it is optimal to request information about symptoms from respondents as close in time to the experience as possible. In this study, respondents were asked to recall their experiences over the course of a year. Memory does not produce a photographically "pure" record of experience under normal circumstances and may be even less reliable when the person is recalling particularly painful events (Herman 1992; van der Kolk and Kadish 1987).[7]

A final challenge to the positivist assumptions presented by this study has to do with using DSM-III-R symptoms rather than a standardized instrument to assess LGBs' responses to Amendment 2. Standardized instruments are favored for a variety of reasons, not the least of which is that they are considered to be optimally capable of making valid and reliable assessments (in positivist terms) of the reality of people's experiences.[8]

The net effect of each challenge to positivist assumptions in this study is a dilution of the clarity with which the findings can be viewed. In combination with the mix of negative and positive outcomes, these challenges offered a suggestive but inconclusive picture of the complex and perplexing psychological consequences of Amendment 2 on Colorado LGBs. Clearly, more was needed to understand how the campaign and election had affected bisexuals, gay men, and lesbians.

*A different epistemology.* If we move beyond the positivist framework, new possibilities emerge for understanding Amendment 2's psychological consequences for LGBs. The 496 responses to the single, open-ended question at the end of the survey were the gateway to those new possibilities. That question directed respondents to "Tell me anything else about your response to any aspect of Amendment 2." I included the question on the survey almost as an afterthought. My idea was that a few LGBs might make comments that would add to my understanding of how Amendment 2 had affected them. I initially assumed that I would treat those responses much as I would the quantified items that came before; that is, I would group the comments into areas of concern and tabulate the percentages of respondents who had raised each given concern.

As I received the surveys in the mail, however, I was stunned by the power and pathos of the responses to the open-ended question, and I decided to conduct a full-scale qualitative analysis of them. Whatever the shortcomings of the quantitative data in the study, the comments had much to say; they could expand on and illuminate the quantitative data.

While qualitative approaches to research cover a vast and diverse territory, they are generally characterized by several points of emphasis, including a focus on "the socially constructed nature of reality, the intimate relationship between the researcher and what is studied, . . . the situational constraints that shape inquiry, . . . and the value-laden nature of inquiry" (Denzin and Lincoln 1994b:4).

The notion of a socially constructed reality differs in fundamental ways from positivist assumptions, including the notion that an observable and measurable reality exists and that its parameters can be grasped, and even quantified, by skillful observers using precise tools of measurement. A social constructionist view argues, in contrast, that what we take as knowledge is not a precise description of a free-standing reality. Rather, we inevitably view whatever there is through the lens of our own perspective, so that what seems self-evidently true is actually a hypothesis, a particular rendition of phenomena that might well be understood very differently when seen through a different lens.[9] To say that understandings are socially constructed (rather than that truth is being discovered) is to say that no one has direct access to reality. Access to reality is never perfect; what access we have occurs through the process of interpretation (Schwandt 1994).

The starting point for interpretation is "the historical and psychological reality of the lived experience both of the subject whose expression of experience is being interpreted, and [of] the interpreter herself" (Tappan 1997:649). Meaningful experiences are, after all, socially rather than privately constructed phenomena (Holstein and Gubrium 1994). Consequently, the most promising way to understand how Colorado LGBs were affected by Amendment 2 was not to devise a better quantitative measure but to ask them more directly to describe their experiences. In essence, this is what the open-ended question in the survey did. "Tell me anything else about your response to any aspect of Amendment 2." This approach allowed LGB respondents to define their own concerns (see Brydon-Miller and Tolman 1997). My task as researcher was not a matter of developing more precise measures but of listening well to the words of LGBs in Colorado (Marecek, Fine, and Kidder 1997), while being attentive to the full context in which the experiences they described had occurred. Finally, I neither assumed that it was possible nor strove to conduct research that was value free. There is no "pure" position from which reality is seen— no "god trick of seeing everything from nowhere" (Haraway 1988: 581). Instead, it was imperative that I know as much as possible about where I stood and about the nature of my relationships to the LGBs whose experiences I wished to understand (Sarbin and Kitsuse 1994; Schwandt 1994).

The goal of my research was to make sense of Amendment 2 in terms of the meanings that gay men, bisexuals, and lesbians attached to it. I did not assume that there was a single "truth" to LGBs' experiences of and reactions to the election. Rather, I was interested in the very differences in these experiences and reactions as well as in shared experiences and reactions. Unlike the task that inheres in positivist approaches—namely, generalization toward the ends of prediction and control—interpretive approaches emphasize "generating and refining more interactive, contextualized methods in the search for pattern and meaning" (Lather 1988:571).

If there is a guiding criterion for judging the value of research findings within such a perspective, it is the question of their usefulness. Can the findings help us not only to understand gay people's responses to Amendment 2 but also to do something constructive in light of those responses? This is a question to which we return in the final chapter of this book. First, we need to explore how interpretations of the qualitative findings from this study are to be made and by whom.

2

■ ■　■　■　■　■　■　■　■

# Team-Based Data Analysis

## The Process of Data Analysis

Once I recognized the richness of the qualitative data that emerged from LGBs' responses to the open-ended question, I set about to analyze those data as thoroughly as possible. In many respects, this data set was a perfect one for qualitative analysis. It was large, composed of 496 separate comments, and it offered a diversity of responses to Amendment 2. The emphasis on context that is so much a part of the qualitative perspective was built into this study: here were LGBs reacting to real-life events, reacting to a campaign and to a vote, reacting to voters, some familiar and some unknown. This study brought into focus the elusive intersection between people and their sociopolitical environments, and could capture the voices of members of a marginalized community. All these dimensions are explicitly of interest in qualitative research (e.g., Banyard and Miller 1998).

From previous qualitative endeavors, I knew that it was important to devise a method of analysis uniquely suited to this data set. Although a qualitative perspective gives the researcher broad guidelines for thinking about the data, it does not dictate a specific method of analysis. As Schwandt has made clear, echoing Wolcott (1988, 1992) and Erickson (1986), "methods are the most unremarkable aspect of interpretive work"

(Schwandt 1994:119). The task of interpretation, Schwandt continues, goes beyond methodological questions to the "very condition of human inquiry itself" (Schwandt 1994:119). Qualitative research is rooted in the very old human enterprise of people trying to understand other people's experiences.

The sheer number and variety of the responses to the question made it difficult to get a handle on the data. In my past research efforts, one effective means of beginning to grasp a large volume of complex data was to use codes to demarcate different themes that recurred in the data. This offered the benefit of putatively categorizing the data into discrete themes, thus consolidating several hundred comments into a manageable number of key ideas. By pinpointing such themes, the data begin to tell not one rather overwhelming story but a number of stories, each with a degree of internal coherence. This approach to the data had the added advantage of being amenable to a software program capable of sorting the comments according to the themes and identifying relationships between them.

Here, too, my prior experience with qualitative research was instructive. Although I had been engaged in this study as a lone researcher to this point, I knew that I could gain a more thorough understanding of the comments if I coded and analyzed them with other people. Holstein and Gubrium's (1994) observation that meaningful experiences are socially rather than privately constructed phenomena comes to mind. I would add that the effort to *understand* meaningful experiences is often best carried out as a social enterprise rather than an individual one.

## Advantages of Coding in a Team Context

If we assume that no ultimate truth is accessible it follows that we must use our own interpretive powers—indeed, our own selves (Hertz 1997)—as tools to gain access to other people's experiences. To understand others' experiences, we must strive to enter into their worlds to see the meanings they give to those worlds (e.g., Banyard and Miller 1998; Hamilton 1994; Lather 1988; Marecek, Fine, and Kidder 1997; Schwandt 1994; Tappan 1997). In Donna Haraway's words: "Accounts of a 'real' world do not, then, depend on a logic of 'discovery' but on a power-charged social relation of 'conversation.' The world neither speaks itself nor disappears in favor of a master decoder. The codes of the world are not still, waiting only to be read" (Haraway 1988:593). Our understanding of the experiences of the 496 LGBs who offered their comments, then, can emerge only from an active encounter with the data. This encounter is most successful if undertaken in an attitude of wonder and perplexity and even dread (Charmaz and Mitchell, 1997). Researchers do well to be open to surprise in their relationship to the data. Charmaz and Mitchell echo this sentiment when they assert: "All research beyond the banal begins in uncertainty, where action is unanticipated and anticipations are unrequited" (1997:209).

Each person—each researcher—who encounters the data does so in a unique fashion. In contrast to the relative invisibility of the positivist researcher, in qualitative research the person of the researcher is deemed to be of central importance to the enterprise.[1] Qualitative research takes as a given that researchers' unique histories, values, demographic characteristics, cultural backgrounds, and theoretical orientations influence the way they approach the data and, therefore, what their "findings"— or, more accurately, their understandings—will be (e.g., Banyard and Miller 1998; Bartunek and Louis 1996; Denzin and Lincoln 1994b; Erickson and Stull 1998; Lather 1988; Marecek, Fine, and Kidder 1997). Given the centrality of the researchers' influence on the data, it is incumbent upon them to understand as much as they can about themselves and their inclinations as researchers. The purpose is not to eradicate these inclinations; that is not even possible. Rather, individual researchers should know as much as possible about those influences so that they can track and make active use of them.

My efforts to increase the active use of myself as a researcher have led me to conduct qualitative analysis and interpretation in the context of a group. I share Bartunek and Louis's belief "that the deliberate and extensive harnessing of multiple, diverse perspectives to the task of inquiring and making sense of complex social phenomena can substantially enhance contributions to knowledge and practice" (1996:9–10). Conducting data analysis and interpretation in a group context has a number of potential benefits. Individuals from different backgrounds bring different perspectives (Brewer 1995; Cecchin 1992). If a team is functioning well, the mix of perspectives can produce a synergy that allows for a larger number of and more creative solutions (e.g., Amabile 1983; Bantel and Jackson 1989; Cox 1995; Godard 1985; Murray 1989; Northcraft and Neale 1993; Northcraft, Polzer, Neale, and Kramer 1995; Rohrbaugh 1979).

The inclusion of multiple perspectives could also potentially help each team member to compensate for her or his shortcomings (Larson and LaFasto 1989); seeing differences in others sometimes allows us to see ourselves more clearly (Bullis and Bach 1996; Lorde 1984). In addition, the differences among us often create contradictions (Erickson and Stull 1998) that, in turn, become the basis for better questions both about ourselves and the task at hand. Such clarity in our collective understanding of ourselves may well enhance our ability to understand how we interact with a data set.

A final benefit to conducting research in a group lies in the mutual support that a well-functioning team can provide. One of the difficulties in doing the work in this study of Amendment 2 was rooted in the highly charged nature of many of the comments. Although the confrontation with so many expressions of anger, grief, and betrayal was difficult enough for the members of our team working together, it would have been considerably more difficult for any of us working in isolation. This is in line with Fine's observation that "those of us who do this work need to invent communities of friendly critical informants who can help us think through whose voices and analyses to front, and whose to foreground" (Fine 1994:80). In our case, we needed communities to help us think well and to help us contain the feelings that our respondents offered us.[2]

## The Team of Researchers

The particular collection of people who worked together to analyze and interpret the Amendment 2 data came from different backgrounds and brought varying personal priorities to the project. We all shared at least two things in common: an interest in psychology and a strong belief that Amendment 2 had been a profound injustice. When we began our work as a team, I was the sole collective contact among us. Only two other team members had known each other prior to the project's inception.

Because the researcher is of central importance in qualitative analysis, sketches of all five team members follow. These descriptions are drawn from narratives that they themselves wrote for this purpose. It is important that readers "meet" the team members for two reasons. First, this research assumes that the researcher is not invisible and that information about researchers may be helpful in evaluating the data. Second, one of the goals of this book is to explore the workings of a team; that goal is served by elucidating the dynamics among five individuals as well as by referring to the group or team in the abstract. In the execution of that goal, it makes sense to "hear" the perspectives of each team member. Accordingly, the words of team members are incorporated into this research account at various points. Here are members of the team presented in alphabetical order; their own words are set off by italics.

## Louis Bardach

*I am a Jewish, temporarily able-bodied, gay white male. My mother's side of the family are Lutheran farmers in Kansas; my father grew up on Long Island, New York. I was reared in a middle-class, well-educated family living in many different parts of the United States. I graduated magna cum laude with a Bachelor of Arts degree in psychology from the University of Colorado at Boulder.* Lou was in his last semester of college when he was given one of the surveys from this project. Instead of completing it, he sent me a letter and résumé and asked if I had work for him. Though I had no money to pay him, I did have work for him. He began work on this project by coding and inputting the quantitative data from the survey. He soon graduated to the qualitative team.

## Sylvie Naar

Sylvie came to the project when I was looking for someone to coordinate the input and analysis of the quantitative data. At that time, she was a graduate student in clinical psychology at the University of Colorado in Boulder. In her descriptive comments, Sylvie said she was a *24-year-old, white—sort of—father Egyptian Jew, mother Eastern European Jew.* She grew up in the diverse environment of New York City. Toward the end of her self-narrative, Sylvie noted that she nearly forgot to comment on her sexual orientation. *One of the things I learned from this study is that I am not sure how these labels really work if sexuality is on a continuum. I suppose I am a heterosexual since I am married to a man, but with bisexual tendencies since I find women sexually appealing. That is a very personal statement, but one that is important to recognize since I truly believe that sexual orientation is normally distributed with very few people falling on the ends of the continuum.* Sylvie worked on the project for over a year, after which she left Boulder to pursue her clinical internship in Detroit. Even after her departure, we remained in contact and her influence on the study continued. Sylvie's interest and expertise in trauma, the subject of her dissertation research, were especially relevant to her input into this study.

## Rob Perl

When he worked on the project Rob was a senior with a double major in psychology and anthropology at the University of Colorado. Both during the project and beyond, Rob expressed pleasure at being able to use all of himself in the service of understanding the data. His Sephardic Jewish background was especially important to his understanding of himself and the data from the study. *I was born in 1972 and raised in Chicago in a Jewish, upper-middle-class family. . . . I am heterosexual, but have never felt completely "straight" relative to my peers. Throughout my life, I have had a strong identification with the women in my life, and have never felt comfortable in the stereotypically straight male role.* During his work on the project, Rob was living with a woman, Amy; they later married.

## Sean Riley

Sean was a 27-year-old European American gay male when Lou recruited him to work on the quantitative data input for this study. Having graduated with a B.S. in business from a college in Rhode Island, Sean was taking undergraduate courses at the University of Colorado in psychology in the hope of gaining admission to a clinical graduate program. Sean described his participation in the research as follows: *I became involved with the project after I had been volunteering and working in the field for only a short time. In the two years prior to this project, I had also worked for the local community mental health center in adolescent services and interned in adult services. Having come out approximately three years prior, I was pretty new to queer culture but learned a lot through my experiences with AIDS prevention, political action, and Amendment 2. This project came along after I had seriously set my sights on graduate school a couple years in the future. As it turns out, I had been a respondent to the survey and was very interested in the project when I heard Glenda was looking for some help.*

## Glenda Russell

I am a clinical psychologist by training and an activist by inclination. My professional work has consistently reflected my broad social interests. I received my Ph.D. in clinical psychology from the University of Colorado at Boulder in 1984. Since that time, I have conducted a private practice, carried out research in a variety of topics, and maintained my lifelong involvement in social issues. At the heart of all these enterprises has been a fascination with the intersection of the person and her or his social environment. When Amendment 2 passed, I realized that Colorado's misguided actions could provide me with a compelling opportunity to explore that intersection in a new way.

I grew up in a rural, working-class family in southern Maryland—a background that sensitized me early to differences among people. My Catholic upbringing instilled in me a sense of commitment to social change. Being a parent made the need for social change even more important to me than it was before. My activism over the years has taken both mainstream and nonmainstream directions. For the year leading up to the Amendment 2 election, my partner Karen and I spent much of our time working to defeat the proposed amendment.

## The Insider-Outsider Dimension

Our research team varied along many dimensions of diversity: sex, age, level of education, ethnicity, religion, and family background, among others. In terms of Amendment 2, the most obviously salient personal characteristic among team members was sexual orientation. As I proceed with the explication of our findings, I will discuss some of the ways that sexual orientation became an issue in understanding the data. For now, I want to comment on the insider-outsider dialectic at a more general level.

In broad terms, it seems clear that the diversity on a team influences that team both in terms of process and of outcome (Jackson and Ruderman 1995). It seems likely that, all other things being equal, the perspectives of the insider and the outsider are often different (Bartunek and Louis 1996). Further, it seems clear that these differences in perspective can add strength to the team.

While I accept those statements in the main, it is important to consider a number of qualifications to them. The first has to do with an assumption that frequently accompanies labeling groups as insider and outsider (or, perhaps, labeling groups in any way), namely, an emphasis on between-group differences and a minimizing of within-group differences (see

Bohan 1993; Brewer 1995; Hare-Mustin and Marecek 1988). Individual differences can quickly be obscured as a result, which is a problem in an enterprise where *all* sorts of differences can be helpful.

In addition, the insider-outsider distinction—in this case, LGB versus heterosexual—can become unduly reified. Sexual orientation is but one dimension along which team members differ. At a given time, it may or may not be the most important difference; indeed, it may not even be relevant at all. People have multiple axes of identity and the salience of a particular axis varies across time and context (Ely 1995; McGrath, Berdahl, and Arrow 1995; Nkomo 1995). Though cues in a data set can activate similar responses in individuals with similar characteristics (Bennett and Edelman 1985), and these parallel resonances can be instructive, we cannot rely on that happening. Nor should we allow similarities among us to obscure the differences that so often give rise to new questions and explorations.

Another qualification to the insider-outsider distinction concerns the practice of giving grossly unequal credence to one side of the dialectic, most frequently to the insider perspective. Although an insider's familiarity with a setting or situation can certainly promote greater understanding (Adler and Adler 1987; Feldman 1995), that very familiarity sometimes obscures the insider's view (Adler and Adler 1987). Haraway (1988) warns against totally trusting the vantage point of the subjugated. There is, she says, no innocent position, no position exempt from critical examination. That lesson took our team some getting used to, especially by the two heterosexually identified members who were initially a bit reluctant to "speak for" the LGB respondents to the survey. In order to utilize the group's differences fully, we had to overcome "the discursive construction of 'outsiderness' [that] served to control who felt entitled to speak out and who could be trusted to hear" (Naples 1997:89).

Attending to and using diversity in a team project has many potential advantages. However, team work is not without significant challenges (Bartunek and Louis 1996; Cox 1995; Ely 1995; Erickson and Stull 1998). In the next chapter, we examine the research on optimal team functioning and use the observations of the five members of our research team to illustrate promising approaches to conducting qualitative analysis and interpretation in a team context.

3

. . . . . . . .

# Well-Functioning Teams

*Common Characteristics*

IT IS ONE THING to believe, in the abstract, that there are real advantages to analyzing and interpreting qualitative data as a group. It is quite another to put that belief into practice. The task is as demanding as it is promising. The members of the team that worked on the Amendment 2 data learned a great deal about what enhanced and what hindered a team in its efforts to bring their best to the project. As the idea of my writing this book was taking shape, the other team members and I wanted to find a way to include their perspectives in this narrative. We collectively generated a lengthy set of questions that addressed important aspects of our joint work. Many of these questions dealt with the structure and processes underlying our team's interactions. In this chapter, we examine how our team functioned and integrate those observations with others drawn from the literature, especially that on research teams.

## Well-Functioning Teams

To anchor our discussion of teams, we draw from the results of a qualitative study conducted by Carl Larson and Frank LaFasto (1989). While in the process of developing a measure to evaluate team functioning, Larson and LaFasto interviewed leaders and members of a heterogeneous group of teams. Their teams came from a variety of fields, ranging from cardiac surgery, to mountain-climbing, to McDonald's Chicken McNuggets, to a group of epidemiologists from the Center for Disease Control, to championship college football. Larson and LaFasto identified eight characteristics of effective teams: a clear elevating goal, a results-driven structure, competent team members, unified commitment, a collaborative climate, standards of excellence, external support and recognition, and principled leadership. Many of the issues that the members of our Amendment 2 research team identified as important fit nicely into Larson and LaFasto's typology.

## Clear Elevating Goal

The shared understanding that drew our team of coders[1] together was the belief that Amendment 2 should never have been proposed, much less passed by Colorado voters. Working on the study was a means for each of us to take some action against Amendment 2. The study became more meaningful to us as we became better acquainted with the data. Taken as a whole, the comments were emotionally forceful and intellectually challenging. Looking back on the experience, Rob wrote: *Through my participation in the research, I was able to see the effects of Amendment 2 through the LGB community's eyes. What a sight it was! As an outsider to this community, it was strange, but also understandable, to see the dichotomies: infighting and coming together, motivation and helplessness, fear and bravery, and the pride and self-doubt of LGBs in Colorado.*

As a group, we discussed feeling that we had been admitted to the private experiences of nearly five hundred people at one time. We felt both honored and humbled by the information that had been entrusted to us. We knew that we could develop a thorough understanding of the data only if each of us brought him or herself to the task personally and fully. Reflecting on the project, Lou said: *My own background and life perspective influenced the research, I have no doubt. This phenomenon occurs when one does research of any type. However, the process in this project made these influences more explicit. Indeed, we used these influences to the advantage of [understanding] the data.*

In Sylvie's words, as the project wore on, *We became increasingly close. I'm not sure why—whether it was due to time, or sharing the same experience, or the recognition of our strengths and weaknesses and having shared that recognition from the outset.* Throughout the experience, our focus always returned to the data. Everything we did was done in the service of making sense of how Colorado LGBs had responded to Amendment 2. That was our mission—one to which we were committed and about which we were hardly dispassionate.

## A Results-Driven Structure

There were three major divisions in our work on coding, each directed toward the ultimate aim of understanding respondents' experiences. Although the nature of the work (the content) in each of these three phases differed, our approach to the tasks (the process) was quite similar throughout. At all times, each coder had copies of all the data and was free to make notes or otherwise personalize the data.

*Phase 1: Developing the codes.* We entered this phase of the project with a data set consisting of all the comments arranged in a numbered format, with lines numbered.[2] Our goal was to identify the most salient themes in the data guided by questions such as, What were the emotional, cognitive, social, and political issues that our respondents wrote about? How could we best analyze what was contained in all those comments?

As we read comments from the data at random and discussed the nature of the themes we heard, a list of codes began to emerge. We spent many meetings generating and refining new themes, a process that embodies two critical considerations. The first is to make the definition of the code so precise that the selection of what falls within it becomes clear. The second is to make the code definitions exclusive enough to ensure that there is no systematic overlap between two codes. By way of example, we used three separate codes when a respondent's statement indicated that he or she had received support from other people. The COMM code designated support received specifically from the LGB community. The FAMS code signified support from the respondent's family of origin. The SUPPORT code was used for any other statement of support; the source of support here typically was friends. The fact that a given theme occurred only occasionally—or even rarely—in the data did not mean it could not be used and be useful. In frequently occurring themes there were "outliers"—akin to atypically extreme scores in a quantitative measure—which nonetheless conveyed important information that we wanted to include in our analyses.

Each team member proposed codes for consideration. When someone proposed a code, we would define it and read relevant comments to see how it "fit." We made frequent adjustments to the definitions of the codes. Eventually, we would apply the new code to comments taken randomly from the data in order to see how it seemed to be working. Over time, the number of codes on our list expanded to about forty.

We then submitted this set of codes to extensive pilot testing. We read and coded random comments to test the codes we had generated. In the process, we added more codes, deleted a few, and further refined our understandings of the codes. At the same time, we were coming together as a team. We were acquiring information not only about the codes but about who each of us was and how the group functioned as a unit. We were beginning to formulate shared ideas about one another's backgrounds and ways of approaching the data.

We were also developing norms for working as a group. Everyone was encouraged and expected to enter into negotiations about codes, both in terms of suggesting new themes and in terms of critiquing others' suggestions. We had a rule among us: there was no stupid comment or question. Sean remembered, *We took time to hear clearly other people's ideas even if initially there did not seem to be any substance to them.*

By generating the codes as a group, we all contributed to formulating a shared framework for analyzing the data. Sean described the benefits in this way: *I believe it was empowering for me and for the group to generate a set of codes that felt all-encompassing. It was a time of crystallization for the group and, fortunately, we all seemed to hit it off well. Generating the foundation for the work as a group increased the buy-in and made me feel personally connected to the codes. It also made clear that our meetings would be about what* individuals *contributed to the discussion and that we, as a team, were responsible for the creativity of our work. It was easier to associate to the codes because there was consensus in what they meant. Moreover, that consensus built as we differentiated one code from the next. The codes might not have held as much meaning if [the leader had developed them alone] because in-*

*ternally we each needed to connect the code to some affect that could not have been imported.*

By the end of this phase of our work, we had a long, well-defined set of codes. Those codes, and brief definitions of them, are seen in Table I. Even though we piloted the codes extensively, the final set in Table I includes several that were added during Phase 2 of our work.

*Phase 2: Applying the codes to the data.* For the first time during this second phase, not every coder attended every meeting. Typically, a subgroup of us met twice weekly. I was always in attendance. Depending on schedules, two or three other coders would be there as well. Coders rotated attendance in such a way that, with rare exception, everyone coded at least once a week. One of the questions to which coders responded for the purpose of this summary was whether the staggered attendance interfered with the continuity of the work. All agreed that it did not. Sean added, *I do recall the times when one member was absent and another of us would ask, "What would ___ say if he/she were here?" That reflected the depth to which we came to know, expect, and predict one another's responses.* And, I would add, it also reflected the value we attached to each other's perspective.

Each coding meeting began with a brief set of questions designed to establish where we were in the process. The coders who had been absent from the immediately prior meeting were sometimes told about an observation or question about a code that had arisen at that meeting. Occasionally, we wanted more input from everyone regarding a particularly troublesome coding question about which we had not been able to reach consensus. Sometimes, we just wanted to share some new insight or a bit of humor that had emerged from our interaction with the data in the previous meeting.

When doing the actual coding, we took turns reading comments. This was a useful practice for several reasons. Hearing the comments read aloud made them come alive. It also allowed us to hear the data spoken by different voices—literally—which mirrored the fact that the comments came from so many different LGBs. The practice also demanded each coder's active engagement in the process.

There was no formal process for deciding who suggested a code first. As Sylvie elaborated, *We took turns taking a first stab at the comment. That structure was critical so that each person had a chance to formulate his/her impressions without being influenced all the time by others.* As in Phase 1, all coders were encouraged to critique the suggested codes: "Is this comment only about this code? It sounds more like another to me. I think this comment reflects several different codes." The conversation was sometimes very matter-of-fact, especially when a particular comment was so straightforward that it warranted only one code and that code was obvious. At other times, the conversations were more extensive and complex. Sean described the interaction thus: *The leader often encouraged debate about what code to assign to a comment, and this made it a lively place to toss an idea into the ring and watch it get scrutinized. It was a healthy process of considering others' responses which, by no means, was dominated by one person's "superior" line of thinking. . . . It was not uncommon for the leader to say, "Say more about that" or "You're onto something so keep going." Often we were not in complete agreement and it was somewhat competitive and fun in that way. In the end, the data were well served.*

During this phase, I kept track of the codes we assigned to the numbered comments. I also kept notes on questions about content and on observations about the process of our work. Some coders preferred to keep full notes on the coding while others did not. Each person found a comfortable approach to the work and settled into it for the duration of the coding.

*Phase 3: Reading the coded segments.* Once all the data had been coded, we entered the numbered segments into the computer. We then retrieved all the segments corresponding to each of the codes. Once, when we were retrieving the sets of comment segments corresponding to each code from the computer, Rob joked that we could just weigh each code and report the weights as indicators of the relative significance of each code.[3] It was an amusing thought precisely because assigning significance based on the weights (that is, on a combination of the frequency of and length of text in a given code) ran counter to the immersion into each code that we were about to undertake. On the other hand, Rob's suggestion would have been exactly in keeping with my initial (and more quantitative) expectations for the data analysis.

The actual process of interpreting a code by reading all the comments that comprised it was complex and demanding. For our group, it was also fun. The conversations were often lively. Sometimes, especially as we were immersed in some of the more somber codes, the conversations were quite painful and it seemed important to give time and attention to our own affective responses to the codes. We intentionally alternated reading the heavier codes and the brighter ones in an effort to give ourselves a break from some of the most affectively charged data. That often helped, but not always; sometimes codes that we expected to be more or less consistently optimistic in tone surprised us with more negative content than we had anticipated.

Phase 2's coding of the data allowed us to see the wide contours of the data set—a macroscopic perspective, in effect. During Phase 3, by contrast, we were able to view the data from a much more microscopic vantage point as we examined them systematically one code at a time, trying to understand as much as we could about each code. It is not possible to convey what those discussions sounded like; they varied greatly from one code to another and even within the same code. Our associations to the comments took us in many different directions. The reading aloud of a given comment frequently generated other comments within a code, other codes, theoretical issues, findings from other research, and personal observations and experiences. These associations sometimes led to fruitful discussions in which new understandings, often putative, would emerge. Sometimes our discussions led to dead ends—ideas that had seemed promising but did not stand up to scrutiny. The data were the touchstones to which our discussions always returned; if our ideas did not match what the respondents had written, we discarded them.

Denzin and Lincoln (1994c) have suggested that applied research has links to clinical methods. Sean made this link explicit when he recalled, *Looking back on our meetings, I see that the structure closely mirrored that which is required for ongoing therapy. With a predictable structure, and a predictable leader/therapist, we were able to free up our minds to associate to the comments.* And associate is what we all did—not, of course, for purposes of self-understanding (though that sometimes was a by-product) but to make sense of the data we were reading.

Every coder on our team retrospectively emphasized the importance of these freewheeling conversations. Lou connected them to a sense of community between the five of us: *Another thing which we did that helped to build a sense of community was to allow ourselves to follow tangents that naturally arose. These tangents led to discussions which helped to better define and refine the codes and better understand what they meant. But the tangents also provided the opportunity for individual and group healing as the data applied to our lives.*

Rob expanded on this latter point: *discussions were essential to this work. Not only did they help to round out the group perspective, making [our understanding of] the data more reliable, but they also allowed the weighty issues of research to be handled by a group rather than by a sole researcher in isolation. In the group, we were able to work through some of the issues and emotions that were stirred while reading the data. I could imagine that, if this task were done by only one person, they might feel overburdened by the content and isolated from the support. The discussions served to ease the impact of what we were reading.*

The extent and breadth of our discussions promoted a thorough encounter with the comments. Sylvie, who had originally been referred to me because of her expertise in quantitative analysis, observed: *What surprised me about the data was the variety of responses and the richness of the data. I had no idea that so much clinical information could be obtained from short comments. But the number of comments and the process we used for coding gave one an understanding that would have never been obtained from quantitative research.*

It is difficult to explain why this close-up view of a code would reveal so much more about the data than we already knew from having created the coded segments in the first place. The macroscopic/microscopic analogy conveys some of the difference. In creating codes, one is looking at the data set from above. Think of the photographs of the earth from outer space: broad contours are apparent. Relationships between different topographies become clear. One sees the big picture.

When we moved to reading each code separately, we focused closely on different topographies in succession. We took a journey through a rain forest, and sometimes we examined the soil and leaves there in minute detail. We moved across an ocean in a slow-moving craft, stopping occasionally to dive below the surface and find what was there. We never lost sight of the fact that these topographies were part of, and fit into, that big picture. In fact, our careful examination of each code helped us to understand the big picture more fully.[4]

Keeping a written record of our wide-ranging discussions was primarily my job. Other coders also sometimes took notes but it was my task to compile a written summary of our discussions that, in turn, would be used as the basis for reports of our research. That summary included observations about the content and the process of our discussions about the codes. I will return to that summary and the difficulties we encountered when it was time to report on the data in chapter 10. For the present, I want to focus on Larson and LaFasto's third characteristic of well-functioning teams.

## Competent Team Members

Based on their research, Larson and LaFasto (1989) identified three variables that seem to be common to competent team members: essential skills and abilities, a strong desire to contribute, and the ability to collaborate. The second of those factors—the strong desire to contribute—was addressed when I discussed the importance of a clear elevating goal. The third will be covered when we examine the fifth characteristic of teams, the collaborative climate. In this section, I focus on the first factor, team members' skills and abilities.

Our team was comprised of five members who brought varied skills and abilities to the task. With respect to educational background, the team included one undergraduate; two college graduates, one recent and one longer-term who was returning for coursework in another field; one graduate student well into her clinical psychology training program; and a psychologist who had been out of graduate school for nearly a decade when the project began. These formal indices of educational preparation represented but one aspect of the differences in skills and abilities among us.

Having read all the comments in the data before our group ever assembled, I knew that a significant proportion of them would be understood to reflect varying degrees of traumatic reaction. To ensure that team members were prepared to deal with such content, I asked all the coders to read several books and articles about traumatic responses and to familiarize themselves with DSM-III-R descriptions and criteria for the three diagnoses covered in the quantitative data. This was an unnecessary step for Sylvie who was already well versed in these areas. However, the three other coders used the readings to close a gap in their preparation.

Sean wrote that those readings *set the stage for the comments and provided context for even the simplest one-liners. Some of those comments, without some context, would not have received the degree of attention to their meanings that they deserved.* Sean went on: *Applying the theory to the raw data served to illuminate it. This was not an experience I had had before. It was fascinating to see issues discussed in texts unfold in the respondents to the survey. In short, I came to appreciate research and see the connection between theory and application.*

Sean's statements illustrate how a well-functioning team depends on the initial inclusion of competent people and also increases the competence of team members (see Bartunek and Louis 1996). Among other changes, some members of our coding team needed to believe that they could make a contribution to the work.

Lou detailed his development from the early stages of the project onward. *During this [early] time, I often felt incompetent—fearful that Glenda would discover how little I actually knew. . . . But I also feel that this was a period of trust building. Glenda would learn to trust that I was dedicated to the project, and trust that I was (as she put it) "clinically insightful." I was able to trust that, if I worked hard, Glenda would respect my work. I also was able to trust in myself that I indeed had something valuable to offer to the group. Eventually, the power dynamics seemed to fade away; they became almost nonexistent. When it came to the actual coding process, I felt as though we were all very much on the same level. I even found that I had some useful knowledge to contribute to the group.*

At this point in his narrative, Lou raised several issues in which he had particular interest and knowledge. Although he spoke for himself, his words applied to the whole group as well. What allowed the discussions to be as incisive and wide-ranging as they often were was the variety of interests and knowledge various members brought. Those interests would have been irrelevant to the success of the group had members not pushed themselves to contribute their perspectives.

Another aspect that each of us brought to the project was the personal. With the exception of clinical training for some of us, most of us had not been invited to bring our selves to academic work. In fact, in most academic arenas we had been explicitly encouraged to keep our personal experiences out of the work. Here, the competence of each individual's contribution—and the success of the team's undertaking—depended on everyone using himself or herself fully. Our understanding of the data could be enhanced by the intentional use of our personal and demographic characteristics and experiences. It took time for all of us to believe that this really was the case. Over time, we became better as a group at bringing ourselves fully to the task of interpreting the data, a task that required trust and courage. The reward for doing so was in the quality of our work and in a sense of mutual appreciation. Rob spoke to this: *On the project, I was able to use my experience and perspective. For the first time, I was able to see the salience of my demographics in a group process. I felt that my perspective was a product of my experience, and that it was taken as serious and legitimate.*

When one is bringing so much of the personal to a group project, it is also possible to say things that disturb or annoy other members of the team. That possibility is magnified when the task at hand focuses on homophobia and heterosexism and other phenomena that are frequently socially disruptive (Russell and Greenhouse 1995). Thus, we all had to grow in our ability to talk about potentially socially disruptive issues as openly as possible. That process relied on the development of a high degree of trust among team members over time. It also opened the way to uncomfortable discoveries.

Sean wrote: *A process of personal discovery was welcomed that made it more real. I specifically recall a comment in the data where a woman referred to herself as "very attractive." My first thought was, "Wait, I thought only LGBs responded to the survey!" My own internalized homophobia did not allow for a "very attractive lesbian." I was shocked by my own thoughts and fearfully shared them with a member of the team. He laughed at how "terrible" it was, making it easier for me to accept that I'm human too.* Sean went on to share that experience with the whole team. We all learned something about homophobia and we all knew how accepting our group was. It was this climate that allowed us to be more competent in this task together than any of us could have been alone.

## Unified Commitment

Larson and LaFasto (1989) make the point that it is difficult to know exactly what constitutes a unified commitment to a team. They describe some of the parameters of unified commitment in this way:

> Certainly, it is a "team spirit." It is a sense of loyalty and dedication to the team. It is an unrestrained sense of excitement and enthusiasm about the team. It is a willingness to do anything that has to be done to help the team succeed. It is an intense identification with a group of people. It is a loss of

self. "Unified commitment" is very difficult to understand unless you've experienced it. And even if you have experienced it, it is difficult to put into words. (1989:73)

Our coding team shared a commitment at several levels: to one another, to the task, to the survey respondents, and to the principle of equal rights for all people. At various points in our work together, all these commitments were voiced by different team members. Moreover, the relationship of our work to each of those commitments was made explicit on numerous occasions.

In her narrative of our work together, Sylvie pointed to a number of factors that, in her view, contributed to the sense of commitment. These included: working together to generate the codes, seeing each person's viewpoint as integral to the task, generating new codes after we had a putatively complete list, and allowing the wide-ranging discussions to occur. I agree with Sylvie's list of factors and with another that she added: *we were one another's best—and sometimes sole—sources of support.*

Often, other people in our lives did not understand the nature of the data with which we were working or the intensity of the work experience. Sylvie referred to her relationship with her husband: *I remember feeling frustrated when other heterosexuals, even my husband—the classic white male—could not understand how traumatic Amendment 2 had been. It was almost like, "What's the big deal! It will be overturned."* In response to another question about support, Sylvie wrote: *What helped me deal with the pain and frustration of some of the data? Talking to other team members and the leader's sensitivity . . . I have to admit, I could not really go talk to my usual supports because I felt they could not understand how my reactions could be so intense.*

Our commitment to our work was expressed in many ways. The seriousness with which we took our work and one another was evident. Everyone's contribution was obviously valuable. That fact enhanced our commitment which, in turn, increased the quality of our contributions. We became an interdependent group (see Brewer 1995 and Erickson and Stull 1998 for discussions of interdependence in research groups). Our individual and collective goals became so intertwined that competitiveness was used for the good of the project as much as for any single individual's gain.

This interdependence was reflected in the way we celebrated our successes. Sean described it thus: *I recall how often we celebrated our work, particularly at times when we would find the answer to some nagging question about the material that we had had. Often we'd have to sit with a thought for a while before it would make sense and when it finally did, there was a huge sense of accomplishment in the room. What stands out for me is how we spent days, maybe weeks, wondering what the significance was of adult respondents reporting on children commenting that Amendment 2 was wrong. When it finally dawned on me that it was a form of witnessing that the adults were expressing, I felt very connected to the work and gratified by the team's appreciation for that contribution.*

One final aspect of our commitment to the project that all the coders mentioned as important was our use of humor throughout our work. We genuinely had fun. Some of our fun was undoubtedly a form of gallows humor when we were working with the codes expressing sadness and betrayal. We laughed at ourselves, individually and collectively, a great deal. The humor allowed us to acknowledge painful truths about homophobia in the world and in ourselves.

Lou described a specific form of humorous engagement that probably surprised us almost as much as it amused us: *One community trust-building aid that comes to mind is that we allowed ourselves to laugh. I'll never forget when we started to "act out" or pantomime the data. We became so intimate with respondents' stories that we could mime them and other team members would know exactly to which story we were referring. One might cringe at this, thinking we were somehow ridiculing the respondents and their experiences. But I think our laughter was actually less about the individuals who wrote their comments and more about how each of us related to them personally. I believe it sometimes helps to be able to look at a perpetrator and laugh; it takes his/her power away.*

And so we laughed at the betrayal of Amendment 2 even as we regarded it with dead seriousness. All the while, we did it together.

## Collaborative Climate

Our feeling of being in the task together both reflected and created a collaborative climate. In their narratives about our work together, all the coders agreed that a collaborative climate not only existed but was essential to our work. Underlying this climate was a genuine respect and affection for one another. The collaborative nature of our work and relationships was what made it possible for us to embody one of my favorite descriptions of team research: "Seeing the same thing at the same time, but differently" (Erickson and Stull 1998:38).

Larson and LaFasto (1989) suggest that trust is at the root of the collaborative nature of teamwork. It is, therefore, not surprising that trust has been mentioned in the previous descriptions of team characteristics. An important part of establishing trust was creating a safe space in which we were free to follow the data where they led us, and those places were occasionally sad, provocative, confusing, and self-revealing.

One way the collaborative nature of our work manifested itself was in specific and routine acts of helpfulness. First, we all had to share honestly. As Lou pointed out, *This [sharing] led to an increased sense of vulnerability for each of us.* It also allowed us to learn from one another. We all brought our experiences and insights to bear on the data. The Jewish members of the team, for example, were especially helpful in making sure we understood the implications of the many Holocaust references in the data. The coders who had not been exposed to clinical training reflected on the degree to which they learned how to think clinically—which, I think, means thinking interpretively—about the comments we were reading. This intermixing of information, skills, and perspectives was at the heart of our collaboration.

Relatedly, we helped one another to see that some perspectives were not helpful in understanding the data. We all had a tendency to view the data in particular ways. Most of the time these proclivities were useful; occasionally not. Lou told us of an instance when his ability to see the data clearly was hampered by personal experiences: *There was a period of a few weeks when I kept wanting to use the code SAD. The coding team knew that I had just ended a two-year relationship and asked if that were influencing how I understood respondents' statement. Of course it was, which was valuable to acknowledge, and it forced us, I believe, to be more sensitive to how relationships played a role in the respondents' Amendment 2 experiences.*

As we discussed earlier, team members also helped one another to process our emotional reactions to the data. Sean described this as follows: *Sometimes, dealing with the affect was just too much, comment after comment. It was important to maintain a boundary between identifica-*

*tion and empathy, and being overwhelmed. We spent huge quantities of precious time processing our feelings and responses and, although this slowed things down, it was tremendously important, if not always for the data, then for our own healing.*

Another way the collaborative climate enabled us to help one another related to our negative reactions to comments that reflected a great deal of internalized homophobia and triggered our own homophobia/internalized homophobia. Sean observed: *I was overwhelmed by some of the most traumatic responses. In those cases, I sometimes felt like pathologizing those victims, possibly a mix of empathic failure and my own internalized homophobia.*

At such times—for Sean and for all of us—other team members could offer a different perspective. While we did this in a variety of ways, two in particular stand out. The first had to do with our practice of trying to link a respondent's internalized homophobia to the actual existence of homophobia and heterosexism in that person's external experience—an issue that will be covered in detail when we describe the IHE and IHI codes (internalized homophobia, explicit and inferred, respectively). The other method for helping ourselves to avoid victim-blaming was also rooted in our analysis of the relationship of external homophobia and internalized homophobia that we developed over time. We acknowledged the ubiquitousness of homophobia and reluctantly accepted it as a given, in ourselves and in the study's participants. Sometimes, when we encountered an especially homophobic comment, one of us would remind the others, "We all got some on us!" That helped us to see the root of the problem in homophobia and heterosexism rather than in our respondents.

*Collaboration across the ingroup-outgroup divide.* Any number of differences between and among coders could have interfered with the collaborative environment we had built up. Given the focus of Amendment 2 and the topic of the study, it might be useful to comment specifically on the relationship between LGBs and heterosexuals on the team. Predictably, the dynamics between the two subsets of the group changed over time. Early on, Sylvie and Rob, the two heterosexually identified team members, were concerned that they could not understand the data adequately because the comments represented LGBs' reactions to an anti-gay political act. Even as the coding proceeded, Sylvie said that *once in a while, I did feel like, "How can you possibly understand?" But I am not sure if this came from the LGB coders or from my own guilt as a heterosexual.*

Rob described some of his reactions as follows: *As the only heterosexual man on the coding team, it sometimes was difficult to deal with the fact that the large majority of Amendment 2's perpetrators were also heterosexual men. I remember being ashamed at times, and also embarrassed that these men in organizations like Colorado for Family Values could commit such atrocities. They did not speak for me. I remember feeling as if my rights were being violated even though I was not their target. Reading people's responses was tremendously painful. However, I also recall the reactions of LGB team members and the depth at which some of the data affected them.*

What made collaboration possible was that, on balance, Sylvie and Rob knew that their input was valuable and respected. It is no accident that both of them, in their accounts of our work together, mentioned times when they—the heterosexually identified members—were the first to spot some codes that were very relevant to LGB experience. Rob portrayed that sort of occasion in broad terms: *Sometimes it seemed that too much experience could work against your judgment. For example, there were times when LGB team members would miss a homophobic theme in the data when it was apparent to heterosexual members.* Sylvie details this kind of experience: *Because I was not LGB, formally, I was not able to connect with the experience [of the respondents] at the same level as one who is LGB. This interfered with my ability to pick up on certain codes immediately—the internalized homophobia codes, for example. The objectivity from not being LGB sometimes helped, on the other hand. I remember a time when I clearly picked up a DISC* (denoting an actual experience with discrimination or harassment) *code. The LGB coders did not because it was something they were so used to.*

The dialectic between LGB and heterosexual team members worked from the other direction too. Lou recounted his initial reluctance to give voice to his own internalized homophobia: *I have to admit that, at first, it was hard to be vulnerable about my own internalized homophobia, especially with heterosexual members of the group, for fear they would not "get it." But it seems to me that they did "get it" through their own translations of [their experiences with being a sociopolitical target] and through their understanding natures. They "got it" enough, anyway, that I felt I could be vulnerable to the degree that I was in the coding group.* Sean recalled one of his responses to the mix of sexual orientation among team members: *It was not a big issue for me—except at first, when I found myself identifying with those [re-spondents] who wanted to "blame all heterosexuals." It was difficult to put that feeling together with the fact that two people involved in this project, two people in the room, were straight.*

While the dynamic across sexual orientations was sometimes uncomfortable, at no point did it become problematically uncomfortable. We all shared a basic perspective on the issue of how LGBs should be treated. We all saw examples in the data of how some LGBs reacted to the pain of Amendment 2 by striking out against heterosexuals and how demoralizing and futile that response often was for them. We all adopted a nonjudgmental attitude toward homophobia in ourselves. We all applauded discoveries that members made about their own homophobic attitudes. And we all taught one another. The teaching sometimes took an explicit form, as when Sylvie explained: *The internalized homophobia (IHE and IHI) codes were the best learning experience for me because I had never had any training in that area (surprise, surprise!). The LGBs were very patient in explaining what it was and how to spot it.*

As often as not, the lessons were not explicit. The very presence of people who are different can force us to reevaluate the certainty and security of our own positions and perspectives. The learning went in all directions; it was both obvious and subtle. Some of it continues, as when Sylvie, in her narrative, spontaneously caught and wrote about a homophobic statement she was about to write. The dynamic around differences in the group was not perfect but, as Lou suggested, we all "got it" enough of the time. That is one of the best and most gratifying feelings that I take from the entire experience.

## Standards of Excellence

Standards of excellence are the team signposts that eventually get translated into individual and group performance (Larson and LaFasto 1989). Such standards are relatively easy to meet when the team consists of competent individuals who are committed to a goal that they regard in very positive terms.

The tasks for the Amendment 2 research were demanding; coders were meeting for two hours at least once, and often twice, each week. Sean once estimated that there had been four hundred meeting hours during all phases of the coding, a number that seems plausible. When we were meeting, everyone had to be consistently alert to the task that was occupying the team's attention. In addition, as we have seen, the data were often intensely emotional, and we all needed to be fully engaged at both the intellectual and emotional levels.

I clarified the demanding nature of the work to each coder before we began. Everyone approached the task with a striking readiness to work. In only a few instances did the standards for our work need to be invoked. On one occasion, after seeing a pattern of tardiness emerging in the behavior of two of the coders, I decided to confront them at the start of a coding session that included only them and me. One of the coders responded to the confrontation by saying, in effect, that he had heard this before. The other coder got upset and had to leave the meeting.

The two coders' reactions to that confrontation were the subject of one of the questions for the narratives. One acknowledged that he responded to the confrontation with a need to protect his and my image of him. He reported having felt a decrease in trust during that time. He wished he had confronted me but he felt too intimidated. *Looking back, I feel that if some of the power dynamics had been discussed more thoroughly, this incident might have been avoided or, at least, better resolved.*

The other coder had a different retrospective view: *The confrontation was indicated and important, if not somewhat of a surprise. Glenda just happened to be the person to call a few of us on something I personally had struggled with (as if I've mastered it). I can't see that it needed or should have been done differently; she was protecting the team from coming apart in some way. It probably was affecting our work. I think it was an important move for our team (hindsight is 20/20).*

The differences in the contemporaneous and retrospective reactions of the two coders to this confrontation speak to the fact that teams are made up of individuals. My confrontation about lateness seemed to have been adequate with one coder but not with the other. In looking back, I wish I had confronted the two coders on separate occasions. I think it would have been easier for them to have been confronted singly and I could have better tailored my words to each of them. However, this was one of the few occasions on which I felt a need to invoke the standards that I wanted to undergird our work; most commonly, those standards were met without question. Undoubtedly this was because the team members were so committed and so competent.

*Groupthink.* While discussing the issue of standards, I want to comment on the danger of groupthink and, more importantly, on how I think we avoided it. Groupthink refers to "the mode of thinking that persons engage in when concurrence-seeking becomes so dominant in a cohesive ingroup that it tends to override realistic appraisal of alternative courses of action" (Janis 1978:157)—or, in this case, of alternative interpretations of comments. Obviously, our team worked to arrive at a consensus both about how given segments of data should be coded and how they should be interpreted. We were moving toward the goal of concurrence, in Janis's terms.

At the same time, we did not want to forgo other possible ways of understanding the comments. Several means by which we tried to avoid groupthink have been mentioned. These include: everyone had copies of the data; we rotated reading comments; we varied who spoke first in response to a data segment; we directly encouraged members to bring up alternative interpretations of the data; the only final arbiter for determining whether an interpretation had merit was the group. In collaboration, "no one has the final word" (Hoffman 1992:22).

This last point is critical. I had collected the data set; I knew the most about the subject at hand. For all intents and purposes, I was the team leader. However, in matters of coding and interpretation, I carried no more weight than did any other coder. I have already mentioned times when a subset of coders could not come to a consensus; we waited until everyone was present so that the group could decide. I have no doubt that this arrangement served the data well.

One final practice that mitigated against groupthink in our team was our habit of engaging in wide-ranging conversations. I was surprised by the frequency with which coders explored the importance of those conversations in their narratives. The discussions sometimes began with clear connections to the data; at other times, the associations seemed oblique. Occasionally, they went nowhere; more often, they helped us understand some aspect of the data better. These discussions required a certain patience, perhaps even a little faith. They almost always paid off.

## *External Support and Recognition*

Larson and LaFasto (1989) make the point that well-functioning teams need to receive external support and recognition for their work. This is the only one of their eight criteria on which our team differed markedly from what their research suggests is typical of well-functioning teams. For the duration of the project, we received limited external support and recognition.

We did receive extensive support from one another. We celebrated our work and regarded it as important. At various times, we all remarked on how lucky we were to be working on research that felt meaningful. A related source of support came from a somewhat surprising source—our respondents. In general, the tone of many of the comments indicated that LGBs in Colorado needed to be heard. Rob picked up on this theme in his narrative: *Many of our respondents were unaware of the effect that their voices would have through the research. But they still felt the need to make their voices known.* One specific set of comments—those we coded THANKS— overtly carried this message. In these comments, LGBs specifically thanked us for conducting the research and for hearing their voices. The THANKS code will be covered in detail in chapter 8. For now, suffice it to say that we felt we were performing a service for many LGBs in Colorado, which was gratifying in and of itself.

The question of external recognition comes up in a new form after the coding is completed. Presenting our findings has been a combination of rewarding and troubling to members of the team—a subject explored more fully in chapter 10. At this time, we move on to Larson and LaFasto's eighth principle of effective teamwork.

## *Principled Leadership*

Erickson and Stull (1998) make the observation that a research team's authority and leadership are typically informal. That clearly was the case with our team. One reason for this is indicated in Larson and LaFasto's (1989) analysis: leaders do not so much manage the team as they manage principles, which in turn manage the team. There were several principles that I brought to the team that were probably influential in the work. The first was a commitment to the project. While I knew that this research was one of my ways of working through my own feelings about Amendment 2, I was also convinced that it could have a broader positive effect on LGBs in Colorado and elsewhere. I think this approach was contagious; it quickly spread throughout the team.

The standards of excellence that I brought to the work were also important. I had had considerable experience with qualitative research in general and with team coding in particular. I trusted the process fully. This also seemed to be contagious.

Judging from the other coders' narratives, one of the most important of my leadership tasks was creating a safe space in which we could do our work, a place where we could all speak honestly. Sylvie pointed out that *the leader's modeling of openness and insight was critical to the process.* Similarly, the other coders all pointed to the need for the leader to be sensitive to each individual's engagement with the data and to encourage full participation. While it was important that our discussions give team members room to pursue their associations and to process their feelings, it was also important that we not turn our meetings into a therapy group. I think everyone was careful to avoid stepping over the line into therapy. Sean reminded me, *I recall the leader would often refocus conversations by instructing individual group members to examine their thoughts outside of our meetings, particularly when comments seemed to reflect more about their own process that we didn't have time to get into.* I suspect that the best and most relevant training I had had for walking this line was my work as a clinical supervisor working with less experienced psychotherapists.

Another line—that between being the leader and being a coequal coder—was more difficult to walk. I am reasonably certain that my biggest mistakes as a leader were the consequence of my reluctance to move out of the coequal coder role and take an authoritative position when such a position was warranted. It seems clear to me that such role transitions were the most awkward experiences I had in the process of doing this work. (The most salient example of this awkwardness occurred when the team set out to present our findings to professional audiences, an issue I take up in chapter 10.) In my role as coder I was able to immerse myself in the comments from lesbians, gay men, and bisexuals in Colorado which constituted the heart of the project. In the next chapter, we begin the process of meeting those comments in detail.

Table 1. *Codes*

| | |
|---|---|
| ACFV | anger at Colorado for Family Values, religious right |
| ACHRIST | anger at Christians |
| AG | anger in general |
| AHET | anger at heterosexuals |
| AMEDIA | anger at media |
| APROC | anger at process of campaign/election |
| AQ | anger at gays, lesbians, and bisexuals |
| ASTATE | anger at state |
| BA | against boycott |
| BARRIERS | infighting within LGB community |
| BF | for boycott |
| CCOMP | compliments for campaign against Amendment 2 |
| CCRIT | criticisms of campaign against Amendment 2 |
| CFV | any references, other than anger, to Colorado for Family Values |
| COMM | sense of community with other LGBs, personal or abstract |
| DISC | actual reports of discrimination/harassment at any time |
| FAMR | rejection and other negative reactions from family of origin |
| FAMS | support from family of origin |
| FEAR | any reference to fear |
| GRASP | grasp of homophobia/heterosexism: first-person perspective |
| HOPE | future-oriented statements of hopefulness |
| IHE | internalized homophobia, explicit |
| IHI | internalized homophobia, inferred |
| INSIGHT | self-analysis with insight |
| INVAL | discounts effects of campaign/election |
| ISMS | interconnections between oppressions at social and political level |
| ISOLATE | alienation or isolation |
| JUD | references to any aspect of the postelection legal challenges to Amendment 2 |
| KIDS | any reference to children |
| LEAVE | desire or plan to leave Colorado |
| LOSS | loss or grief |
| MEDIA | any reference, other than anger, to media |
| MOVE | Amendment 2 placed in broader political context |
| NOMOVE | Amendment 2 not placed in broader context |
| NTE | emphasis on need for widespread education on LGB issues |
| OUT | any reference to being out of the closet |
| OUTL | being less out |
| OUTM | being more out |
| OVER | overwhelmed |
| PERSONAL | references to personal responsibility |
| PRIMARY | references to primary responsibility |
| RECOVER | attributions to process or outcome of recovering from Amendment 2 |
| REGRET | explicit regret for not having done enough in the campaign against Amendment 2 |

| REPOC | attribute election results to Equal Protection Colorado's campaign to defeat Amendment 2 |
| RINFO | attribute election results to misinformation/confusion |
| RLIES | attribute election results to lies told |
| RMIS | attribute election results to voter mistakes |
| SAD | depression (including specific symptoms) or sadness |
| SHOCK | surprise at the election |
| SUPPORT | support from friends (not from family or from community) |
| THANKS | gratitude for research study |
| TRAUMA | references to past traumas, images of trauma, symptoms of trauma |
| TRUST | references to trust of any kind |
| VWP | references to victims, witnesses, and/or perpetrators |
| WAR | statements using war or fighting imagery to describe aspects of Amendment 2 experience |

## 4

■ ■  ■   ■   ■   ■    ■     ■      ■

# Early Reactions to Amendment 2

WE WERE CHALLENGED to make sense of a large and disparate group of responses by people who ultimately may have shared only one thing in common: that they had all identified as LGB and been victimized by Amendment 2. Our team of five coders started this project with comments by 496 gay, bisexual, and lesbian Coloradans. Responses ranged from a single word to several paragraphs; all but two fit on the half page allotted to the open-ended item. The typical response length was three to five sentences or several statements separated by bullets. The large number of contributions and their variability added diversity and texture to the study.

In chapter 3, I outlined the structure we used to frame our work. To summarize: (1) we read random comments about which we had no demographic information; (2) from those we generated a preliminary set of codes; (3) we then piloted the codes, during which process we analyzed and refined them by using them in conjunction with more comments; (4) once we had a final coding schema (table 1, chapter 3), we read and coded the entire set of comments; and (5) we entered those codes into the computer. The output from the computer consisted of segments organized by code, which (6) we read and discussed, often at considerable length, in order to get a microscopic view of each code.

The more we learned about the whole set of comments, the more we understood each individual code. The converse is also true: the more we understood each code, the greater was our understanding of the entire set of comments. As we completed the six steps outlined above, we discussed how we should organize the data so they would make sense to us and, we hoped, to those to whom we would transmit the data in written or oral presentations.

Unlike positivist approaches which assume that data are self-evident and "reveal" the facts to researchers, qualitative approaches demand that researchers actively make sense of and interpret the data. In such studies, data analysis and interpretation are neither self-evident nor absolute endeavors. A given data set could be understood in multiple ways, none of which is absolutely "correct" or absolutely "wrong." The criteria for legitimacy applied by such studies to data analysis and interpretation include the questions, Is the outcome coherent, reasonable, and/or useful?

## Framing the Data

### Trauma Theory

As we approached the end of the six steps summarized above, we considered three major ways to frame the data, each of which had some merit and some drawbacks. First, we viewed this data set in terms of the research and clinical literature on trauma. We examined three possible constructions based on the trauma literature. One of the frameworks we considered adopting would have entailed a division of the clinical symptoms common to traumatic reactions. A second approach would have involved dividing the data into three categories, reflecting the three actors in traumatic situations: victim, perpetrator, and witness (Herman 1992). Finally, we discussed the possibility of dividing the data according to the major dimensions in Janoff-Bulman's (1992) synthesis of research on the cognitive substrates of trauma.

All these trauma-based frameworks were potentially worthwhile. The data were loaded with indications of trauma—symptoms, references to iconic images of trauma, statements about all three members of the trauma triad, and comments demonstrating the kind of cognitive meaning making in which traumatized individuals engage. At the same time, adopting any of these trauma-related frameworks seemed to exclude too many comments. We were concerned that using a trauma structure might distort the data by forcing them into this particular framework.

## Grief Theory

A second framework we considered would have been rooted in an exposition of the grief process, which entails a bereaved individual's movement through a variety of affective experiences. In many respects, a grief framework would include considerably more of the data than would a trauma framework. The grief process includes many of the feelings and experiences—shock, sadness, anger, and resolution—that we found in the data. However, some comments would have had to be forced to fit a grief structure. My personal resistance to using a grief framework also derived from a general antipathy to stage theories, particularly as they are apt to be employed in a highly reified fashion and as they imply a "normal" outcome.[1]

## An Alternative Framework

While the coding team was actively discussing ways of framing the data, Sylvie left town for a brief time. We talked by phone during her absence and she suggested a third framework, which we eventually decided to use. It is possible that Sylvie's distance from the data offered her a different perspective that allowed her to see the overall pattern of the data in a new way. Her framework represented a more commonsensical, phenomenological (rather than theory-based) rendition of the data set. Not only could it accommodate most codes well but it stayed very close to the comments of respondents as we were reading and understanding them. This framework divided the comments into three groupings: (1) immediate reactions to Amendment 2; (2) the cognitive processes that LGBs used to make sense of the amendment; and (3) factors related to risk, resilience, and recovery. Any code might include aspects of immediate effects, efforts at meaning making, and/or factors related to risk, resilience, and recovery. The three categories offered a structure for understanding the data without forcing them into any theoretical system, such as trauma or grief. At the same time, the relevant theoretical literature could be invoked to illuminate any of the three divisions within a code. A brief description of these three dimensions follows.

*(1) Immediate reactions to Amendment 2.* The comments in this division of the data were characterized by an immediacy and an emotional charge. As a group, they illustrated how people often think and talk in the midst of great distress. The language of many statements in this division was harsh, while other comments had a disturbingly poignant tone. Typically, these initial reactions were brief and affectively sharp; they made little or no effort to make sense of what had happened. When coders referred in their narratives to comments that evoked a strong response on their part, they were frequently referring to LGBs' immediate reactions to the passage of Amendment 2.

*(2) Meaning making.* In contrast to immediate reactions, the meaning making comments were focused on respondents' efforts to make sense of Amendment 2. In the broadest sense, of course, the entire data set reflected LGBs' attempts to understand Amendment 2 in all its personal and sociopolitical ramifications. Within the domain of the meaning-making division, as we employed it, the focus was on the specifically cognitive aspect of dealing with a highly disturbing event. In this division, we were interested in individual LGBs' efforts to get beyond their immediate reaction to the situation and to reformulate a view of reality that could account for Amendment 2 and its effects and, at the same time, offer them a view of the world that was not entirely threatening.

The data that fell into these categories revealed a remarkable variety of efforts to make sense of Amendment 2 and its effects on respondents. As in any response to a disruptive situation, a given individual's meaning making will have more or less adaptive or functional value. The individual is juggling competing considerations: the need to appraise the external world with as little distortion as possible on the one hand, and the need to feel that one can act on one's own behalf and still remain as safe as possible on the other.

*(3) Risk, resilience, and recovery.* This final division of the data concerned those factors that appeared to influence how effectively Colorado LGBs dealt with and recovered from the negative effects of the campaign for and passage of Amendment 2. As the name of this data division suggests, some types of responses and external circumstances were especially problematic for LGBs while others seemed to insulate them

against negative consequences and/or helped them to recover from a negative impact. One code is especially relevant in this division; the RE-COVER code contained comments in which LGBs specifically identified factors that helped them regain their equilibrium in the aftermath of the election. As we see in chapter 8, RECOVER, like so many of the codes, was more complex than we anticipated when we defined it.

## The Codes

As we move into an exposition of the codes that the team devised, it is important to recall briefly the context described in chapter 1. Amendment 2's passage represented the end of an acrimonious campaign. During the year-long campaign preceding the election, LGBs had been objectified and vilified, and countless distortions had gone virtually unchallenged. Public figures in the state had been split on the amendment, and the support that did exist was inadequate to overcome the intersection of the anti-gay campaign rhetoric and long-standing, if sometimes unstated, homophobia and heterosexism. The quantifiable effect was an election result in which 53.4 percent of the voters in a general election essentially endorsed the opportunity to discriminate against lesbians, gay men, and bisexuals.

We were less interested in those statistics than in the psychological impact of the vote. This is what we sought to explore in our coding. Each code represented a significant theme in our analysis of the comments by participants in the study. In what follows, we will consider several aspects of each code. We will look at how our team defined the code, and also examine various dimensions of each code as we came to understand them over time. Three of these dimensions fall within the divisions noted above: immediate effects; meaning making; and risk, resilience, and recovery. However, these dimensions will not be used for every code. Rather than forcing the code to fit a preformed structure, the discussion will follow the phenomenology of the comments as much as possible. In some cases, I will make reference to the relevant theoretical and research literature. More importantly, the codes will be illustrated by letting the gay, bisexual, and lesbian respondents to the survey speak for themselves. Direct quotations from the data are presented in italics. In addition, respondents' descriptions of their personal demographics—especially of sexual orientation and race and ethnicity—will be presented in their own language. Doing so is predicated on the belief that people need to have the fundamental power to name themselves and that the way people name themselves may convey valuable information about their perception of themselves and their world.

A comment is warranted about the order of the presentation of the codes. Broadly speaking, the order reflects two considerations. First, it *generally* reflects their most common sequence in the experience of people who have gone through a crisis. Having said this, it is important to say that, in fact, people in crisis manifest no particular order and there certainly is no "right" or "appropriate" sequence. The second consideration has to do with the degree to which the three divisions—immediate reactions, meaning making, and risk, resilience, and recovery—are relevant to the phenomenology associated with a code. *In general,* the codes proceed from more immediate reactions to those that entail significant meaning making to those involving relatively greater considerations of recovery. However, I want to underscore that the two considerations noted here are broad and inexact. The order as a whole is neither indicative of a linear sequence of responses to the election nor of the importance of the codes.

Relatedly, the exposition of codes should not be read as a "model," "synthesis," or "conclusion" about the psychological consequences of Amendment 2 on LGBs in Colorado. Each code is a theme derived from the data. In contrast to some research methodologies that effectively summarize all the data (or the "average" response), the desired outcome in this qualitative study is a rendering of important themes, any of which may be relevant to other instances of anti-gay political activities and none of which has the final say about how the election affected gay people. Here, as in qualitative research in general, the aim is not to distill a typical or average set of experiences related to Amendment 2 but to depict the diversity of LGB responses to the amendment.

## Response Codes: I

### SHOCK

The SHOCK code referred to the deep sense of surprise and dismay that many LGBs experienced in reaction to the election outcome. Comments in this code encompassed elements of immediate reactions, meaning making, and risk, resilience, and recovery. The language of the SHOCK code tended to be affectively strong and to convey a sudden and pro-found realization of the kind that shakes a person's world. In fact, for many, SHOCK indicated that they had been forced to reappraise them-selves and their place in the world. At worst, the shocked state signaled a person's entry into a full-blown traumatic response. Even in the absence of meaning making (which typically comes later), SHOCK carried an implicit recognition that something that the individual had understood and accepted had been profoundly challenged. SHOCK represented the edge at which assumptions about the self and the world were shattered (Janoff-Bulman 1992).

*SHOCK as an immediate reaction.* Participants in the study used a variety of linguistic expressions to convey SHOCK, including *appalled, shocked, stunned, astounded, blown away,* and *dumbfounded.* LGBs made use of fa-miliar metaphors to communicate the forcefulness of their surprise; they compared the passage of Amendment 2 to "a slap in the face" and to get-ting "hit by a Mack truck." In most cases, the shock related to the unex-pected passage of Amendment 2. In far fewer instances, respondents coun-terbalanced their reaction to the election with another unexpected—and often positive—observation. One person, for example, wrote: *Some feeling of surprise both at the amount of virulent homophobia, as well as surprise at some of the heterosexuals who support gay rights.*

*SHOCK and meaning making.* The language of SHOCK inherently sug-gests that one's view of self and/or others and/or the world has been forcibly altered. One reaction to that forcible change is denial. The fol-lowing respondent, a 37-year-old white lesbian from Colorado Springs, looked at her own denial: *At first after the election I felt a great sense of de-nial—don't talk about it, don't acknowledge the pain and disbelief. I avoided discussions with all friends about it. I am processing it better now.*

For some LGBs in the survey, allowing the fact of and feelings associ-ated with Amendment 2 to surface gave rise to a new and deeper under-standing of themselves. One respondent, a gay man in his thirties, wrote: *I was very naïve before—almost childlike in my faith in understanding and equality. There are no stars in my eyes anymore. Voters say they don't hate me, but a year's worth of hate proves them wrong. I will carry this hurt for a life-time. After the vote, a friend said I looked older.*

For others, the forced change in perspective had to do with the way the world and its people looked different. One woman reported: *I felt I had been living in a dream world after the election. I was shocked at the hatred and violence people felt toward gays and lesbians. I really thought the issue was more resolved and that only a small fringe of right-wing religious really objected to gay rights.* A 34-year-old Hispanic gay man wrote: *I think that there are a lot more people out there that do not understand or like homosexuals than I believed previously. I am more awake and sensitive about being homosexual. I wish that individuality rather than sexual orientation was more important to heterosexuals.* These descriptions of an increased understanding of what one respondent called the *extent of homophobia among [the] "grass-roots" population* overlapped considerably with the code GRASP, which indicated a new comprehension of homophobia, and which we discuss later. Interestingly, SHOCK was also frequently cross-coded with REGRET, in which participants expressed their regret at not having worked harder—or sometimes not worked at all—to defeat Amendment 2.

SHOCK was one of the codes we used most frequently in analyzing the data. At one level, this is hardly surprising given that polls taken prior to the election had indicated that Amendment 2 would not pass (Finley 1992; Zeman and Meyer 1992). However, the fact that the passage of Amendment 2 shocked so many LGB Coloradans speaks to other considerations as well. Ronnie Janoff-Bulman (1992), in her extensive review of studies related to the cognitive substrates of trauma, points out that there is a high degree of resistance to changing—and even to questioning—basic assumptions about reality. Janoff-Bulman goes on to discuss three basic assumptions that most people carry with them. The first, that the world is benevolent, was shaken by the experiences of the campaign and the election. As long as LGBs could take comfort in the preelection polls and assume that CFV was a fringe group, they could hold on to the belief that the world in general was benevolent. But once the amendment passed, LGBs were forced to acknowledge that CFV's campaign rhetoric had been persuasive for a majority of the voters. Moreover, it was clear that the voters saw fit effectively to legalize discrimination against LGBs. Given the direct contradiction between these acknowledgments and the assumption of a benevolent world, the frequency with which we saw the SHOCK code in the data became understandable.

The second core assumption, according to Janoff-Bulman, is that the world is meaningful. A meaningful world is one in which there is a relationship between what people do and what happens to them. Put another way, in a meaningful world negative things happen only to people who are bad, and only positive things happen to good people. The experience of Amendment 2 challenged Colorado LGBs' assumption that the world was meaningful. On the one hand, LGBs were lied about and vilified—certainly bad things; they were regarded as bad, immoral, and dirty by much of the campaign rhetoric. On the other hand, CFV, which disseminated the distortions about LGBs and worked to legalize discrimination, was rewarded with a victory at the polls—a seemingly positive consequence for such negative acts. Again, the contradictory nature of these two events contributed to the frequency with which LGBs were shocked by the election outcome.

The final basic assumption in Janoff-Bulman's typology is the belief in oneself as worthy. This understanding encompasses a view of oneself as "good, capable, and moral" (Janoff-Bulman 1992:11). These and other dimensions of self-worth were challenged for many LGBs by the campaign and election. They had been told they were bad and not deserving of basic human rights; many LGBs were in pain and afraid; none had been capable of countering CFV's anti-gay attacks sufficiently to defeat the amendment.

Thus, one way of understanding how shocked LGBs were by the election is to realize that many of their experiences during the campaign and election directly interfered with their ability to maintain a firm grasp on a sense of the world as benevolent and meaningful and of themselves as worthy. Another level at which the success of the amendment contested their view of the world had to do with misperceptions about how much and how pervasively homophobia and heterosexism existed in their world. We will discuss this issue more extensively when we focus on the GRASP code.

*SHOCK and risk, resilience, and recovery.* By definition, shock is the first step in the process of responding to unexpected events. As such, the content of an initially shocked reaction may foreshadow areas which an individual will need to review when engaging in meaning making later on. The degree of shock and the pervasiveness of the beliefs that were challenged by the amendment might serve as a clue as to how psychologically disruptive the experience might be for a particular person. In general, it seems plausible that the greater the shock, the greater the disruption. However, many other factors are involved in a person's response to a surprising and negative event. Expecting the worst does not automatically offer protection against distress. As one lesbian resident of Colorado Springs wrote: *I was surprised at how depressed I was by the outcome. I thought I was steeled to losing, but found the actual results devastating.*

## OVER

The OVER code was used to indicate explicit or implied references to feeling overwhelmed or devastated by the Amendment 2 experience. While comments coded OVER sometimes carried a measure of surprise, they went beyond the SHOCK comments in terms of their intensity and their references to debilitating effects on the person. We used this code when respondents seemed to be overwhelmed to the point where their ability to draw on their internal or external resources, to make meaning, or to engage in productive problem solving was either limited or entirely absent. In most of the OVER comments, this extreme state was referred to in temporary terms. In a smaller number, the state seemed more enduring.

*OVER as an immediate reaction.* The immediacy and emotional charge in the language of the OVER comments were somewhat similar to the language of the SHOCK comments. Among the descriptors were *powerless, outnumbered, devastated, demoralized, blown away, sick to death, overloaded, and fatigued,* and, of course, *overwhelmed.* Respondents also spoke of being *burned out, too exhausted to get into it, too intense at times, worn down and tired,* and *tired of justifying my existence.* One word that came up frequently in these overwhelmed comments was *rejected.*

*OVER and meaning making.* As we look at the subthemes in the OVER code we begin to see how some LGBs experienced Amendment 2, especially in the early postelection days. Comments in this code were characterized by a profound sense of powerlessness. The following two comments by white gay men are emblematic of this powerlessness. The first was by a 25-year-old from Fort Collins: *After the amendment passed, I felt like it was me against the world, and that was a pretty unfair competition.* The other was a 40-year-old from Denver: *Often completely powerless re:*

*Amendment 2. I feel we're outnumbered and I often feel that no matter what we say in our defense, people won't believe us. I feel that the proponents of Amendment 2 have "tunnel" vision and refused to see it any other way than as a "special rights" issue.*

The powerlessness that some LGBs felt in relation to Amendment 2 was evidenced by the frequency with which they invoked death imagery in their comments. One 34-year-old lesbian Indian from rural Colorado said: *People will die. . . . What is the value of life? How do you bring someone back when a wrong is committed?* One gay man from Colorado Springs made reference to the suicide of another gay man in his city just after the election: *It was a physical blow. I knew Marty Booker, saw him two days before the election, he committed suicide because of election. I switched my phone message machine to screen calls, and would not answer the door unless I got a call first. I had an increasing sense of dread, by mid-December I felt overpowered by dread. I had to leave. Just before Christmas, I left Colorado to spend the winter in Florida. At the New Mexico state line I felt a great weight released . . . I put my property up for sale in December. When it sells, I will leave Colorado as I do not want the stress of being gay in Colorado.*

The depth of powerlessness and dejection in the comments coded OVER apparently generated varying degrees of impaired functioning in some LGBs. One white lesbian in her midthirties in the Denver metropolitan area described a sense of powerlessness and inefficacy that continued for weeks after the election: *[My partner and I] were devastated with the Amendment 2 passing. We totally were in shock—could not function for about three days. I am a faculty member at [a university] and students came in to talk—papers I was supposed to grade piled up—I couldn't get any work done—I was like a zombie. I went to work but felt like nothing ever was accomplished. I was not able to get my priorities set. Everything was too huge to do. I was constantly late, I was constantly fatigued, I was constantly overwhelmed, I did not call friends, I did not write Xmas cards. I was alone and isolated.*

Another woman, an Anglo lesbian from the western part of the state, detailed her own overwhelmed response to her daughter's efforts at problem solving: *I was devastated after the election and could not go to work the next day—I rarely miss a day of work. I just couldn't stop crying and have never felt so devalued. I felt as though my citizenship had been revoked. My/our seven year-old daughter just panicked listening to the election re-*

*sults*—*"What are we going to do? You could say you are sisters and one of you was married so you have different names."* It broke my heart that a child would even need to consider such things. But, of course, a child does have to consider such things when her mother has been devastated.

*OVER and risk, resilience, and recovery.* Even as some of the LGBs in the study were struggling in the aftermath of the election, the comments offered some clues as to what was and was not helpful. One of the responses that did not seem helpful was internalizing the messages of the CFV campaign. For some, the internalized message was quite specific and drew directly from campaign rhetoric. For example, one 38-year-old white gay man in Denver wrote: *Amendment 2 was like a communal punch in the stomach. During the first week, I was devastated—as were all of us—that we are not deserving of protection from discrimination.* This comment was striking in that its author did not distinguish between what the vote said and his broader conclusion that LGBs generally were not deserving of protection against discrimination. It was difficult enough to acknowledge that a majority of Colorado voters in this election were willing to permit anti-LGB discrimination; but it was much worse to conclude that anti-gay discrimination was acceptable—with no qualification as to who subscribed to such a belief.

The internalization of anti-gay rhetoric occurred in much broader forms, as when a homosexual white man in his early thirties from Durango wrote: *The outcome of the election confirmed every bad thought that I ever had about myself. I feel certain now that there is really no hope for humankind and we will all (humankind) die in a nuclear holocaust. No doubt.* The catastrophic nature of having all his bad thoughts about himself confirmed apparently led almost inexorably to the notion that a nuclear holocaust was inevitable.

Just as a nuclear holocaust is not something over which most people have any hope of control, the same can be said for other kinds of fears voiced by respondents whose comments were coded OVER. One 35-year-old bisexual man wrote: *Immediately after vote results, felt some sense of formless threat, unreality as I moved through Boulder streets.* It was equally difficult to respond to the threat embodied in this 32-year-old gay man's understanding of the problem: *The biggest reaction I had was an overwhelming sense of dread and sadness. I just kept thinking, wherever I go, the*

*majority of people hate me, even though they don't even know me. The major-*
*ity of people I run into today hate me, are scared of me. I almost couldn't leave*
*my house, the feeling was so strong.*

Both the impersonal quality of the fear expressed in the first response and its personalization in the second one seemed to engender a kind of paralysis. These comments stood in contrast to ones in which the writers were able to distance themselves from the problem through analysis, thereby also seeing the problem in specific (and thus presumably more manageable) terms. We discuss this sort of analysis more extensively when we refer to the GRASP code. The following comment came from a 50-year-old white lesbian who identified the problem of homophobia and heterosexism but without thoroughly personalizing it nor entirely escaping the sense of being overwhelmed. *I feel "family values" have become code words for prejudice, conformity, hatred, intolerance, and injustice; and I am totally and completely tired of the issue, the debate, the protest, and the position of challenge, protest, and defense that is expected as a lesbian. I really would prefer not to have it in my face most every day, I would die for my rights but I don't want to live each day as a warrior over them.*

Overwhelmed individuals also seemed to become paralyzed by focusing on things over which they had no control rather than on areas where they did. The extent to which the former can leave one feeling trapped was exemplified in this dilemma described by a gay man: *I hate feeling like the supporters of [Amendment] 2 have the upper hand. If we act out of anger or fear they will point and say "See how they behave," on the other hand if we do nothing they are still getting what they want—for us to remain in the background, out of sight, out of mind. Trying to reason with them doesn't seem possible either because they are reacting to their fears and myths about homosexuality.*

With dilemmas of this sort and the paralysis that results, it is hardly surprising that some overwhelmed individuals saw withdrawal as their only reasonable course of action. For some, this meant literally leaving the state, as we saw in the example of the man from Colorado Springs. For others, withdrawal was less absolute, but no less compelling or attractive a choice. The following comment also came from Colorado Springs, from a 21-year-old lesbian: *When the Amendment first passed I responded with shock, anger, disbelief, and intense work on the issue. I felt the world crash. Since then I have been losing the energy to fight this thing. The larger issue is homophobia and it's looming ever larger. I feel the need to withdraw from all this political mayhem but still feel the need for a sense of community. Because of Amendment 2, I feel hate and fear directed against me personally. I feel very out of synch with the mainstream.*

Across the state, in Rifle, another lesbian voiced her need to withdraw: *I am so tired of all the negative stories, editorials, and television blurbs about gays and lesbians. It seems as if I am constantly bombarded everywhere I turn with "how sick, immoral, and dangerous" gays and lesbians are. I'm worn down and tired. I've quit watching any television programs about gays and lesbians because I end up angry and depressed (same with newspaper and magazines).*

Some LGBs who were overwhelmed by the election and the events surrounding it found ways out of their desperation. Sometimes the way out came in the form of external intervention, often through support from family members, an issue we explore further with the FAMS (for family support) code. For the aforementioned faculty member whose work was impeded in the election's aftermath, the external encouragement came from a very different source: *The best thing was that right after the election our landlord called and in his own way said he was sorry about the results of the election and we don't have to worry about being kicked out. We were very worried about that.* The injunction against the enactment of Amendment 2 by a District Court judge on January 15, 1993 (M. Gallagher 1994) brought great comfort to many LGBs and, to varying degrees, helped them out of their desperation. The meaning that LGBs in our study gave to the injunction is explored in the discussion of the JUD code in chapter 8.

Another avenue opened up when LGBs took more active personal control over their lives. For some, this involved intentionally attenuating the psychological overstimulation caused by the political situation. A Fort Collins man described his efforts to counter the "chaotic" aftermath of the election: *In mid-December, I checked out and crashed at friends in the mountains to detox: no newspapers, no media appearances, no meetings; we banned A2 talk and conversation! By mid-January, I was starting to feel alive again. I still fatigue politically fairly quickly, and am cautious of both the media and "well meaning" liberal straights, I'm willing to slowly re-engage in the process!* A less systematic effort to counter the overwhelming nature of his experience was made by this 19-year-old homosexual male: *I feel so burned out about Amendment 2. I have really withdrawn a lot of the work that I used to put in down in Colorado Springs. But I feel good just taking some time to relax and spend time with my boyfriend. I am starting to feel like a person once again—and not like a machine. The injunction was great news! I still put in my share of work, but over all of this mess I have finally learned to just relax and enjoy any quiet time I have with myself and my boyfriend.*

One final positive step respondents took to deal with their overwhelmed reactions to the amendment was to personally acknowledge manifestations of their own internalized homophobia that had been awakened or exacerbated by the election. The next comment, in which a Denver lesbian in her midthirties forcefully described the overwhelmed experience, also touched on areas over which she could take some control, although it was not a simple or easy task: *I want it to be over. I want to be asleep for the next twenty years while this is all getting ironed out. Many of my decisions are being affected—where to live, whether to have children, to stay self-employed or not, look for "regular" job—but where? Everything feels affected—all of the old unresolved shame about being different has surfaced—about not fitting in—no matter how hard we try—or how honest we are with ourselves, our community, our neighborhood. (Scream here.)* This comment had much of the overwhelmed quality, but it also held out the promise that it is within one's power to change things, given introspection and insight. The significance of this observation will become clearer as we develop the story of Amendment 2's effects on our respondents in subsequent codes.

## *AG*

The AG code referred to a generalized anger expressed by some LGB respondents. This code stood in contrast to seven other codes in which anger was targeted against something or someone in particular. In AG, typically there was no identified target; the anger seemed more global in nature and lacking in focus. In addition, the AG comments were characterized by less meaning making than were the anger codes that pinpointed specific targets.

Significant subthemes in the AG code corresponded to issues about which LGBs were angry. These issues included feeling betrayed; being lied about; feeling powerless, tired, and let down; feeling defeated by the majority; feeling frustrated; and wanting to fight back. The code had a striking number of scatological references, perhaps not surprising as an expression of anger that was ill-focused and fueled by frustration.

*AG and meaning making.* One of the most vexing dilemmas for the respondents was what to do with anger that resulted from their having been outnumbered by voters whose opinion not only differed from their own but felt demeaning and even dangerous to them. One mode of venting that anger was through the use of insults directed toward those voters. One 31-year-old lesbian from a rural area criticized society in general: *Depressed, surprised that it had passed, frustrated with how stupid society is to think gays choose to be gay. Frustrated with a society that cannot comprehend that gays are from all backgrounds and walks of life. We are born and raised in small rural areas as well as large cities. They (society) do not realize we are their children, brothers/sisters, friends and neighbors and coworkers.*

A 54-year-old lesbian described her efforts to work with anger in this way: *Immediately after the election and for about a week thereafter I froze, then experienced extreme anger. Finally found the way to become active which best suited my talents and personality, and since then, although frequently tired from doing so much, am much better able to handle the effects of Amendment 2. It was fortunate that I did not run across some militant group; my anger was so intense I could very well have done something dangerous and stupid with little urging. I still look about me and realize one out of four voted against us, and despise them for it, but the nearly overwhelming anger has cooled. Somewhat. (They're still a bunch of hetbreederassholes, though).*

This statement was one of several that contained thoughts of violence. Some LGBs identified such impulses in very personal ways. One Hispanic homosexual man said he was *walking around with a chip on [his] shoulder* and, though he *hated to admit it*, he seemed *to be looking for a fight.* Other participants' violent impulses were stated in broader terms. One woman described her reaction after leaving the gathering where she learned the amendment had passed: *I wanted to see a riot except that seemed irresponsible.* A gay man in his forties described his violent impulses in the context of a more general anger: *I find it hard to discuss this issue like at work, because I find myself getting extremely upset. My first response to the passage of Amendment 2 was to go overturn and burn every cop car like they did in San Francisco. I still find myself having violent reactions toward people who supported Amendment 2 like [a spokes-woman for CFV who lived in his town]. Because I prefer that my sexual orientation not be open, it's hard to suppress the anger and hard to figure out what to do.*

Despite these avowals of a violent impulse, no actual act of violence was reported. One man made a point of distinguishing between impulse and act in his comment: *Since [date of election], an almost chronic feeling of rage and betrayal by the community at large. This includes frequent thoughts—but not intentions—of acts of violence toward the bigots who perpetrated this.* The most explicit act of hostility reported by a respondent came from a gay man in Denver. In fact, it was not coded AG but ACFV (for anger at CFV). I include it here because of its relevance to the impulse-action link: *I was depressed the night of Amendment 2's passage, but the next morning I called up CFV, got their answering machine, left a blistering angry message, and got over it.*

In contrast to the direct relationship between the angry impulse and the hostile act in this example, much of the global anger expressed by partici-pants seemed to go nowhere; at least it went to no external place. One woman wrote of spending *a lot of mental time writing letters to the editor in my head, holding imaginary debates, etc.* A man described *periods of ob-sessional worry, "need" to write to respond to every homophobic letter in news-papers (didn't beyond a point though).* Much of the anger described in the AG code was of this sort: ruminative, often unspoken, usually not enacted. The language of this unfocused anger was more passive than that associ-ated with most forms of anger, as for example, when one 24-year-old bi-sexual woman's entire comment consisted of this simple sentence: *I find myself feeling angry.*

*AG and risk, resilience, and recovery.* While much AG anger was character-ized by an unproductive quality, some respondents were able to make im-portant connections for themselves in the midst of their anger. One bisex-ual woman in her twenties described a series of reactions that showed her increasing insight into herself and her social situation accompanied by in-creasing anger: *My response to having my basic rights protected by some is gratitude. Kind of like a starving dog being thrown a bone. And then I get mad—why should I feel gratitude toward those who believe I'm a person who deserves to have these rights?* A Jewish lesbian in her thirties had a parallel reaction to the injunction against Amendment 2: *The injunction felt great on one hand, yet on the other I still felt like shit because here were all these people having to work so hard so some straight white man could "grant" us an injunction. I'm angry because I'm supposed to be "happy" and "hopeful" from a crumb.*

For some respondents, the postelection anger was of sufficient intensity to warrant their seeking professional help. One 24-year-old white homosexual man from Fort Collins reported: *I sought psychotherapy because I have all this indirect anger concerning #2. I found I was often anxious and on edge, and I'd often lash out (verbally) at the slightest provocation. All my feelings seemed so intense and out of control.* Some LGBs used the anger associated with the amendment to positive therapeutic ends. A lesbian in her forties reported: *The therapy I am currently doing is primarily concerned with relationship and incest issues, however, we have spent some time dealing with my reactions to the Amendment 2 nonsense. . . . My response to Amendment 2 of anger and rage has in some odd ways helped me face and deal with my incest experience and my own internalized homophobia.*

This woman certainly was not alone in seeing the relationship between Amendment 2 and a negative prior experience. A Colorado Springs man in his early forties described how the election had affected him at a deeply personal level: *Alternately enraged and very depressed (suicidal). I hadn't ever been depressed at all in the previous five years, so my extreme reaction to Amendment 2 was startling. It resonated for me with childhood sexual victimization, there was the same feeling of injustice and powerlessness. After a month, the anger and depression ended and I was able to recommit my energies to fighting Amendment 2.* This man's comment exemplified the value of an individual's making connections between his or her own history and the present. From reading so many comments of this nature, our team observed that when LGBs drew clear connections between their reactions to the amendment and earlier experiences, their statements often ended on a positive note.

We saw a similar pattern with respect to participants' ability to draw connections between their personal rage at the election results and social analysis and/or a commitment to activism. A 41-year-old Anglo woman who lived in an unincorporated mountain area demonstrated this connection between her activism and her being out as a lesbian: *The result of Amendment 2 has strengthened me in my resolve to include gay/lesbian/bi issues in my continuing human rights work. Before, I was willing to focus on issues of racism and sexism and let homophobia sit on the back burner. I'm no longer willing to do that, I am now out virtually everywhere I go, and despite the (alternating) rage, anxiety, pain, [I] am feeling empowered by this.*

The theme of increased commitment to being open about sexual orientation occurred repeatedly in these comments. A 47-year-old lesbian in Grand Junction drew the following link between her anger and her decision to be more out: *I can't tell you exactly what happened to me when Amendment 2 passed, but I have taken a big step out of the closet. At first I was appalled, in shock. Then I became extremely angry. I used to just accept that I had to hide my life—that's the way it was. I can no longer do that. It is not okay to make people live in closets. . . . Grand Junction has found its gay community and I am part of it. I want more now than I ever dared hope for before Amendment 2.*

Predictably, there were LGBs whose desire to be more out was inhibited by personal and/or professional considerations. Dilemmas of this kind were often expressed in tandem with AG codes. A Boulder lesbian in her early thirties said: *I changed careers in 1990. My new career necessitated a return to "the closet." I have grown increasingly angry about the battle for equal rights for gays and lesbians, and frustrated that I must hide my sexuality and stay away from lesbian social and political events to keep my job and to be successful professionally.* A white homosexual man, also in his early thirties, wrote of the dilemma throughout his comment: *I am considered to be a very calm and objective individual. I cannot recall any issue that has angered me as does "Amendment 2." My desire to fight back openly is stifled by my fear of personal and professional loss. Unfortunately, I'm sure my feelings are shared by many gays and lesbians who do not fit the stereotypes and are assumed to be "straight" by those around them. I wish there were enough of us with "guts" to show the state that a gay man or woman is not what CFV would have you believe.*

In the absence of an ability to relate feelings about the election to a larger personal and/or political plan of action, LGBs who were globally angry sometimes found it difficult to move out of their anger. Such was the case with this 27-year-old gay man: *The reason I became more agitated and frustrated about this issue even after [the injunction] is simply the passage of time. Time in which it is okay for the gays of our community to be harassed, and bashed—with little or no recourse.* Not surprisingly, the perception that one was a target, of harassment or otherwise, also promoted fear, the subject of the next code.

## FEAR

Statements comprising the FEAR code varied widely. In the milder versions of FEAR, LGBs referred to themselves as being *on edge, uneasy, nervous*, and *not always comfortable*. Increased levels of fear were expressed in statements about *having to look over my shoulder* and *feeling paranoid*. In some cases, the fears were conveyed in far more serious terms: respondents reported *chilling fear* and being *scared to death*. In addition, some images of fear were iconic in nature. They followed familiar fear-inducing forms including, most prominently, *the Holocaust* and *Nazi Germany*. These images were often expected to speak for themselves; little or no explanation was given, and none was necessary.

*FEAR and meaning making.* As our team began to read the segments of the data we had coded as FEAR, we asked ourselves several questions. The first question was also the most obvious: what exactly do these participants fear? The responses to our query ranged over a vast territory. Some LGBs did not identify specific fears; rather, they spoke of fear in global terms. Among these were fears of *what might happen, of the future*, and of *future actions/reactions*. It was striking to us how unmanageable these global fears must have felt to participants. One can scarcely take measures to protect oneself if the source of one's fear cannot be identified.

Most FEAR-coded comments did mention specific objects of fear. LGBs in the study feared some of the very things that antidiscrimination ordinances were designed to prevent: loss of jobs, loss of housing, and discrimination generally. Many wrote that they feared being harassed. For many, the focus was physical harassment and assault; a far smaller number of respondents had psychologically based fears—being *demeaned* and being *rejected*, for example. As a coding team, we frequently had to remind ourselves that the psychological fears deserved as much credence as did the physically based ones. Even among our psychologically minded group, we risked minimizing the significance of fears of psychological damage in LGBs' lives.

It was striking to see the avenues through which the broadly social phenomenon of Amendment 2 had been transformed into an explicitly interpersonal phenomenon for some gay people. A number of LGB parents expressed fears about the effects of the amendment on their children. Similarly, some respondents were concerned about how it was impacting their partners. Some reported being afraid of their families of origin.

On the other hand, many respondents' fears were centered on the political sphere. There were numerous concerns about the power of the religious right, the degree of ignorance and mean-spiritedness in people, the apparent ease with which CFV had swayed the voters, and the pervasiveness of homophobia and heterosexism in the population. Some participants also voiced concerns about the LGB community, fearing that LGBs would *adopt extreme tactics, escalate tension,* and have a *low sense of community.*

Some participants in the study wrote of their struggle to define an appropriate or realistic level of fear. They reasoned that Amendment 2 had changed the climate but they couldn't be certain as to how much it had changed or precisely what the parameters of danger and safety were now. It seemed that the rules for determining rational outness (Bradford and Ryan 1987) had changed and it was no longer clear to LGBs what measures were necessary to protect themselves from danger. The change in climate, and the resulting confusion, were evident in this comment by a lesbian schoolteacher: *I work for Boulder Valley Public Schools and have felt safe and secure the past four years or so. I still am not concerned about my lesbianism becoming an issue within the school district, but am very concerned that it has become a topic of conversation and discrimination among students and parents (even though I don't discuss it with students and rarely with parents). I feel that I could lose my job due to the CFV backlash, despite the fact that I have had excellent performance evaluations. I have been called in by my principal to discuss what he perceives as victimization of me due to my sexual orientation; I do not feel victimized, however.* This teacher's response was different from that of other teachers in our study. In general, respondents who identified themselves as teachers were particularly fearful of the threat to their jobs in the aftermath of the election.

*FEAR and "OUT" codes.* When we examined the FEAR comments for broader trends, one of the most prominent themes to emerge was the connection between fear on the one hand, and being open about one's sexual orientation on the other—which we referred to as the fear-out connection. This theme came into play most especially with regard to the fear of physical harassment and assault. LGB individuals' risk of harassment and assault generally increases as their visibility as gay people increases. This relationship created a dilemma for many LGBs; there were realistic fears of assault if they were out. These fears were probably magnified for Colorado LGBs in the wake of Amendment 2, since the risk of harassment and assault increased for LGBs at that time. Certainly for this sample, the fears of the possible consequences of being out increased. (See Appendix C, Table IV.) With escalated fear and increased risk, the issue of being out became more of a dilemma than it had previously been for many LGBs. To complicate this issue further, paradoxically many LGBs were prompted to be even more open as a result of Amendment 2. Together, these reactions point to an intensification of conflict regarding being out, and practical difficulties in determining what constitutes "rational outness"—that is, being as out as possible and as closeted as necessary (Bradford and Ryan 1987).

*FEAR and COMM.* Related to the fear-out conflict was the issue of LGBs' access to LGB communities. A number of respondents indicated that they avoided LGB events due to fears of being harassed there and of having their sexual orientation discovered. Avoidance of the gay community often carries a heavy price for LGB people, especially when they are dealing with the stresses associated with anti-gay politics. The LGB community—or communities (see Bohan 1996)—provide a significant buffer against various stressors (Adam 1992; Dworkin and Kaufer 1995; Paul, Hays, and Coates 1995). When contact with the community becomes dangerous, LGBs may lose one of their most useful resources.

*FEAR and TRUST.* Another theme that emerged in this code was the relationship between FEAR and TRUST, a code that highlighted LGBs' sense that their trust in others had been violated. For many LGBs, increases in fear were secondary to their perception that they had been betrayed by heterosexuals, whether strangers, friends, or colleagues. A 41-year-old Denver lesbian commented on this relationship as follows: *I am shocked with what the vote turned out to be. I look at people in automobiles and know they'd probably harass me if they knew my orientation. My trust for heterosexual community has greatly decreased. I feel threatened by my own fear and the reality that 50+ percent of Colorado would discriminate against me and gay/lesbian/bisexual persons.*

The data suggested that the connection between mistrust and fear was especially strong when LGBs brought no sociopolitical analysis to bear on the situation. In the absence of an analysis of homophobia and heterosexism, LGBs ascribed the passage of Amendment 2 to their own heterosexual neighbors and personal contacts.

*Fear and risk, resilience, and recovery.* While fear can limit people's mobility and engagement with their world, it exacts a psychological cost as well. Some LGBs wrote that their fears made them feel that they did not have *enough guts* or even that they were *worthless*. Fear can also increase people's sense of being immobilized and powerless. For LGBs in Colorado after Amendment 2, fear sometimes became manifest in or engendered suspiciousness or hostility toward other LGBs. The link between fear and this intragroup hostility was usually not made by the respondents; rather, our team inferred the link from respondents' comments. Illustrative exceptions to that trend occur in the following two comments, both written by lesbians in their forties.

The first comment concerned tensions between out and closeted lesbians: *Have become increasingly aware of, disturbed by, angered by homophobia within the lesbian community. Have witnessed and experienced an increasing number of incidents of more closeted lesbians wanting more "out" lesbians to "be discrete," and the more "out" lesbians wanting the closeted lesbians to respect them for being as out as they want to be. Lots of survival related fear issues being exaggerated and tactlessly expressed.* The second comment also defined a root problem: *There has been a huge increase in homophobic behavior among this neighborhood of lesbians. Horizontal discrimination and oppression increased dramatically. Fear is the motivator and it's not pretty.*

One factor that seemed to have a positive impact in decreasing participants' fears—and, indeed, ameliorating many of their negative reactions to Amendment 2—was feeling supported by others, including both heterosexuals and other LGBs (see codes FAMS, SUPPORT, and COMM). In many of the comments, receiving support from others seemed to constitute a turning point or at the least to counterbalance troubled reactions. The interplay of fear and support, along with the fear-outness dilemma, were evident in the following comment made by a bisexual Asian American woman in her midtwenties: *I find the passage of Amendment 2 deeply troubling and frightening. Because the issue has taken on a more high profile, I have also become more open about being in a gay relationship. I have found that the openness brings a somewhat more open and deeper understanding on the part of others—it also often makes me feel very vulnerable. But I feel it is necessary to educate folks on who gay/lesbian/bisexual people really are. I do not regret becoming more open and involved—I only hope I do not suffer discriminatory consequences for it. I have found to my great happiness and relief, that so many heterosexual people find that my relationship is as valid as any other and that I am as much a "person" as they are. Suffice it to say that I have thus far been very encouraged and have shared my sexual orientation with those who are open— the tougher challenge comes when I share myself with those who are more likely to espouse the values of CFV!*

## SAD

The assignment of a comment or segment to SAD was based on expressions indicating a state of sadness and symptoms of depression. Not surprisingly, the two often occurred together. If we had taken Rob's advice and analyzed the codes on the basis of the relative weights of the computer output of each code, SAD would certainly have ranked near the top in terms of importance.

One could not read SAD statement after SAD statement and not be affected by the content. This was one of the times when working as a group helped us all to maintain our stamina in the face of what, at times, felt like nothing short of a collective heartache. Respondents described themselves as *devastated, discouraged, let down, disappointed, sickened, saddened, anguished, embarrassed*, and *heartbroken*. Some wrote of feeling *weary* and *weakened, dismayed* and *distressed, demoralized* and *discouraged*. One man from Castle Rock said he was *tired of justifying [his] existence*. A lesbian from Granby said she felt *drained of [her] creativity* and *robbed of [her] emotional well-being*. Some LGBs used the language of *depression* and *depressed* quite explicitly. Some of the depressive symptoms were: short-term memory loss, frequent teariness or crying, fatigue, trouble with concentration, irritability, anhedonia, and sexual dysfunction. Several LGBs also reported feeling suicidal in response to the election.

*SAD and meaning making.* Participants responding with SAD statements drew on powerful imagery in an effort to convey the effects of the campaign and election. One lesbian in her forties made a comparison with death: *It's like with a death. After the initial shock and funeral, no one thinks to note you're still in pain.* A 32-year-old gay man described his sense of victimization in these terms: *I have been attacked and mentally raped by CFV and the voters. The injunction reaffirms my belief in the rule of law, but doesn't erase the hurt—the scars.* A bisexual woman wrote that the amendment, along with the public reaction to the proposal to end the ban on gays in the military, *left an indelible mark.*

It was in the SAD code that LGB participants often revealed what the election had meant to them at a personal level. One lesbian felt as if her *citizenship had been revoked.* Another felt more like a *second-class citizen and unwelcome in Colorado.* A self-defined WASP wrote that she felt *very sad to think that I am so hated by the community in which I live.* A bisexual woman said she felt *less like [she] belong[ed].*

The statements contained in the SAD code seemed to exemplify the construct of shattered assumptions drawn from the literature on the cognitive substrates of trauma. The desire to see the world as a meaningful place (Janoff-Bulman 1992) where good is rewarded and evil is punished was violated by the passage of this amendment, which most LGBs viewed as unfair. More specifically, the election starkly contradicted what Lerner has called the "just world theory," the belief that the world is just and that people are treated fairly and in accordance with their actions (Lerner 1980; Lerner and Matthews 1967; Lerner and Simmons 1966). Many LGBs in the study specifically referred to being judged by people who did not know them. A 34-year-old Mexican American lesbian expressed her depression and an angry reaction to being judged by strangers as follows: *After amendment 2 passed I was very depressed and I'm still having difficulty retaining sexual interest in my partner of 5 years, which I attribute to those fucking Christians and their smear campaign. Don't they have anything better to do? What happened to saving souls? It's very disgruntling hearing that over half the people in this godforsaken state hate me, and don't even know me!*

For many, the assumption that strangers would give gay people a fair hearing was violated. A related assumption was that those who knew individual LGBs as decent and good people would treat gays well. Specifically, many Colorado LGBs assumed that people who knew them would reject an amendment based on misrepresentations of their qualities. Not only was this belief widespread during the campaign, but it held (and still holds) a prominent position in LGB political rhetoric extolling the merits of LGBs' coming out. Indeed it is not without empirical support. According to Herek, a variety of studies have "consistently shown that heterosexuals who report personal contact with gay men or lesbians express significantly more favorable attitudes toward gay people as a group than do heterosexuals who lack contact experiences" (Herek 1996:213–14).

However, this assumption—which we called the "if they know us, they will love us" assumption—was violated for many LGBs whose heterosexual family, friends, or colleagues voted for the amendment despite contacts with gay people. For many survey participants, this was a significant source of sadness. One woman from Grand Junction wrote: *It hurt to know that my vote in opposition to #2 was canceled out by members of my own family.* A 39-year-old lesbian from a rural town responded with pain and anger to the votes of coworkers. *Hard to realize that nice people I work with—who see me and know I'm a good person—voted yes and still wouldn't change their vote. Realized there is still an overwhelming stigma about our lifestyle—Just hurts so bad—People know I'm a lesbian yet still choose to believe we're somehow deviant—"different from normal people," so frustrating. I get angry.* One bisexual woman, also from a rural area, stated quite explicitly: *I no longer assume that people will come to accept me once they get to know me.*

In some cases, respondents generalized from the sadness associated with learning that friends, family, and/or strangers had voted for the amendment to much broader arenas. One respondent, after commenting on voters' hateful motives, declared: *My sense of the world as essentially a safe and beautiful place has been shaken to the core.* Another respondent spoke of feeling profound sadness and grief about the election and went on: *Incredible sadness for the state of the human race and the lack of compassion and understanding.* One participant concluded a statement about fearing *this Nazi mentality* with: *Overall, I have a general sense of hopelessness for the human race, and it saddens me.*

*SAD and risk, resilience, and recovery.* As with many other codes, SAD comments often included references to supportive acts made by heterosexuals. Apparently some LGB respondents interpreted these actions as a form of witnessing (Herman 1992). In such cases, LGBs had felt victimized by the campaign and election. When heterosexuals, who were not themselves targets of the amendment, took a stand against Amendment 2, LGBs often felt that their victimization had been acknowledged and even denounced by people outside the LGB community (see SUPPORT code). They felt supported and less isolated as a result of such witnessing, and probably felt less outnumbered and, therefore, less vulnerable as well. Some respondents with SAD aspects to their comments made note of witnessing by public figures, including Colorado Governor Roy Romer and Denver Mayor Wellington Webb. Others described witnessing by family members, friends, and colleagues. References to feeling witnessed were often the only bright spots in otherwise grim statements. This comment was made by a 34-year-old white lesbian who engaged in and felt empowered by extensive campaign work: *I have been devastated and demoralized by the passage of 2, and only slightly encouraged by the injunction. My family has surprised me with their support, but overall I feel very discouraged by the process.*

A related source of help for some LGBs was having contact with the LGB community. The multifaceted value of such contact is discussed in detail in the COMM code (for community) in chapter 8. For some, the fact that the LGB community organized was a direct antidote to depression: *I was surprised at how depressed I was by the outcome. I thought I was steeled to losing, but found the actual results devastating. The depression was bad until the glb community started to organize so much. So many people came out.* Some participants in the survey found that the act of coming out in particular served as an egress from sadness or depression. A 40-year-old Denver lesbian wrote: *The day after the election, I was definitely depressed. I felt as if I'd awakened to Nazi Germany. In the next few weeks, I experienced some fear but eventually I did begin to feel a sense of empowerment. I decided, as others have, that the best way to fight Amendment 2 is to be more open and to come out to more people—and I have.*

Often implicit in the decision to come out was the expectation that doing so would have some future impact. Focusing on the future was helpful to some study participants, allowing them to look beyond the painful reality of the present. As one respondent told us: *Most frightening and depressing days were, for me, one week prior to election day, election day and a few days after election day. Afterward, started focusing on future and on working positively toward better future.*

Many LGBs in the study seemed to be fighting against internalizing the negative messages about themselves that were promulgated by CFV and through media coverage of the election, among other things. Participants seemed to have varying degrees of awareness about the dangers of internalizing those negative messages. Some LGBs demonstrated very little distance between themselves and the homophobic campaign messages. A 24-year-old lesbian from a suburb of Denver, for example, stated: *[T]he biggest sense of helplessness/hopelessness I have is in relation to those [CFV] who would assume they know me—sexually and otherwise and with no respect to me, assume that I have chosen deviance to purposely "eat away" at the family institution. I also feel very displaced from the Colorado Gay and Lesbian Community as many of these people's actions have set us back, not thrust us forward. We cannot command respect as long as we cannot give it.* Her statement suggested that she had not challenged aspects of CFV's messages; she appeared to accept the description of her lesbianism as "deviance," and her observations about the gay community echoed CFV rhetoric.

Other LGBs were quite aware of the effort it took to refuse to internalize CFV's (and others') messages. This statement, by a 40-year-old lesbian from Denver, serves as an example: *I avoid reading the papers and exposing myself to people's ignorance. I used to be able to not know about people's homophobia because the subject didn't come up. Now that it does, it is very painful to hear all the horrible stuff. I find it extremely hard not to let it bring down my feelings of self worth.* One 30-year-old lesbian's struggle against internalizing CFV's message was evident in her comment: *I'm a good person. I've done a lot of work to be a good person. It is clear that CFV is trying to convince me I'm not okay. They are bigots. It is their loss. After this fight I hope their bigotry will be recognized. I'm hurt and angry. How can they think they're not hating? How can they believe what they believe?* While her comment ended on a note of some bewilderment, she had not moved at all from her position of knowing herself to be a good person. She located the source of her confusion in CFV rather than in LGBs, including herself. In so doing, she externalized the source of Amendment 2 problems, which appeared to be associated in the data with moving out of depression.

## LOSS

The code we designated as LOSS was closely related to the SAD code. While similar themes emerged in both, the LOSS code was more circumscribed. We used it to refer exclusively to statements about a specific loss as a result of the Amendment 2 experience. Comments in the LOSS code expressed grief in unmitigated terms.

*LOSS and immediate reactions.* Descriptions of loss do not usually arise immediately after a negative event. Although the feelings of loss may arise immediately, there is usually an interval—both of time and of meaning making—between the affective experience of loss and the cognitive process that transforms that experience into words of loss. It is one thing to know that an event or situation has evoked considerable pain; it is another to be able to say, in more precise terms, what the pain reflects and what it means. In the process of looking back on their experience in order to make sense of what they had lost, some respondents located the sense of loss in their immediate reactions to election day. A Glenwood Springs lesbian referred to her *evaporated, naïve faith in [her] neighbors.* A 32-year-old gay man from Boulder described his election night reaction in these stark terms: *I was shocked at the outcome. My 32 year love affair with Colorado died that night—a loss I'll never regain. The beauty of this state (which I often gain spiritual strength from) is smeared black by naked hate and bigotry.*

*LOSS and meaning making.* Specific descriptions of what had been lost as a result of the election were numerous and varied. The two most frequently mentioned were the loss of a sense of safety and the loss of a sense of home. With respect to the former, respondents identified a decrease in psychological as well as physical safety. One white lesbian from a Denver suburb explained her fears in the context of her privilege: *I'm in a very secure position—I own my own home, I'm in business with a good partner (not gay) who is supportive, I'm a partner in the business and it's one I'm fairly secure in—medicine. The passage of 2 brought fear home for one of the first times. I had never worried about being fire bombed or killed before.*

A 37-year-old homosexual man from Pueblo explicitly linked Amendment 2 and his fears of violence: *I go places now, with my friend(s) and find myself wondering if any homophobic person or group will now feel encouraged to harass me and/or my friends. I believe it is a disgrace that gay and lesbian people must live in fear for their physical safety. . . . Amendment 2 will allow and promote gay bashing, anytime, any place, anywhere.*

Perhaps it is not surprising that, fearing for their safety, many respondents also reported feeling displaced—a phenomenon to which we on the coding team referred as psychological homelessness. One gay man described *a sense that for me, personally, the social fabric is irrevocably torn.* A 61-year-old lesbian wrote that she *felt let down by [the] home state populace.* For some, the feeling of having lost a sense of home was rooted in relationships to specific groups rather than to Colorado and its people collectively. One respondent, after stating that the election had had a negative impact on his self-esteem, went on to discuss his work group: *It's frightening that with the debates related to Amendment 2 at the water fountain, etc., how many mean spirited persons there are. How can it not affect a person!*

Some participants attributed their loss of a relationship to a campaign that had heightened previously minor conflicts; people who had managed to get along formerly despite differences of opinion about gay rights could no longer escape a direct confrontation once the issue became polarized. One 31-year-old homosexual woman reported the *loss of a friendship with a straight coworker who voted yes* on the amendment. A 40-year-old lesbian described how her relationship with a business partner was affected: *My business partner and friend of seven years voted yes on 2. He's a fundamentalist Christian and pointed his finger at me and quoted the Bible. That was Thursday after election. The following Monday I moved my things out of the office and left. I lost all my clients.*

For some LGBs, Amendment 2 represented just one among a host of other losses. One respondent saw the election as the most recent negative LGB experience: *I think my major emotion has been one of loss, another one in the long list that gays, lesbians, and bisexuals experience in our lives.* Several explicitly compared this loss with that associated with death, including assertions that the loss was permanent in some respect.

*LOSS and risk, resilience, and recovery.* The LOSS code was notable in that it had few implications for risk and resilience. In reading all the comments in this section, we surmised that working with loss was an end in itself.

That observation is in keeping with the views of many students of trauma and grief who have emphasized the importance of mourning as a means of working through the loss and resuming life to the fullest (e.g., Herman 1992; Lifton 1980; Shatan 1973). One gay man observed some resistance among LGBs to mourning: *There was a subtle pressure among many gays and lesbians to look on the bright side of things and to feel optimistic about all the benefits that could happen. I didn't feel that it was okay to grieve the loss openly and even those who did discuss their grief did so quickly and then seemed to get over it. I felt a lot of denial as a community about what Amendment 2 really means.*

When the coding team read all the LOSS comments together, we noticed that they came from LGBs throughout the state with the exception of one city, Colorado Springs, where a large number of religious right groups, including CFV, were headquartered (Bull and Gallagher 1996; Gottlieb and Culver 1992; Lowe 1992). Many LGBs regarded Colorado Springs as a particularly difficult place for them to live. For LGBs in that city, Amendment 2 represented but a single stressor in a whole series of anti-gay phenomena, and at the time of the study LGBs in Colorado Springs were very much in the middle of an extremely anti-gay environment. One might have expected that LGB residents of the city would have experienced many losses. Thus, we were surprised by the absence of Colorado Springs LGBs from LOSS comments. For a putative explanation, we returned to the trauma and grief literature which suggests that one must have a sense of safety for the work of mourning to occur (e.g., Herman 1992). We wondered whether Colorado Springs felt so unsafe to its LGB residents that they were inhibited from acknowledging and making sense of their losses. Perhaps LGBs there had not been able to acquire the distance and the perspective necessary for them to mourn. We cannot know if our explanation is "accurate," but it is clearly consistent with other observations about Colorado Springs covered in chapter 7.

## TRUST

The TRUST code, which included statements indicating betrayal of trust, forcefully demonstrated the relational nature of the Amendment 2 campaign and vote. While many voters may have perceived the vote as an impersonal act, it was experienced as a deeply personal betrayal by some members of the target group. Comments bearing the TRUST code often embodied what might be heated statements yelled over backyard fences by neighbors who had once been friends but no longer would be. They spoke about relationships that had undergone a significant and negative change.

*TRUST and meaning making.* By far the most prominent focus of state-ments about changed relationships were heterosexuals, which made sense for several reasons. Heterosexuals were, socially speaking, the counterpart to the gay targets of Amendment 2; as LGBs became the focus of the amendment, so did heterosexuals become the focus of LGBs' resentment about their unfair treatment. The election infringed on the rights of LGBs and left heterosexuals' privileges not only intact but more explicit than be-fore. In addition, heterosexuals (and perhaps some LGBs) had voted for the amendment in numbers sufficient to ensure its passage. Finally, even heterosexuals who had not supported Amendment 2 had failed to prevent its passage. Thus, heterosexuals as a group were invoked in the TRUST code as the privileged, as the oppressors, and as failed witnesses.

Other groups—fundamentalist Christians, for example—could have been seen as privileged oppressors as well. Indeed, some respondents did implicate Christians in general as sources of oppression; however, that re-action surfaced far more often in the anger codes (which we examine in the next section) than in the TRUST code. Underlying the TRUST code was a sense of *personal* betrayal because a previously positive personal relation-ship had been damaged.

While a few respondents felt betrayed by Christians or by the state as an entity, most LGBs identified heterosexuals in general as their betrayers. The state, after all, was as abstract an entity as a collection of people. Close relationships with Christians, especially those identified with the religious right, could be avoided by many LGBs. But most respondents could not avoid encounters with heterosexuals. Moreover, most LGBs had hetero-sexuals in their lives whom they liked and loved. It was the presence (and loss) of those affective bonds that underlay the sense of betrayal described by so many participants.

Virtually all LGBs knew some heterosexuals well and had enjoyed preelection relationships with them. For many LGBs in the study, rela-tionships with heterosexuals were disrupted as a previous level of trust was challenged. In a few instances, respondents spoke of their mistrust of heterosexuals as applying to specific individuals or to members of small groups—of colleagues, for example. Most often, though, mistrust was expressed toward heterosexuals as a group. Our coding team noticed that when LGB respondents talked about heterosexuals as an amorphous and negative group, their descriptions appeared to parallel—or to counterattack—the stereotypical pejorative images of gay people presented during the campaign.

Two of the comments, given below, illustrate the changed nature of respondents' relationships with heterosexuals. A 41-year-old white lesbian offered this assessment: *I feel very suspicious of most straight people after the election because I realized "they" were not truthful in stating opinions when I did phone banking and because many were verbally abusive when I did campaign work near the polls or while holding a "No on 2" placard on election day.* A 45-year-old gay man was more blunt: *I feel like I can't trust heterosexuals to tell the truth—friends, family members, or anyone else. They are selfish, greedy, dishonest, and spiteful people.*

Some respondents were more modulated in their views of heterosexuals and seemed to struggle against the impulse to regard and treat all heterosexuals stereotypically. A homosexual Hispanic man reported that *I find myself constantly "analyzing" people and wondering or trying to guess how they voted. And based on what I believe to be their bigotry I also can develop animosity toward them without a real reason. I find myself uncomfortable around heterosexual people/situations or people/situations I believe to be heterosexual.* A white lesbian wrote: *I felt very let down by the straight people of the world—I was pretty indiscriminate about who let me down. I was very unsocial for weeks. Fuck them! was always in my head.*

The four comments quoted above locate the basis of mistrust of heterosexuals in heterosexual privilege and active oppression of gay people. Other statements held heterosexuals accountable for their failure to provide adequate witnessing for LGBs. A woman in her midforties illustrated such criticism: *I am deeply concerned about the lack of support from straight people who say they are in favor of Civil Rights for gays but seem not to be willing to act on their beliefs and give active support.*

*TRUST and risk, resilience, and recovery.* One of the difficulties associated with a breach of trust in any relationship is ambiguity as to the future of the relationship. Such ambiguity appeared to characterize relationships between LGBs and heterosexuals after Amendment 2. It was not easy for LGBs to decide how to proceed in the face of what had felt like a betrayal. Some respondents said they felt a need to evaluate their day-to-day encounters with other people; in particular, they did not know which heterosexuals to trust.

One gay white man from Boulder reported: *Increased suspicion of all strangers regarding homophobia. Anticipating hostility toward "stereotypical" heterosexual personality types.* A black homosexual man from Pueblo spoke of his reaction when he visited the next major city north, Colorado Springs: *Every time I'm in Colorado Springs and see a white, over-50 male looking at me, I wonder if he voted yes on Amendment 2 to oppress me. I don't like Colorado any more and plan to move away.* A young Latino gay man from Fort Collins wrote that, although he continued to be vocal in his opposition to Amendment 2, *I am also more worried and tend to be more careful than before. I catch myself feeling like people are talking about me when I pass them while wearing my pride buttons. Also, I feel like I'm looking over my shoulders, especially when walking alone, a lot more than before—even during the day.*

One arena in which the ambiguous nature of postelection relationships between gay people and heterosexuals was played out was in the decision to disclose sexual orientation. Even LGBs who had been comfortably out before the election encountered more internal conflict in maintaining their outness in the aftermath of Amendment 2. A 28-year-old, Native American/white lesbian from Denver who illustrated this conflict unambiguously concluded: *I am so far "out" I'm practically falling off the edge. I have never been frightened about being a lesbian. I've always known and been comfortable. But now I am uncomfortable. I think twice about who I come out to; I still come out to new acquaintances but I stress more about it. But this will not put me in a closet!*[2]

It is easy to imagine that LGBs who viewed heterosexuals collectively as untrustworthy felt outnumbered and unsafe. In reviewing the TRUST-coded comments, one means of moving out of the intense mistrust of heterosexuals seemed to be through an explicitly political analysis of Amendment 2—which corresponded to the GRASP code discussed in chapter 5. In the absence of a political analysis of the homophobia and heterosexism underlying Amendment 2, participants seemed more likely to view and respond to the election as a personal affront. A white homosexual man's comment illustrated this sort of response: *I really didn't think it would pass, and I was very upset and felt backstabbed personally, when it did.* Even a limited analysis of the amendment moved this Hispanic-Swedish lesbian toward a less stereotyped view of heterosexuals: *Worried that good people can buy into the fear perpetrated by causes/groups such as CFV.* While political analysis of the amendment certainly was no guarantee against LGBs feeling personally affronted by the election, it did seem to help them form a more heterogeneous picture of heterosexuals. This view of heterosexuals, in turn, allowed LGBs to see—and perhaps to welcome—the possibility of positive support and witnessing from truly supportive heterosexuals.

Our reviews of the TRUST code led us to another observation about the nature of the relationship between LGBs and heterosexuals during the campaign and after the election. This was a subtle observation and one that could easily be misconstrued. Therefore I must first state our team's unequivocal rejection of Amendment 2 and everything associated with it. That said, Amendment 2 was viewed in vastly different ways by LGBs and by those who voted for it. Our data indicated that LGBs saw the amendment in terms so deeply personal that I expect most pro-Amendment 2 heterosexuals would have serious doubts about the results described in this book. Many would wonder how LGBs could possibly have felt so personally injured by the campaign and election, which to them reflected nothing more than a question of protecting "equal rights."

As we discussed this disjunction of perceptions about Amendment 2, our coding team began to make sense of how different the two campaign messages were. The slogan adopted by EPOC, the organization heading the anti-Amendment 2 campaign, was the now familiar "Hate is not a family value." CFV's campaign slogan was "No special rights." The EPOC slogan spoke directly from the hearts of LGBs, who experienced the amendment in personally demeaning and destructive terms. In contrast, the CFV message was political, not personal, in nature. CFV's slogan was rooted in homophobia and heterosexism and its success owed much to the homophobia and heterosexism of voters. Bias and prejudice both underlay the votes in favor of Amendment 2 and influenced voters to ignore the nature of the message that their votes would convey to LGBs. The ability to ignore the personal and political implications of one's actions against a stigmatized group is one of the privileges of being a member of the dominant group (Batts 1989).

Nonetheless, personal antipathy toward LGBs—that is, hate as a family value—may not have been uppermost in the minds of most voters who endorsed Amendment 2 on election day. In effect, those who voted for the amendment could view their actions in purely political terms, thus denying that they were acting unfairly—despite LGBs' sense that the vote conveyed hatred.

That so many LGBs felt horribly betrayed by the vote is not surprising. Neither, however, is it surprising that many heterosexuals who voted for the amendment never understood why LGBs felt personally attacked. This disjunction alone may explain the intensity and pain that characterized so many comments in the TRUST code. In many respects, of course, this is another instance of one group's seeing another as "the other" (Batts 1989; Bullis and Bach 1996; Kitzinger and Wilkinson 1996; Staub 1993).

## INVAL

We used the INVAL code to designate statements by LGB respondents that invalidated, discounted, or minimized any negative effects from the campaign or election. Our coding team became interested in this theme because we wondered why some respondents, when offered the opportunity to comment on their reaction to Amendment 2, essentially said that they had no reaction.

*INVAL and meaning making.* In reading the limited number of comments that seemed to minimize the effects of Amendment 2, we encountered a range of rationales. Several LGBs indicated that other stressors—illnesses, financial problems, and dissolutions of relationships, for example—were causing them more significant distress than was Amendment 2. Several other respondents indicated that the amendment was just one in a series of oppressive challenges. One lesbian from Glenwood Springs wrote: *Amendment 2 concerns me—but it is not affecting my life a whole lot. I have always been concerned about discrimination—I have lost a job in the past in Iowa—and know that this Amendment is a real threat. Is it possible I have gotten used to this life? Yes, I believe so.* An unusual response came from a 27-year-old white gay man from Boulder: *It was not a priority issue for me in the election. If I was straight I'd have voted for it. No one should have special rights.*

In addition to these subthemes within INVAL, we made several other observations about the code. Generally, the comments in the INVAL code contained little or no affective expression; this stood out in a data set that on the whole was quite emotionally charged. These comments also contained a preponderance of externalizing references as opposed to internalizing ones—that is, INVAL comments typically focused on the world and on other people and considerably less on the respondents themselves.

In addition, INVAL comments frequently had a defensive tone—an understandable response when a person who felt unaffected by Amendment 2 encountered (and filled out) an eight-page survey largely focused on the amendment's negative effects. The introspection apparent in the comment (mentioned above) by the woman who wondered if she had grown accustomed to living in threatening circumstances was an exception to the externalizing tendency.

*INVAL and risk, resilience, and recovery.* One final quality about the INVAL code caught our interest: INVAL frequently occurred alongside codes signifying internalized homophobia (IH). While the IH code will be discussed more fully later (see chapter 6), one element of internalized oppression may be especially relevant to the INVAL code. Valerie Batts (1989), in a treatise on internalized racism, has postulated that one of the manifestations of internalized oppression is a "lack of understanding or minimization of the political significance of racial oppression" (1989:16). Some of the INVAL statements, especially those that were also coded IH, may have reflected a similar process; some LGBs refused to recognize the political significance of the amendment (that is, the homophobia underlying it) and therefore had limited reactions to it.

More broadly, how any individual LGB saw the election depended on virtually limitless factors. As a rule, we expect a range of cognitive appraisals of any given event; the spectrum of these appraisals for the same event may extend from benign to awful (see, e.g., Newberger and De Vos 1988). The meaning that a person gives to an event usually carries as much psychological weight as does the event itself. While some studies suggest that accurate cognitive appraisals help people manage stress (e.g., Beardslee 1989), the ability to maintain and utilize illusions (as seen in INVAL comments) often serves as a buffer against stress (e.g., Taylor 1983). The INVAL code, then, is a provocative invitation to further exploration.

Where an individual is especially resilient, we may be able to learn more about factors that promote resilience. In other cases, where the INVAL position reflects denial of a real phenomenon in LGB persons' worlds, this position could be dangerous in that it prevents LGBs from assessing potential threats realistically.

5

■ ■　■　■　　■　　■　　　■　　　■

# Efforts at Meaning Making

IN OUR EXPOSITION of major themes in the data thus far, we have
been focusing on codes in which participants have generally turned their
attention inward. Respondents have described their shock and betrayal,
their grief and sense of loss. In this chapter, the respondents direct their attention outward in an effort to understand the sources of the disruption
associated with the campaign and election, and pinpoint those who seem
to have been responsible.

## Anger Codes with Specific Targets

When we explored the AG code earlier, we saw that it portrayed immediate reactions that contained very little meaning making. We turn now
to six other codes that are angry in their orientation, but differ from the
AG code. Instead of being characterized by global and unfocused anger,
these codes identified the perpetrators of Amendment 2. The very act of
pinpointing a person or organization as responsible for a hurtful event
involves meaning making; the person who feels victimized is making an
effort to sort out the source of his or her victimization. The ability to
identify the perpetrator is often the first step toward reestablishing a
sense of safety.

The codes in this section identified six different entities as responsible for the passage of Amendment 2: (1) ACFV held Colorado for Family Values (CFV)—or sometimes the religious right more generally—responsible for the amendment. We included angry comments about particular individuals associated with CFV in this code; most frequently, that was Will Perkins, a Colorado Springs car dealer who was named as CFV's Executive Board Chairman in CFV literature. (2) The ACHRIST code included comments with angry content directed toward Christians in general or toward any subgroup of Christians (for example, fundamentalist Christians). (3) AHET was a code in which heterosexuals in general were the targets of anger. (4) In the AMEDIA code, anger was directed toward the media, usually in global terms and only occasionally focused on specific media outlets. (5) The APROC code included statements expressing anger about the process by which the campaign and election (but especially the former) were carried out by CFV. Finally, (6) ASTATE consisted of comments in which anger was focused on Colorado as a state and/or on Coloradans as a collection of people. One other anger code, AQ, in which anger was directed toward other LGBs, is not included in the present discussion. It is presented later in the context of codes representing LGBs' relationships with one another (chapter 6).

In looking at these six codes in which respondents directed their anger against specific people associated with Amendment 2, several general observations can be made. First, when anger was directed at CFV (a Christian-identified group) and at Christians in general (ACFV and ACHRIST, respectively), respondents' statements quite often included the language of good and evil, right and wrong, or love and hate. This was notably not the case when LGBs turned to heterosexuals, the media, the process of the campaign, or the state.[1] As we tried to make sense of this difference, we concluded that respondents seemed to be reacting to Christian-based arguments in a fashion that exactly paralleled those very notions. Specifically, LGBs saw Christianity and CFV (as a Christian-based organization)[2] as heavily emphasizing understandings of right and wrong and good and evil, and, indeed, some of the campaign literature used the language of right and wrong. Thus, when LGBs turned their anger on Christians and on CFV, they did so in a way that was strikingly consistent with the religious tenets of good and evil.[3]

The following comment by a 29-year-old Fort Collins lesbian illustrated this tendency for angry statements about Christians and CFV to mirror LGBs' perceptions of Christianity's basic attitude: *I feel genuine hatred for CFVers who continue to lie and distort statistical information. Any concept of organized religion makes me sick.* Another lesbian, a woman in her early fifties, seemed to suggest that the conflict between good and evil existed in herself as well as in the world: *I'm still very angry at CFV for the lies they wrote about us and how they got away with it, are still doing so. Love is the answer but their kind of what they call love is hypocrisy!*

The AHET (anger at heterosexuals) comments expressed the disappointment and betrayal that we saw in the TRUST comments relevant to heterosexuals, a personal disappointment that was not generally evident in the other anger codes. Anger toward heterosexuals was often stated in global terms and only occasionally directed toward specific people. This 31-year-old homosexual woman's comment contained both: *Some animosity toward heterosexuals. . . . Strained/loss of a friendship with a straight coworker who voted Yes.* The following Grand Junction lesbian's anger focused on her frustration at having to explain things to heterosexuals, an act which she viewed as care taking: *Blown away that there is still so much fear, ignorance and hate—but glad that it is being discussed openly—even though I am SICK TO DEATH of taking care of heterosexuals' fear, ignorance and hate. Explain, explain, explain. Are they ever going to just "get it" and then move on?*[4]

The ASTATE (anger at the state) code was striking for the number of sarcastic and disparaging remarks about Colorado and its residents. One homosexual man, for example, made this criticism: *Tremendous frustration over "special" rights thing. It's like the majority of Coloradans are brain dead. But I really wanted special rights! Close-in parking, etc.* The ASTATE comments often made references to what we described earlier as the sense of psychological homelessness. A 43-year-old lesbian expressed her anger in this fashion: *I think Colorado is a horrible place to live. It went from being beautiful to a sordid trash heap in my mind. I'm still thinking of moving away. Constitutionality of proposed laws are checked out in many other places, Why not here?*

The APROC (anger at the process) code contained, as its central feature, frustration at being powerless to change a consummately unfair situation, whose most obvious negative manifestation was the passage of a law that, if enacted, would have legalized discrimination against LGBs. More subtly, APROC statements suggested that the election had also damaged some respondents' sense of self-worth and self-efficacy.

A subset of the APROC comments concerned themselves with the unfairness of the campaign. Respondents were especially angry about CFV's "special rights" campaign slogan, CFV's simplistic emphasis on a "gay lifestyle," and the reduction of LGB orientations to sexuality and sexual expression. The most frequently cited basis of anger among APROC comments was the political situation in which the majority voted on the rights of the minority. One 25-year-old gay man wrote of it in these terms: *I also feel angry over the fact that basic rights are even voted upon. They should not be handed out on the pretense of being a privilege.* Comments about this aspect of the process often suggested that some respondents' anger was rooted in a perception of gross unfairness that violated the assumption of a "just world" (Lerner 1980).

AMEDIA-coded comments carried a special power. In contrast to the identification of CFV, Christians, heterosexuals, the campaign process, and/or the state as perpetrators, the anger reserved for the media was something of a surprise for our coding team. Several different views of the media emerged. Among other things, they were seen as the battleground where the fight over equal rights for LGBs was conducted. Belief in the power of media outlets was implicit in many of the AMEDIA comments. Some of the anger at the media derived from the perception that they had failed to provide adequate witnessing for LGBs. Specifically, some respondents charged that the media did not contradict erroneous and misleading information promulgated by CFV. In some comments, what began as anger at the media for their failure to witness gay people turned into anger for their having become a perpetrator, as in this statement by a bisexual woman: *I felt frustration that the media misrepresented the amendment and related issues (saying that it would prevent "special rights" rather than pointing out that it removes the right to sue for discrimination).*

*Anger codes and risk, resilience, and recovery.* One of the most obvious observations about the anger codes was the size of the entity perceived to be behind Amendment 2. CFV was a relatively small, religiously based political organization. Although it had ties to other radical right groups around the country, CFV was not menacingly large (even if it was clearly menacing). At another level, seeing all fundamentalist Christians as the source of one's political problems was different from seeing all Christians as the perpetrators.[5] At an even broader level, the view that the perpetrating entity for the election consisted of all heterosexuals or of all Coloradans enlarged the scope even further.

The perceived size of the perpetrator group has at least two consequences. The larger the perpetrator entity, the more outnumbered—and, likely, the more powerless—LGBs (or any other oppressed group) are likely to feel. In addition, LGBs' perceptions of the perpetrator entity could have influenced their ability to see and make use of allies—for example, the Christians who were against Amendment 2.[6] This constricted vision might also have contributed to a greater sense of powerlessness on the part of some gay people and inhibited LGBs' ability to receive support at both the interpersonal and political levels. In the extreme, this view interfered with their ability to build political coalitions.

In addition, at a process level, identifying perpetrators was important because such identification had important implications for (re)establishing safety. When people feel victimized, the perpetrator(s) often looks more powerful than is the case. Indeed, many of the participants viewed the perpetrators of Amendment 2 in extreme terms—testimony to how badly victimized they felt. This sense of victimization limited LGBs' ability to solve the problem, because it hindered them from making a clear and accurate appraisal of the perpetrator(s).

Another implication of making such an appraisal had to do with political analysis of Amendment 2, which enabled gay people to see that the problem resided in the homonegativity that characterizes much of society rather than in themselves. This analysis also allowed LGBs to see variations in the degree of homonegativity in a given person or situation, which in turn allowed them to appraise the parameters of their oppression more accurately, to feel less overwhelmed, and to identify potential sources of interpersonal and political support.

*Changing focus.* We can look to APROC and ASTATE for an illustration of how one's analysis affects what is seen and what its implications seem to be. Most of the comments coded ASTATE saw all inhabitants of Colorado as the agents of LGBs' victimization. This was a large group indeed. Identifying so large a group as the perpetrators was overwhelming and offered no solution about how to defend against such victimization. On the other hand, identifying the process of the campaign as the source of victimization (APROC) narrowed the scope of the perpetrator group and implicitly offered a means of countering the victimization—for example, by disallowing the votes of the majority about minority rights or by educating the public about gay peoples' experiences. None of these remedies guaranteed an end to victimization, of course, but taken together they offered LGBs something beyond the overwhelming feeling that the entire state was against them.

While our team saw differential advantages in the designation of perpetrator(s), angry responses to Amendment 2 were not necessarily negative. On the contrary, anger is a healthy response to the experience of violation, which is what Amendment 2 was for LGBs in Colorado. In addition, many of the angry responses seemed very energized, as though they had the potential to move beyond victimization and engage in productive action. The gay man who made the following statement was not at all explicit as to what occurred for him over time, but it would not be surprising if the anger described in the first sentence were a necessary step toward the acceptance described in the second: *Lots of anger towards heterosexual friends for "getting it" too late. Finally, acceptance of their support.*

## REGRET

The REGRET code moved the postelection analysis of the outcome to a very personal level. Comments in this category included individual expressions of regret about not having been more active—or not having been active at all—in the campaign to defeat Amendment 2. This code is notable for reports of considerable affect and very little action. Some comments in this category expressed regret in very simple terms: LGBs were sorry they had not worked during the campaign. A few added, by way of explanation, that they had assumed the amendment would be defeated on election day—an expectation supported by polling data, as mentioned previously (Finley 1992; Zeman and Meyer 1992). Some respondents regretted not having been more out as LGBs. Several said that they had begun to come out to more people in the aftermath of the election, particularly in their place of work.

*REGRET and risk, resilience, and recovery.* Regret can reflect a useful recognition that one needs to change one's behavior, or it can be a tool with which people berate themselves. When regret is acknowledged but does not lead to new action, it is probably not useful. Some respondents seemed stuck in (and with) their regret, as in this comment by a 35-year-old bisexual man: *I often feel guilty I am not doing more to support opposition to "2" but remain relatively uninvolved.*

Other respondents, in contrast, utilized their guilt as the basis for change. One reported: *I felt shocked at the passage. Guilty that I wasn't more "out" and have since been more vocal at work and feel better about that.* Another respondent spoke of her movement in the following terms: *As a lesbian therapist, I was devastated by the passage of Amendment 2 for both myself and my patients. I was surprised at the intensity of my reaction and at the guilt I felt and the personal responsibility I felt because I did not actively work on the campaign. I am currently working to change that, beginning with my own internalized homophobia. Becoming active has had a healing effect on me.*

At their worst, some respondents seemed immersed in their internal experience of regret and unable to find an outlet to work out their guilt in some productive way in the world. On the other hand, when LGBs were able to find a personal basis for action, very positive changes became possible.

## GRASP

The GRASP category included some of the more compelling comments in the data set. Taken collectively, they demonstrated that Amendment 2 represented a definable historic moment for many LGB people in Colorado, the moment when denial about the still extant presence of pervasive homophobia and heterosexism was challenged—when LGBs grasped this fact. For some, the denial ceased altogether. It is not easy for people to understand that their group membership sets them apart as targets for moral and social disapproval; it is, in fact, often a painful and frightening realization. As we shall see, it may also represent an important step toward empowerment for some LGBs.

*GRASP and meaning making.* The significance of the GRASP code can be understood only in the context of the denial of homophobia and heterosexism by many gay people (Garnets, Herek, and Levy 1992). This denial is adaptive in many respects (see Wortman 1983). It allows LGBs to go about their lives without focusing unduly on what Herek (1992b:89) has described as "an ideological system that denies, denigrates, and stigmatizes any nonheterosexual form of behavior, any identity, relationship, or community." However, when LGBs do not acknowledge that heterosexism is pervasive in society, they may be at risk for a shocked and overwhelmed response to direct encounters with heterosexism, and may have difficulty understanding such encounters as societal rather than purely personal in nature.

Amendment 2 involved a direct encounter with homophobia and heterosexism for many LGBs in Colorado (Donovan and Bowler 1997; Linde 1993). The campaign and election vividly demonstrated to LGBs how they were seen by many of their fellow Coloradans, precisely because it tapped into the homophobia and heterosexism pervasive in society (Fernald 1995; Gibson and Tedin 1988; Herek 1992a, 1996).

Some respondents reported their newfound grasp of homonegativity in straightforward terms with no apparent affect. A 45-year-old Denver man referred to conversations with friends: *When talking with gay friends, we are all more aware that gay acceptance is more isolated than we imagined, and conversely, homophobia is alive and well.* However, other LGBs reported that their confrontation with homonegativity had been decidedly painful. One 37-year-old lesbian from Greeley wrote that she was shocked when the amendment passed and went on: *I am more painfully aware of the anti-gay sentiment in this state and world.*

For others, understanding the homophobia underlying the election made them feel hated for their identity. One 40-year-old woman described these feelings in the context of many others: *I have felt incredible rage, frustration, sadness, fear—I am so appalled at the hatred directed at gay people— it seems so senseless, inexplicable. . . . I'm shocked, finally, after deflecting the hatred and indifference all these years by what it feels like to let it hit me, full force.* Such feelings often contributed to the decreased trust that LGBs felt toward heterosexuals—a diminished trust often reported in other kinds of victimization (Bard and Sangrey 1979; Garnets, Herek, and Levy 1992).

Other participants in the study moved from their grasp of homonegativity to a sense of quiet hypervigilance or even to outright fear. A 21-year-old white gay man in Boulder expressed both the sense of being hated and his own fear in this statement, already seen in the OVER code: *With the passage of Amendment 2, I began to see the reality of this country. I was ignorant [of] homophobia, not really believing it to be in existence. Certainly now I feel much different. The biggest reaction I had was an overwhelming sense of dread and sadness. I just kept thinking, wherever I go, the majority of people hate me. The majority of people I run into today hate me, even though they don't even know me. The majority of people I run into today hate me, are scared of me. I almost couldn't leave my house, the feeling was so strong.*

*GRASP and risk, resilience, and recovery.* For many respondents to this survey Amendment 2 marked a turning point, as they saw the effects of homophobia and heterosexism in their lives for the first time. In some cases, this emerging realization sounded strikingly similar to descriptions of the reactions of gays and lesbians who have been victimized by hate crimes (Garnets, Herek, and Levy 1992). It is difficult to move out of denial and the sense of security and well-being that goes with it, and into a fuller appreciation of the homonegativity in the social environment. The coding team was not surprised that the GRASP code often accompanied the two codes alluding to trauma: VWP and TRAUMA.

One manifestation of the difficulty in moving from denial to understanding centered on respondents' conflicts over the role of homophobia in the election outcome. A bisexual woman alluded to this conflict in the context of a much longer statement: *At first I believed it passed due to misunderstanding of the amendment's true meaning, purpose, and intent, and ignorance of who and what gay people are . . . I've since come to believe that it passed and would pass again out of sheer stubborn hatred and willful misunderstanding.* This conflict was also apparent in the words of a 23-year-old lesbian, whose entire comment can be read as a dialectic between the two poles—a grasp of homonegativity on the one hand, and a wish to minimize its influence on the other. *Generally, I am consistently upset by Amendment 2. I never had any incidents of a negative nature until Amendment 2, now it seems that I'm hearing about it and seeing ignorant behavior everywhere. I am trying to balance my disgust in mankind with an attempt at forgiveness. I realize that the percentages that were reflected by Colorado's Amendment 2 were slightly incorrect due to Colorado for Family Value's brilliant job of confusing the voters. However, I didn't think that even one-half of the public could be misled. Or perhaps they weren't. Judging by the increase in hate crimes (it seems we know more now who our enemies are, and our friends).*

A number of respondents drew on their personal experiences with other forms of oppression in order to come to terms with the homonegativity apparent in the campaign and election. Their comments resonated with the heterosexually identified members of our coding team, who used their own experiences with other forms of social oppression to understand homophobia and heterosexism. One Jewish respondent drew an implicit parallel between anti-Semitism and homonegativity: *I fail to understand why it ever became an issue. When it did I was taken aback by the amount of hatred and judgmental positions that came to light. Also, being a woman, a lesbian, and Jewish—mostly the last item—I understand where this could have gone, if it wasn't addressed as aggressively as it was.* A Latina lesbian drew a more explicit parallel: *As a woman of color, now I feel more vulnerable because I will no longer know whether people are discriminating [against] me for being Latino or because I am gay—also, I have experienced discrimination for so long as a person of color, that I am not at all surprised by the consequences of Amendment 2. Racism, oppression, and discrimination are not new items for me to deal with, they've been in my daily agenda for many years and I have learned some valuable skills to cope with it.*

This last comment underscores one of the values of understanding Amendment 2 as a form of oppression, a perspective that sometimes allowed respondents to apply skills acquired from other oppressive experiences. This was but one potential advantage of participants' increased understanding of homonegativity. At the individual level, it is important for people who feel victimized by an event or situation to be able to name it (e.g., Herman 1992; Root 1992). In addition, naming the source of one's victimization is akin to identifying and outlining the parameters of a problem, a necessary part of optimal coping (Pearlin and Schooler 1978; Wortman 1983). It is in this sense that grasping Amendment 2's homonegative roots was potentially helpful to respondents for better problem solving.

Acknowledging the homonegativity in Amendment 2 allowed some LGBs to make sense not only of the amendment but also of their feelings about it. Garnets, Herek, and Levy (1992) suggest that insidious "psychic scars" may result from anti-gay verbal harassment, in part because targeted LGBs are unable to connect their negative reactions to their prior histories of victimization. Hence they are mystified by their own pain. A similar dynamic seems to have been evident among some LGBs in Colorado. We return to a gay man who made this observation implicitly: *I felt that after #2 passed, there was a subtle pressure among many gays and lesbians to look on the bright side of things and to feel optimistic about all the benefits that could happen. I didn't feel that it was okay to grieve the loss openly and even those who did discuss their grief did so quickly and then seemed to get over it. I felt a lot of denial as a community about what #2 really means.* Another gay man noted more explicitly that the election could have an unnoticed negative impact on LGBs: *I've had to remind many people that Amendment 2 might be affecting their performance in school, on the job, etc.*

The reality of seeing the homophobic underpinnings of the amendment also allowed some LGBs to counter some of its impact. This statement by a 34-year-old white lesbian illustrated a moment when this potential was actualized: *Through my work with my therapist currently I have discovered/uncovered my own homophobia. I understand in a new way the ways in which homophobic messages have impacted my sense of worth, my self-esteem, my experience of myself, and many of my decisions through the years.*

Moving the analysis from the individual to the social level, an understanding of the homophobia underlying the election allowed some LGBs to make sense of the horizontal oppression that occurred (in apparently increased measure) after the amendment's passage.[7] In the following comment (which we have seen before), a lesbian made the link between the amendment and horizontal oppression: *There has been a huge increase in homophobic behavior among this neighborhood of lesbians. Horizontal discrimination and oppression increased dramatically. Fear is the motivator and it's not pretty.*

With respect to the social level more broadly, when individual LGBs understood that other gay people had similar reactions to Amendment 2 and that it was homonegativity that underlay all these reactions, a new vision emerged. This vision changed the definition of the problem from the personal to the sociopolitical, and promised to transform personal experiences into collective voices. Resistance to the sociopolitical problem consequently became possible (Bullis and Bach 1996; Collins 1991; Scott 1985, 1990). Thus, some LGBs, seeing the election through the prism of societal homonegativity, no longer viewed it as a purely personal problem but as a sociocultural phenomenon that could be changed through activism. A gay Hispanic man from Denver moved directly from his new understanding of homonegativity to his own personal transformation and political vision: *Although I have become cognizant of the bigotry, I have also become so much more aware of my own inner strength. I feel that perhaps the passing of Amendment 2 may in the long run work in our favor—it symbolizes a renewed opportunity for all Americans to do battle against all bigotry, but it also symbolizes an opportunity for us gays and lesbians to destroy the stereotypes by coming out and speaking out against all infractions to civil rights, not just those that are convenient for us.*

On the other hand, some LGBs, understanding the intensity and pervasiveness of homophobia, found it not just painful, but overwhelming. The problem seemed so large that they felt there was little they could do to diminish it. A 40-year-old homosexual man from Denver commented: *Coming to the realization that these debates will go on forever. This question seems to engender the same anger that the abortion issue does. We might as well get used to it.* A 26-year-old homosexual woman also expressed the sense of being overwhelmed by her hopelessness in the face of homophobia and heterosexism: *My conclusion is that the people in the state voted on Amendment 2 not because of ignorance, but because of a feeling of moral superiority and self-righteousness based on deeply ingrained religious dogma and rhetoric. People knew exactly what they were voting for, I don't believe for a minute that people were "confused over the issue." At first I vowed to fight, but now as time passes, I see that I won't change people's attitudes toward us. The court might overturn #2, but people's homophobia, bias, and hatred will remain. That is the most depressing thought of all. I'm looking forward to moving out of state this summer.*

Despite the hopelessness voiced by these respondents, there were many times their number who felt personally and/or politically activated. Several factors seemed to have stimulated an activist response, including seeing the struggle for equal rights for LGBs in terms of a long-term movement, feeling a sense of community with other LGBs, and feeling witnessed by heterosexual allies.

## *ISMS*

The ISMS code, which refers to comments containing references to forms of social oppression other than homophobia and heterosexism, was in some respects an extension of the GRASP code. Respondents often mentioned anti-Semitism and racism as parallels, occasionally referred to sexism, and made rare references to other forms of injustice. Comments coded as ISMS were disappointing on account of their infrequency and limited depth of analysis. We had hoped that more gay people would have developed clearer and more sophisticated analyses of the linkages between various forms of oppression. Indeed, a good many of the ISMS comments with references to anti-Semitism did not explore the parallels between anti-Jewish sentiment and homonegativity so much as draw parallels between aspects of the trauma of the Holocaust and their own trauma in response to Amendment 2.

*ISMS and meaning making.* Very different themes emerged in the ISMS comments from white respondents than from those from LGBs of color. Comments from people of color focused largely on two issues. The first was the observation that LGBs of color had had extensive experience with social oppression, while white LGBs had had the privilege of ignoring such oppression. A Latina lesbian asked: *Why are whites surprised about discrimination? Is it because it's just knocking at your door for the first time? It's been on my steps forever. Hope you can finally see and realize that oppression should not be experienced by any human being—to be stripped or robbed of culture, language, sexual and cultural identity are emotional rapes that people (gays and lesbians) of color experience on a daily basis.* In similar vein, a 50-year-old American Indian lesbian wrote: *Since some people of color feel we have lived in a "police state" for some time now, I guess we shouldn't be so surprised about the passage of Amendment 2—it is sad that people (some) can't seem to adopt a "live and let live" attitude.*

The second prominent theme among the few ISMS statements from respondents of color was their stated new intention to include gay issues in their human rights work. An Asian American bisexual woman explained the amendment's impact on her: *Its passage compelled me a bit further out of the closet—which is hard for a very private person. Am generally a human rights activist (racial justice primarily) and now am even more intentional, vocal, blatant about an inclusive agenda.*

Among white LGBs, two major themes emerged in the ISMS comments. The first had to do with the connection—often implicit, but occasionally explicit—between homonegativity and other forms of oppression. A bisexual woman in her thirties wrote: *Found with discrimination I am reminded often of the hard struggle black Americans continually go through fighting discrimination.* A European American lesbian in her thirties drew a connection between homonegativity and a number of social injustices: *For me this amendment is tied to a long line of anti-gay politics and feelings, as well as racism, sexism and a general sense of the greed and power of the "haves" against the "have-nots."*

One subgroup of the white respondents whose ISMS comments focused on the relationship between homonegativity and other social prejudices identified themselves as Jewish. A Fort Collins woman who referred to herself as a lesbian-identified bisexual ended a statement on homophobia with the sentence: *I'm Jewish and Amendment 2 has a special horror for me—anti-semitism, Holocaust.* A Colorado Springs lesbian was somewhat more explicit but conveyed the same message: *I've felt rising feelings of similarity between the Holocaust and the religious right and threats to me due to my sexual orientation.*

The second substantial theme in ISMS comments made by white LGBs was that Amendment 2 had taught or inspired them. A 17-year-old wrote that, in addition to coming out more since the election: *I've learned a lot about tolerance of others and I've also learned how to educate others.* A gay man concluded a statement largely focused on his fears with: *Greater understanding (?) of oppression of women, ethnic groups.* A lesbian from Pueblo spoke of her changing perception: *I'm beginning to understand what black people had to go through to get their basic American rights. Nothing like being a "second class" citizen.* A lesbian from the Denver area wrote of having been active in the effort to defeat the amendment, and then: *Mostly, the ignorance about Amendment 2 confirms my feeling that most people are passive about something until it directly affects them. It simply adds more fuel to my anger at any social injustice—racial, sexual, or civil. Fear and silence are what keep people in chains.* This ISMS comment stood out from others by white LGBs as one in which the respondent seemed likely to go beyond a better understanding of the connections between forms of oppression and actually act on that understanding in a new way.

As noted, members of the coding team were disappointed by the small number and analytic limitations of the ISMS category. When given the opportunity to comment on Amendment 2, most respondents said very little about the connections between oppressions. Sadly, this was probably an accurate reflection of where the gay community was in terms of being inclusive—a subject to which we return when we discuss codes focused on LGBs' relationships with one another (chapter 6).

## Codes Related to Election Results and the Campaign

Several codes reflected attributions regarding the election outcome. These codes referred to causes more proximate and concrete than the presence of homophobia and heterosexism in the culture. The first four codes in this subset posited reasons why Colorado voters might have endorsed the amendment at the ballot box, reasons having nothing to do with antipathy toward LGB people. The final two codes included comments about the campaign conducted by EPOColorado, the pro-gay organization that unsuccessfully attempted to defeat the amendment at the polls. None of these codes included more than a handful of comments. Their infrequency, coupled with their limited importance to our understanding of the psychological effects of Amendment 2 on LGBs, leads us to discuss them in collective terms.

The four results codes identified four distinct factors as influencing the election outcome. First, the campaign organization, EPOColorado—EPOC for short—was sometimes held responsible for losing the election; these comments were coded REPOC. One respondent said that EPOC had been unsuccessful in countering the "special rights" campaign promulgated by CFV and picked up by the mainstream media. Two other respondents thought that EPOC had lost the campaign on purpose because campaign organizers wanted to raise money and visibility for national gay organizing.

The RINFO code was by far the largest in the "results" subset, with three times the number of comments as the next largest result code. The RINFO comments attributed the election outcome to misinformation fed to the voters. CFV was often cited as the party responsible for this misinformation, though a number of references were made to the media as well. One campaign theme singled out numerous times was the notion of "special rights." In reality, that slogan has been the centerpiece of other antigay campaigns and a difficult one to counter effectively, not only in Colorado but also elsewhere (Bull and Gallagher 1996; Herman 1997; Keen and Goldberg 1998; McCorkle and Most 1997a, 1997b). The other notable theme in RINFO was the ambivalence of respondents in assigning blame for the election loss. Several comments contained an internal debate: were the public misinformed or did they simply dislike gay people that much?

RLIES comments attributed the loss of the election to lies told by CFV. RLIES was unique among the results codes in containing both more affect (notably anger) and more personalizing statements than the other three. It is hardly surprising that LGBs would have been personally touched by and angry, given their perception that CFV was lying about them.

In the RMIS code, respondents attributed the election outcome to mistakes made by the voters at the voting booth. This code emphasized that some were confused as to the meaning of voting "yes" or "no." The RMIS and RINFO codes frequently overlapped.

*Codes focusing on the campaign.* The two "campaign" codes also contained relatively few comments. The CCRIT category involved criticisms of the campaign waged by EPOC. It was cross-coded with the REPOC category in most instances. Criticisms of EPOC's campaign centered on two major issues. One had to do with questions about campaign strategies. Respondents particularly found fault with EPOC's failure to mount an effective analysis of and counter to CFV's special rights slogan and its failure to undertake a broad-based statewide educational campaign.

The second critique of EPOC was more complex in nature, going beyond questions of strategy to more abstract visions of the campaign. One version of the criticism expressed the conflict between organizing a campaign and building an LGB community (Nash 1999; Pharr 1993). Respondents were critical of the campaign organization for not being inclusive, notably along dimensions of class and race. In addition, some respondents saw EPOC, a Denver-based organization, as having usurped power and disregarded the input of rural parts of the state during the campaign.

The second "campaign" code, CCOMP, which was small and limited in scope, expressed approval of EPOC's campaign. One woman acknowledged her gratitude toward people who had tried to defeat Amendment 2 at the polls. One man suggested that the postelection criticisms of EPOC were akin to victim-blaming in cases of rape.

*Results and campaign codes and risk, resilience, and recovery.* In analyzing the campaign and election results, respondents were attempting to explain an unpleasant election outcome. Conclusions about the campaign offered the possibility of regaining a sense of control and the promise of winning future elections. One gay man suggested that, in the aftermath of the election, *CFV has recently shown its true agenda and some people realize it now. We'll get an accurate vote next time.* By "accurate," we took him to mean a vote favoring LGB rights in a future election. To the extent that these attributions identified realistic problems in the campaign, they could be of future use. Unfortunately, many of the comments in this subset were posed in all-or-nothing terms and were therefore probably of limited use. (This all-or-nothing approach to evaluating campaigns makes sense in light of the all-or-nothing quality inherent in elections; there are wins and losses and little is left to ambiguity.) In addition, as a coding team, we often speculated that the defensive tone of many of the comments in this subset reflected respondents' desire to avoid a confrontation with the reality of homonegativity. They were also valid criticisms of a campaign facing overwhelming odds.

## DISC

With the DISC code, which we constructed for descriptions of specific experiences with discrimination, we move to a more global perspective on the problem of Amendment 2. The amendment's legal effect, had it been instated, would have been to exclude LGB sexual orientation from the protection of antidiscrimination laws at any level anywhere in the state. To CFV, that meant denying LGBs "special rights"; to most of the LGB population of the state, it meant legalizing discrimination against them. It is not surprising, then, that a fair number of respondents described specific experiences with discrimination, most of them first-person ones.

*DISC and meaning making.* We included in the DISC code instances of verbal and physical harassment as well as experiences with discrimination. When the timing of such an event was specified, it usually occurred after the election. However, nearly half the respondents who reported discriminatory incidents did not include information that would have allowed us to determine whether these events had occurred before or after the election. The language of the code suggested that in general respondents were arguing that Amendment 2 had created a hostile climate for LGBs, one in which incidents of discrimination were on the increase. A few participants made such observations explicitly, as this Anglo bisexual woman from Denver: *It seems that bigots have been given permission by the election results to come out of their closets, and I've heard commentary that shocked me.*

The nature of the discriminatory experiences reported by LGBs varied. By far the most frequent were cases of verbal harassment.[8] Following well behind verbal harassment and occurring with equal frequency were reports of violence against property, physical assault, and discrimination in employment and public accommodations. Many of the DISC comments included descriptions of affective responses to the victimization. A set of fearful reactions—from cautious to terrified—was most prominent; such reactions were cross-coded with FEAR.

One group of DISC responses came from LGBs who had been physically assaulted in the past. Memories of these past experiences were sometimes revived by the passage of Amendment 2. A 30-year-old Hispanic homosexual reported: *My biggest fear, post-Amendment 2, is the fear of being physically assaulted. I was attacked and assaulted eight years ago. At that time, I was not out to myself or others. One of my biggest fears when I came out was being assaulted again. I figured it was a chance I had to take. Now that I am out and after Amendment 2, those fears are once again of concern to me.* A 40-year-old white homosexual man reported that his survey responses were influenced by an assault history. His use of third-person language made us wonder whether he were trying to distance himself from the memory he was describing and its associated feelings: *These responses are from an individual who has been a victim of assault and near death due to being gay. These responses could reflect some paranoia and anger from this unpunished assault. These responses are also from one who finally got tired of being completely closeted and decided in 1992 he was deserving of happiness and started being gay/seeking gay relationships openly.*

*DISC and risk, resilience, and recovery.* As the foregoing quotation suggests, these comments frequently highlighted the relationship between experiences with harassment or discrimination and decisions about how out to be. Sometimes respondents chose to limit their disclosures around sexual orientation. Work was frequently mentioned as a place where LGBs did not feel safe about being open. Teachers, in particular, seemed caught in this dilemma: *I am a teacher in the public schools. Consequently, fear of being "out" is an everyday reality. Amendment 2 has heightened that fear. Discussions about Amendment 2 (at work) have made me very uncomfortable. I'm sick and tired of listening to homophobic comments from adults and students alike. I feel like my hands are tied. I have to sit and listen or speak very carefully when the issue comes up. I never know how far to push my defense on 2. I'm afraid I'll implicate myself. It's very frustrating.*

Some respondents were wrestling with conflicts about remaining closeted, wanting on the one hand to be more open but dissuaded by their observations of LGB coworkers who were more out. This comment by a white gay man (who notably did not indicate his city or town of residence in the survey's demographics section) was representative: *The biggie for me has been the huge guilt I've been feeling because I'm not out. I'm well liked at work but only the other gay workers know I am gay too. Keep trying to be open but see how fellow workers treat other gay folks and I don't want to deal with that. I'm a firefighter and the guys can be so cold and nasty. Gonna keep working on it and see what happens.*

Other respondents chose to be out despite encounters with harassment. This 37-year-old white lesbian made her resolve to be out quite clear: *I have a very visible job within the gay and lesbian community and am therefore really out there. Right after the election . . . my rear windshield was shot out. I also receive threatening phone calls at work, etc. Not fun, not easy, but I couldn't live my life any differently. My life depends on my being involved— nobody is going to do it for me. Some days [are] harder than others, but "a girl's got to do what a girl's got to do."*

In addition to the question of how out to be, LGB respondents who had experienced harassment and discrimination had to contend with the disruption to their sense of safety in other ways. A lesbian in her thirties succinctly wrote: *I was physically assaulted since the election and demeaned. So now I do fear much more, frightened and closeted.* Another lesbian, also in her thirties, reported: *There was an incident when my vehicle was vandalized. Now, I worry when driving my car—am I safe due to my overturn #2 bumper stickers? I've even thought on one occasion I was being followed.* The safety issue caused LGBs to question not only their own actions, but, as we see saw in the previous comment, their own role in their victimization (Garnets, Herek, and Levy 1992).

A related ambiguity had to do with the question of how to define a situation that could be, but perhaps was not, harassment or discrimination. Ambiguous situations lead LGB persons to question not only the situation but sometimes themselves as well. A white lesbian from Colorado Springs illustrated how the changed postelection climate affected LGBs' responses to specific incidents in their lives: *Since A2 passed, we have received harassing and obscene phone calls, and our house was vandalized. We fear for our own safety and for the safety of our children. Recently we called the city gas folks about a smell. They said it was not gas, but did smell it outside, and it smelled like kerosene. Scary stuff.* A gay man in his forties from a Denver suburb wrote: *I lost a job one week after Amendment 2 was voted on. The [name of hotel chain] said they were consolidating my job with the general manager's. But one month later, they replaced me with someone to do the same job but with a new title.*

Experiences of harassment and discrimination may be seen as stressors in the lives of LGB people (DiPlacido 1998; Garnets, Herek, and Levy 1992; Root 1992, 1996). The results of such experiences are often complicated by their association with the sexual orientation of the victims. At its worst, the sexuality and sexual orientation of victims of harassment and discrimination may become entangled with the victimization, resulting in an association between sexual orientation and victimization rather than in an association between homonegativity and victimization (Garnets, Herek, and Levy 1992). A variety of factors, both intrinsic and extrinsic to the individual, may influence their resilience in the face of such victimization (DiPlacido 1998). Accordingly, victimized individuals need to understand the nature of their victimization in the broader sociopolitical context (Garnets, Herek, and Levy 1992; Root 1992).

## WAR

Under favorable circumstances, LGBs understand that the stresses associated with being members of a marginalized group are an outcome of tensions between different moral and social belief systems in society. Such stresses challenge LGBs on an ongoing basis. However, under special and less favorable circumstances, gay people may encounter new levels of tension. In the extreme, these tensions have been referred to as "a cultural war" (Buchanan, quoted in Bull and Gallagher 1996:88). Amendment 2 represented a major battle in that war. Not surprisingly, then, the imagery of battles and wars was scattered throughout the data set from this study.

The WAR code was designed to explore and study this imagery. It was not in our original set of codes when we began formal coding. We added it later along with a handful of other codes, and recoded all the comments, being struck by the use of war imagery. Lou in particular noticed it when we were deep into the data.

War imagery was used to refer both to LGBs and to others. With regard to the latter, CFV and the radical right more generally as the enemy or opposition. They felt *outnumbered* by what one self-described Christian lesbian sarcastically referred to as *Christians on a mission for God*. One respondent noted that Amendment 2's most profound effect on her was to change her attitude toward radical religious right groups: *I was tolerant of them and their beliefs prior to the election. I now feel like they are "the enemy" and are a real danger and a threat to my very existence.* The references to CFV and the religious right in the WAR code tended to view these entities in one-dimensional terms, a perceptual inclination common in times of war.

However, when respondents referred to themselves and other gay people within the WAR theme, their references were considerably more complex. In fact, these references were subdivided into two very distinct subthemes—one focused on being victimized and the other on being mobilized, but both in warlike circumstances. Many comments in the data set referred to feeling victimized. In their effort to indicate how negative the Amendment 2 experience was, respondents used a number of familiar and strong images to convey its quality and intensity. These images included the *Holocaust, rape*, and of course *war*. War references included feeling *shell-shocked* and *under siege* and being *assaulted* by the campaign and election.

The second subtheme, which referred to gay people's being mobilized, was by far the larger of the two subthemes of war imagery applied to LGBs. Comments in this area emphasized an engagement for battle in the aftermath of what had been a defeat at the polls on election day. Indeed, one respondent compared the election to the lost battle that would turn out to have been a prelude to victory in the wider war. Respondents clearly saw their engagement as a necessary defense to unprovoked aggression by CFV and the religious right.[9] They spoke of mobilization as an individual and a community action. One Pacific Islander (Chamorro) lesbian described her individual acts of mobilization as a crusade: *As a result of the passage of Amendment 2, I have been on a crusade to "out" myself to everyone at work, as well as those whose businesses I frequent (i.e., dry cleaners, tailor, etc.). I have also been more visible among the college population with whom I work regarding my sexual orientation.*

A 44-year-old white gay man saw his individual mobilization in these striking terms: *I strongly believe that I was placed on this earth—at this time, in this place—to fight for gay rights. Amendment 2 woke me up. In retrospect, Amendment 2 may be the best thing to ever happen to gays/lesbians/bisexuals of this country.* For all but two respondents, the mobilization at the individual level focused on increasing their visibility as gay people, education, and political activity. The exceptions were a white gay man who reported that he had purchased *equipment/books on defense/assault material in anticipation of the "Gestapo,"* and a white lesbian who had purchased two guns.

The many comments about mobilization at the community level often emphasized *solidarity* with other gay people. One lesbian in her fifties described the mobilization in these terms: *I feel the results of Amendment 2 [have] brought us together to fight for ourselves in ways we haven't ever done before. Hopefully it (the result of our coming together) will help present and future generations to be treated in a more humane way. It isn't easy for anyone, but change never is. I would hope we would maintain a peaceful but effective approach to all that arises from Amendment 2 and hopeful we will reach levels of equality that have been impossible in the past. Viva the Revolution!*

Two other themes emerged in the WAR code. One had to do with the resources being used to fight the amendment that otherwise could have been used to fight *the battle over AIDS/HIV.* The other had to do with divisions within the LGB community. In the context of the WAR code these divisions were spoken of as ruptures in the community's ability to mobilize against Amendment 2. In one case, a gay man referred to gay publications, *with their car ads and overt sexual overtones [as] the enemy within.* Such divisions within the LGB community are explored more fully under the BARRIERS code in chapter 6.

## CFV and MEDIA

The CFV and MEDIA codes focused on two large entities—Colorado for Family Values and the media—frequently mentioned in the data. An earlier version of our coding system included the codes ACFV and AMEDIA (discussed above) which picked up on LGBs' anger at CFV and at the media, respectively. In one of our pilot runs with the coding system, several coders noted that a significant number of comments about CFV and the media were not always angry in tone. After some discussion, we decided that some nonhostile comments about CFV and the media did, in fact, convey information that was important to our understanding of how the election had affected gay people. Consequently, we added the CFV and MEDIA codes for references to the two entities that were not explicitly angry. When we began using these two codes we knew only that both were perceived to have played key roles in the campaign and election. CFV had been viewed as the perpetrator, at least within a trauma framework. The media, on the other hand, had been described as a perpetrating agent by some respondents and as a witness by others; sometimes, the line between the two was elusively thin.

## CFV

The CFV code included nonangry references about Colorado for Family Values and the religious right, two groups that ran together in many respondents' minds. Among the comments coded CFV, three distinct themes were especially prominent.

The first focused on the motives that, in the respondents' judgment, had led CFV and the religious right to promote Amendment 2. While a fair number of comments dealt with these issues, there were more questions than answers. One lesbian from Pueblo reflected the confusion of many respondents: *I don't understand why it's such a big deal.* A gay man from Durango expressed his confusion about CFV's motives: *I find it very hard to even imagine being as closed and self-righteous as many of those working on the Amendment 2 campaign (CFV), even despite trying to take into consideration upbringing, etc. Also, why is it so difficult to successfully divide church/state? I long for the day that we can let each other live without imposing our views/beliefs—moral, religious, political—on others.* For the few respondents who ventured an answer to the question of CFV's motives, their answers varied: CFV and the right *have to hate someone and need gays as a basis for their own fund raising.* The efforts to assign motives to CFV were notable in expressing fear of CFV and the religious right.

A second dimension to the CFV comments was the way respondents perceived the nature of the relationship between themselves (and, by extension, LGBs more generally) and CFV. Their remarks strongly suggested that they viewed CFV and the religious right as having victimized them. Their references to CFV in these comments seemed to reflect their effort to make sense of their experiences of Amendment 2 by naming the perpetrator behind the campaign and election. Respondents not only knew and referred to CFV by name, but they also knew the names of major figures within the organization. Sometimes, the name of CFV came so easily to respondents that they had to remind themselves to tell the reader who they were writing about, as in this comment by a rural lesbian: *Their campaign was so unfair and unjust. I feel frustrated that people would rather believe their (CFV) sensational lies than trust in objective studies and statistics that say that we're no more dangerous than anyone else.*

Many of the references indicated that respondents saw CFV and the religious right as both powerful and dangerous to LGBs. These perceptions were often expressed in direct and very personal terms, but perhaps none more so than this statement by a 17-year-old white gay man living in Denver: *My family kicked me out and took everything I had and/or wanted. The gay community in Denver became my home and my family. Now that is under threat from CFV. I take that very personally.*

As our coding team noticed the intensity of respondents' fear of CFV, we explored a third dimension of the code—the specific dangers that LGBs attributed to CFV and the religious right. While a few comments referred to specific personal concerns—fear of job loss being the most frequent—most of the danger-specific comments focused on lies that had been perceived to have been part of CFV's campaign. For many respondents, the impact of such lies went considerably beyond the psychological insult of being lied about, and included concrete dangers in their daily lives. The danger was almost palpable in this comment by a 51-year-old Colorado Springs lesbian: *I've always been cautious concerning my lesbianism but now I am terribly afraid. Amendment 2 and what is happening toward gays is always on my mind now. Before Amendment 2, most everyone in Colorado seemed to tolerate each other but Colorado for Family Values has turned people against us with their lies. So much that I fear for my professional job and my safety. If I become personally targeted, I'm afraid there will be no one to help me.*

*CFV and risk, resilience, and recovery.* The power that respondents seemed to ascribe to CFV and the religious right varied considerably. Typically, as we have noted already, CFV was seen as a dangerous and powerful instigation of Amendment 2, with the possibility of more victimizations to come. In addition, a few comments in the code acknowledged CFV's power from a very different perspective. These LGBs viewed CFV as responsible for positive growth and change, both in LGB individuals and in the LGB community. It did not surprise us that LGBs regarded the Amendment 2 situation as the source of positive change at both the individual and community levels. The observation occurred in different ways throughout the data set. Indeed, an important premise of this book is that a complex, paradoxical nexus of changes occurred in the aftermath of Amendment 2. But it is one thing to acknowledge such changes in general or, for example, to recognize that they occurred as a function of the way LGBs handled Amendment 2; it is another matter to see those changes credited to CFV and its spokespeople.

The following comment by a Denver homosexual man illustrates the mix of important personal and community growth and gratitude to CFV, in the person of Will Perkins, CFV's board chairman at the time of the election: *Although I was initially stunned, depressed, and demoralized by the passage of 2, my response to this was to form an organization to fight for the well-being and uplift of the community. As a result, I now feel more empowered as a gay man and as a multi-dimensional person than I ever have in my life. I expect some day to write a thank you letter to Mr. Perkins, et al., because I believe that—contrary to their mean and perhaps evil intentions—they have coalesced the gay community, opened our eyes, brought the issues around gay and lesbian people and our integration into the mainstream.*

Some of the CFV-coded comments tended to mirror CFV's rhetoric, using the opposed absolutes of good and evil, for example. Our coding team was curious as to what it meant when people who felt victimized used the language and constructs of the perpetrators of the victimization. As a team, we often felt a sense of relief when we came upon a comment whose author seemed to avoid thinking and talking in terms akin to CFV's rhetoric. This 27-year-old Mexican American homosexual exemplified the ability to create an important boundary between the victim and the victimizer: *Felt like I should do more to educate people on homophobia. Tried not to use the same tactics CFV used and tried to be equal to others, no matter what their race, religion, or sexual orientation.* Such a boundary seems to help LGB persons to live their own lives rather than to live in reaction to CFV and other anti-gay entities.

## MEDIA

It was hardly surprising to read references to CFV throughout the data. However, the number and variety of references to the media exceeded our expectations. As a group, comments about the media were more complex than were those about CFV. Whereas CFV caught LGBs' interest as the source of their victimization, the media served multiple roles in the campaign. In addition, while CFV as an organization had been founded recently for the sole purpose of promoting Amendment 2, the media had been present and influential in the lives of LGBs long before the campaign. Individual respondents related to the media as a multifaceted collection of communication outlets that had preceded and would endure well beyond the campaign.

Our coding team identified a number of separate dimensions used by respondents to describe the media. The first group of comments suggested that respondents believed that the media had provided objective reports of information about LGBs to the public at large and, therefore, that LGBs were wholly responsible for images of gays in the media. The view of the media as an objective reporter occurred only in the context of references to LGBs. Here, respondents expressed concern about how LGBs had conducted themselves and how their behavior would be communicated to public audiences. All comments in this dimension stated or implied that LGBs should not act in ways that would confirm gay stereotypes to the public or otherwise cast LGBs in a negative light.

A related dimension in MEDIA comments credited the media with providing images of LGBs to the general population. This set of comments focused on the media's ability to render gay people more visible than they had been in the past. Comments in this group contained, explicitly or implicitly, a sociopolitical analysis: Amendment 2 and the media attention it generated had countered years of LGB invisibility in mainstream media outlets (Fejes and Petrich 1993; Gross 1991; Moritz 1992). A 42-year-old lesbian expressed this understanding: *I believe that CFV has done more to help us by keeping gay and lesbian issues "up" in the news, and in people's awareness. . . . More people are coming out. This crisis serves us. The invisible minority becomes visible! Yes!* Like many others, her statement combined observations about the LGB community's visibility with observations about individual LGBs coming out.

Another MEDIA dimension focused on the media as avenues through which LGBs acquired information about CFV, the religious right, and those associated with them. The media served as a significant source of input into the meaning making that LGBs did in the aftermath of the election. They used the media to understand what CFV and the religious right were and what further steps they might be expected to take.

An important dimension in the MEDIA code related to the media's role as witnesses. At times, the media were said to have acted as successful witnesses, especially when they portrayed LGBs and their issues in a nonbiased or a positive light.[10] On the other hand, the media were often portrayed as failed witnesses as for example when they appeared to accept and transmit CFV's campaign rhetoric without any critical analysis. This comment by a gay man was illustrative: *I'm tired of the lies CFV says and the media not trying to verify or disclaim them.* More generally, comments in this dimension expressed LGB's concerns about media portrayals of them. This homosexual man's comment left unanswered the question of who was to blame for LGB images that he did not like: *Concerned that current media bits create militant image that is ultimately unfavorable—no place for just ordinariness.*

When the media's witnessing was particularly troublesome, the media were said to have slid into another dimension and become perpetrators themselves. Rather than merely failing to challenge anti-gay rhetoric, the media were seen as participants in its creation, an observation that mirrored some professional media observers at the time of the election (Ostrow 1992).

Some LGBs saw the media as a source of overload for themselves. The media coverage of Amendment 2 occurred not only prior to but for weeks after the November election; it overlapped with extensive national coverage of the debate over gays in the military that began soon after Bill Clinton was elected president in November 1992 and peaked after he assumed the presidency the following January. Many respondents reported feeling overwhelmed by the change from minimal visibility of LGBs and their issues in the media to a barrage of such coverage. One 38-year-old gay woman described her anxiety and fear after the election and went on to write: *Many of these same reactions have also occurred in response to the intense scrutiny and discussions and media coverage of the ban on gays in the military—being constantly exposed to the homophobic, bigoted, ignorant, vitriolic, diatribes by the military "experts," the religious right ("wrong"), and the general public has been horrible.* A number of LGBs not only blamed the media for their sense of being overwhelmed but went on to say that they had discontinued contact with media outlets in an effort to reestablish their psychological equilibrium.

The final dimension of the MEDIA code was LGBs' participation in the media as a way of finding their own voices. This code was strikingly different from the others because it was the only one in which LGBs described themselves as agents rather than as objects of action. One Hispanic Irish homosexual told of being profiled with his lover for a television news spot. Saying that the Amendment 2 situation had *brought me out to a level I never would've expected*, he added: *I don't think I could be more "out" than proclaiming it on TV—it's a wonderful feeling!* In similar vein, a number of respondents had been able to find their voices by writing letters to the editor. This activity allowed them to express their ideas in a public forum, which represented—and represents—a move from personal invisibility to visibility for many gay people.

6

■ ■   ■   ■   ■   ■     ■       ■         ■

# Internal and External Dimensions of Trauma and Oppression

IN THIS CHAPTER, we examine some of the most poignant and expressive comments in the entire data set. The first two codes in this chapter, TRAUMA and VWP, went to the heart of the pain that many LGBs in Colorado experienced during the campaign for and passage of Amendment 2. Subsequent codes in this chapter address how these experiences influenced LGBs in their relationships with themselves and with other gay people.

## TRAUMA

TRAUMA, whose referent is self-explanatory, was one of the most complex codes in the data. This is not surprising in view of two observations. First, trauma itself is a construct of great breadth and depth. Second when 496 people describe their reactions to an event that many of them experienced as traumatic, one can expect considerable variation and complexity in their descriptions. TRAUMA was in our set of codes as we initiated our pilot effort at coding the data. We had not gone far when we realized we would need at least one other trauma-related code. The VWP code—signifying references to victim, witness, and perpetrator perspectives—was born of that realization.

Our understanding of the TRAUMA code included a number of distinct dimensions. One of the most obvious was the high number of references to what we came to call iconic images of trauma. Iconic trauma images are those that are so much a part of the popular discourse that their significance is immediately comprehensible to others. They serve as a sort of shorthand to convey a lot of information in a brief package. By far the most frequent iconic image in these data was the Holocaust, references to which were made in a number of ways, including *Nazi mentality, Gestapo, Nazi Germany,* and the *Nazi/Hitler thing.*

Some respondents were careful to make specific parallels between their Holocaust imagery and Amendment 2. In other remarks, respondents made the Holocaust reference without elaboration, apparently assuming the image was strong enough not to need any. And, of course, it was, as can be seen in this comment: *The day after the election, I was definitely depressed. I felt as if I'd awakened to Nazi Germany.* Several other iconic images of trauma emerged in the data, including rape, racism, genocide, and ethnic cleansing. None occurred with anything near the frequency of the Holocaust.

The advantage of iconic images is that they carry a broadly understood generic package of cognitive and affective information quickly. Their disadvantage is that the precise meaning of the respondent's message may not always be clear to the reader. As a team, we occasionally wondered to what degree LGBs understood the parallels between the Holocaust and Amendment 2—and the limits of those parallels. As we saw in the review of the ISMS code in chapter 5, the analysis of the linkages between different forms of social oppressions was neither extensive nor refined in these data.

Whatever our participants' understanding of Holocaust imagery, other dimensions of the TRAUMA code offered more precise descriptions of LGBs' responses to the election. A second TRAUMA dimension tracked symptoms associated with post-traumatic stress disorder (PTSD).[1] There are three general categories of symptoms associated with PTSD, including expressive or intrusive symptoms, avoiding or numbing symptoms, and symptoms associated with increased arousal. Respondents indicated the presence of symptoms in all three of the categories. Indeed, very few DSM-designated symptoms in these three categories were not mentioned.

At one point in the process of coding, Sylvie commented that many of the participants' statements represented the way real people spoke about traumatic reactions when not asked to do so and when they were not necessarily aware that that was what they were addressing.[2]

*Intrusive symptoms associated with PTSD.*[3] In the words of van der Kolk, "the response to psychological trauma has been described as a phasic reliving and denial, with alternating intrusive and numbing responses" (van der Kolk 1987:3). In our analysis, the intrusive symptoms included in DSM-III-R (American Psychiatric Association 1987) were subdivided into four separate categories. All but one of those categories were described in multiple comments in the data. One included intrusive recollections of respondents' reactions to Amendment 2. One woman wrote: *I think about Amendment 2 frequently. Every day, I mull and think and talk.* Another lesbian wrote: *When someone tries to defend amendment 2, I spend the next few weeks going over and over out loud to myself with the reaction I wish I would have had the courage to have said. It almost consumes me.* Interestingly, a number of the comments describing intrusive recollections focused on the lies about LGBs that respondents perceived CFV to have promulgated.

Some respondents also reported frequent dreams related to the campaign and the election. Many of these dreams included iconic traumatic images. The following statement by a 25-year-old bisexual woman was typical: *Right after the election, I had several dreams about being grouped with other gays/lesbians/bis and persecuted—being forced to wear triangles like with Hitler and World War II.*

In part because respondents were more likely to describe their avoidance behavior than to say exactly why they felt the need to engage in that behavior, it was not clear how many respondents had actually had experiences with reliving the campaign and election. There were some hints in the data. One 21-year-old gay man was clear about what underlay his avoidance behavior: *I felt much anxiety right after election day but soon grew tired of hearing about the issue. I still feel anxiety when I think about it, but just don't care to think about it much.* A 30-year-old lesbian was succinct in stating the reason underlying her avoidance behavior: *I really don't like to hear or talk about CFV. It is upsetting.* A lesbian from Colorado Springs identified the effect exposure to the media discussions had on her more precisely: *I find the Amendment 2 stuff is radically reducing my in-*

*terest in sex. The barrage of media "sinner" stuff is getting to me! Filling this [survey] out is depressing. I guess I use denial to cope. This questionnaire is just another stressor and reminds me of all the shit we take from all the jerks.*

In a very different vein, a gay man from Boulder happened to encounter a university football coach who had been a public proponent of Amendment 2. Seeing the coach evoked a strong reaction in this respondent, reminding him of the negative stimulus of Amendment 2: *I ran into Coach Mac one day on the creek path—just the two of us. In fact, it was on Nov. 4. I was feeling ill and left work early to walk home. As he passed me, our eyes met for just a second. I screamed at him as loud as I could "You fascist pig." God, it felt good!*

For some respondents, the survey itself evoked old and difficult feelings associated with the campaign and the election. Our team was saddened to read the handful of comments—including the one cited above from the Colorado Springs lesbian—telling us that completing the survey had given rise to intrusive thoughts about the election. In the following comment, one respondent made a clear linkage between his election night experience and his completion of the research survey: *Sitting in a room full of gays and lesbians watching the returns—as the support for Amendment 2 grew, I felt more and more alone. Filling this out brings up all those feelings or rage and sadness that my sexuality is up for public vote. Fuck 'em.*

*Avoidance and numbing responses.* The traumatic responses in this subcategory seemed to be related to the effort to reduce the intrusions or hold them at bay. Doing so may have offered the traumatized person a greater sense of control (Herman 1992; van der Kolk 1987). However, it may also have constricted the person emotionally and isolated him or her socially as well. The comments in the data set included numerous and varied accounts of LGB efforts to avoid thoughts and feelings associated with the election and situations connected to it. As we have already seen, some respondents tried to avoid thinking about or engaging in discussions about the amendment. The most prominent focus of participants' avoidance were media outlets. Many comments referred to the avoidance of newspaper and television news discussions of gay people. Perhaps none made as great an effort to avoid any source of recollection as this 38-year-old man: *Bought a whistle to carry in my pocket after election. Have felt like crying—started crying at work. . . . Have started Prosac anti-depressant. . . . Have stopped taking the paper, have stopped watching the news on TV, have stopped listening to the radio (NPR). Also have "unsubscribed" from computer bbs (Internet).*

There were other indications of constriction and numbing in the data. One woman described her state during the campaign: *I felt as though I was in a psychic fog during most of the campaign. The fog lifted after the election when our side of the argument came out more.* For others, including this man, the election was the beginning of the experience of numbing: *For almost two weeks after the election, I was almost catatonic—walking around as if in a dream.* Many respondents spoke of feeling estranged and alienated, experiences sometimes understood to be symptoms of constriction and numbing. Some of the respondents spoke of estrangement in very specific terms. One woman's estrangement was tied to her sense of others' hostility: *In the aftermath of the election, I felt very sad to think that I am so hated by the community in which I live.* Another wrote: *I feel less like I belong.* Still another respondent wrote: *I feel alien here in part due to the passage of 2 and in part due to our failure to mount an effective campaign against the religious right.*

A number of respondents' statements reflected the sense of a foreshortened future characteristic of the constriction of traumatic responses. We have seen examples of this phenomenon previously, as when a homosexual man declared his certainty that all of humankind would die in a nuclear holocaust. The sense of a foreshortened future was also apparent in this statement by a 41-year-old lesbian: *Although it's brought both my partner and me out of the closet and closer in our relationship, I do feel fearful for us. I worry about losing my freedom, having to give her up or being forced apart. I fear this Nazi mentality. Overall, I have a general sense of hopelessness for the human race, and it saddens me.* A 25-year-old woman expressed herself thus: *I am more depressed about being bisexual—I don't understand all the hate, and I don't like being an object of hate. It's scary. It makes me more depressed about the whole world.*

Perhaps the sense of a foreshortened future was nowhere more apparent than in the small number of references to suicidality in the aftermath of the amendment. In most cases, respondents who described suicidal ideation after the election indicated that they had moved beyond such thinking. Nonetheless, it was striking and sad to see that the election had caused such pain and disruption in the lives of even a handful of LGBs.

While we have discussed the intrusive and constricted symptoms of trauma separately here, they were sometimes described together in the data. As mentioned earlier, the two types of symptoms do tend to occur as members of a biphasic pattern in some people who have been traumatized (Herman 1992; van der Kolk 1987). Some respondents spoke of the two sets of symptoms interacting with one another, producing something of a *roller coaster* effect. Others spoke of one or both of them as separate entities.

*Symptoms of increased arousal.* Increased arousal signals that the traumatized person has gone into "permanent alert, as if the danger might return at any moment" (Herman 1992:35). After the passage of Amendment 2, the danger had indeed not gone away for Colorado LGBs; the legal implications of the amendment would hang over their heads for several years. Moreover, the vote had exposed the pervasiveness of homophobia and heterosexism in general. For many individual LGBs, the picture of homophobia had touched them in a deeply personal way, and the dangers associated with homonegativity did not disappear even after a district judge granted an injunction two months after the election.

In their comments, participants described all the common symptoms of hyperarousal, including difficulty sleeping and trouble concentrating. The hypervigilance and irritability associated with hyperarousal were featured in many statements, including this one by a white homosexual man from Fort Collins: *I sought psychotherapy because I have all this indirect anger concerning #2. I found I was often anxious and on edge, and I'd often lash out (verbally) at the slightest provocation. All my feelings seemed so intense and out of control.*

A white/American Indian lesbian in Colorado Springs described hypervigilance as a paradoxical expression of the fear of and the wish for some external intervention, terms familiar to clinicians who have handled traumatic responses (Herman 1992; van der Kolk 1987, 1996): *There is great expectation that something blatant will happen. When it does not, there is almost a feeling of disappointment in that there is no release from the constant expectancy.*

*Other phenomenological elements of trauma.* In addition to the symptoms of trauma found in the DSM nomenclature, respondents described a number of other reactions, among them helplessness, self-blame, and a diminished sense of self-worth. In Judith Herman's words, "Helplessness and isolation are the core experiences of psychological trauma" (Herman 1992:197). Feelings of helplessness and powerlessness were reported by respondents throughout the data. Often these feelings were expressed in statements coded as GRASP, OVER, or TRUST. This statement by a homosexual woman conveyed both the helplessness and the isolation: *Surprised, appalled, frustrated, anxious, tired, angry, let down, fearful of ignorance, helplessness, small in comparison to the "system," hands tied, uncomfortable at times at work because I learned after the election that most, if not all my coworkers voted "Yes" on 2. Not at ease with many heterosexuals in daily life—since November, 1992.*

Self-blame, which occurs frequently among traumatized people (Herman 1992; Janoff-Bulman 1992; Marmar 1991), was also a common characteristic in many of the TRAUMA responses. We saw some indications of self-blame previously when reviewing comments in the REGRET code. In cases of LGBs' regretting their absolute or relative lack of involvement in the campaign, there was a realistic, identifiable action that might have been taken but was not. In some instances of self-blame, however, respondents seemed to be holding themselves accountable either for actions they could not have taken in the first place or would probably have had a negligible impact. Self-blame of this sort sometimes seemed unreasonable and unhelpful. It made sense only by reminding ourselves how painful it is to feel genuinely helpless: "assuming responsibility for the trauma allows feelings of helplessness and vulnerability to be replaced with an illusion of potential control" (van der Kolk and McFarlane 1996). In some cases, respondents' self-blame for the loss of the election extended to blaming other members of the gay community, an issue to which we return later in this chapter.

Diminished feelings of self-worth also occur quite frequently in some individuals who have been through traumatizing circumstances. Some of the reduction in self-worth is rooted in helplessness and self-blame; some comes from the effort to reestablish the belief that the world is predictable and just (Janoff-Bulman 1992). Much of the campaign rhetoric around Amendment 2 had been explicitly or implicitly disparaging of LGBs (Douglass 1997; Eastland 1996b; Pharr 1992, 1993). Further, the trauma of the election was inextricably linked to LGB individuals' sense of sexual identity. When traumas are linked to personal characteristics, especially to those that feel deeply a part of oneself, challenges to self-worth are common and understandable (Garnets, Herek, and Levy 1992). This 23-year-old lesbian's comment illustrated how diminished self-worth was part of a complex of reactions: *After #2, felt very isolated, some homophobia, and lots of concern for my physical well being. Burnt out on politics. Less understood by parents. Insecure and decreased self-esteem. Was reasonably well adjusted before all this.*

The following comment by a 27-year-old gay man serves as a more subtle example of the way the experience of Amendment 2 influenced many LGBs' sense of self-worth: *When the Amendment passed, I was angry, hurt and fearful for my future. I knew I couldn't run since I knew the Amendment would follow me wherever I would go. I felt very closed-in since everyone now knew I was gay and they knew my disappointment. I felt on-stage, under pressure, and wondering why and who of my friends, co-workers and family members voted against me. I took it very personally.*

*TRAUMA and risk, resilience, and recovery.* One final dimension of the TRAUMA code had considerable implication for risk and resilience. This dimension touched on respondents' experience with prior victimization. Interestingly, the comments of respondents with such histories suggested that previous victimization could weigh in either as a risk or a resilience factor.

Some LGBs indicated that unresolved issues from prior experiences of victimization had fueled their reactions to Amendment 2, rendering those reactions both more complex and more intense than they might otherwise have been. This comment by a lesbian in her fifties described the intersection of the stress of the election outcome and childhood experiences of rejection. The event occurred on the evening of the election at a gathering of opponents of Amendment 2. *On November 3, I walked five blocks from my chorus' rehearsal to Mammoth Gardens—and, before we sang, I tripped and fell on some cable and injured my knee quite badly. I directly asked [five separate people] for help. I needed an Ace bandage, not an ambulance. I was turned down (rejected) by all I asked. We sang—the [election] returns got worse—I was in a lot of pain and worried about my stand-up-all-day job. I couldn't connect with people. So, I walked back to where I was parked—in a panic. I was feeling this "adult" rejection of my lesbianism—and as I walked up Colfax, I cried and screamed, "I'm sorry, I'm sorry" in my little girl voice (about five years old). The pain in my knee and my fear of injury allowed me to get in touch with rejection presented by Amendment 2 via some old rejection by adults.*

A gay man in his twenties had a different though parallel set of stressful experiences: *I am a Naval Reservist who was recalled to active duty in support of Operation Desert Storm. Even though the events of the recall and the election are in no way related, my feelings were very much the same. I felt a great deal of fear, shock, hopelessness, etc.* This man went on to detail some of his dreamlike symptoms after the election.

A white/American Indian lesbian related her own experience as an adolescent to her empathy for LGB youth dealing with Amendment 2: *I have thought a great deal about the adolescents who are gay/lesbian and their feelings about Amendment 2 (two teenagers committed suicide here in unrelated cases). It is a great sadness to me and has made me really miss my own teenage years when I was so in love with a woman but could not share that with anyone else. I wish there had been someone then who could have understood.*

For a few respondents, their past personal histories followed them right up to the election. A lesbian in her thirties wrote about a difficult interaction with a woman she had known in college; she described her as *one of my very best friends in college, who had had a lesbian relationship once in her life and with whom I had fallen in love (if I even knew what love was then).* The respondent went on, *I allowed her comments to "destroy" me after the November election. I called her to see how she voted on 2. She was always extremely religious; now she's a CFV "person." She told me I was sinning and most likely would go to hell but that she wouldn't because she had repented.*

The intersection of the election with difficult past experiences was not a universally negative one. A number of people—especially women with incest histories—reported that they had been able to deal with the amendment more effectively because they were able to apply lessons they had learned from the earlier stressors. This comment by a lesbian in her thirties exemplifies this "crisis competence" (Kimmel 1978): *My work on my incest issues has helped me to more effectively channel anger over these social injustices such as Amendment 2.* Another lesbian respondent reversed the more familiar model in which insight gained from earlier experiences is used for later ones. In this instance, she used Amendment 2 to clarify an incest history: *My response of anger and rage to Amendment 2 has in some odd ways helped me face and deal with my incest experience and my own internalized homophobia.*

This woman's statement also illustrated the fact that many LGBs used Amendment 2 to push the personal issue of being open about sexual orientation. This somewhat surprising consequence of the election is pursued more fully below under the OUTM (out more) code. This respondent's comment demonstrated how some LGBs used the negative aspects of Amendment 2 to their ultimate benefit: *The one reaction your questionnaire didn't really deal with is the positive aspects of being forced farther "out." My family has known almost as long as I have—but I have never confronted my born-again Christian sister with her homophobia. Painful, yes! Ultimately honest and freeing—yes!*

Situations that challenge people sometimes also move them to make important positive changes in their lives (Tedeschi and Calhoun 1995; Tedeschi, Park, and Calhoun 1998). The crisis situations do not "cause" these positive changes to occur. Such situations, of course, often leave people feeling helpless and isolated for extended periods of time. Rather, the means by which some people manage crisis, including the kinds of support they have, sometimes "cause" positive changes in trauma's wake. Several other respondents made note of significant life changes (besides coming out) that they had made after the election. Participants mentioned changes in jobs and career paths with particular frequency. Painful though the amendment was for many LGBs, it served as what one lesbian who left the teaching profession called a *catalyst* for positive change.

The occurrence of positive changes in a person's life does not necessarily mean that she or he had a less traumatic encounter than others. In fact, the severity of the reaction to the crisis and the presence of positive, post-traumatic growth occur independently of each other. Many of the respondents to this survey were quite negatively impacted by Amendment 2 but still managed to generate significant growth and positive change in their lives.

Before we leave the TRAUMA code, I want to make one final note. Optimal management of the crisis by LGBs almost always involved support of one kind or another from other people. Managing and surviving crises—not to mention learning from them—are not typically done in isolation. From simple ways to very complicated ones, other people

exerted a profound influence on the way respondents managed their reactions to Amendment 2.

## VWP

The VWP code emerged after our team was well into the pilot coding of
data. It was born of our frustration that the TRAUMA code, as we had
defined it, was not able to capture some important trauma-related issues
in the data. As we discussed the matter, we realized that many of the elements we were missing could be subsumed in a category corresponding
to the three actors or participants in every trauma—the victim, the witness, and the perpetrator. Once we included VWP in our pilot coding,
we found that this code identified new aspects of the trauma experience.
While the TRAUMA code had focused on the phenomenology of post-
traumatic responses, the VWP code was more attentive to the active
meaning making that respondents undertook in an effort to make sense
of the Amendment 2 campaign and election. Our decision to develop
and use the VWP code illustrates the importance of being open to new
possibilities emerging from the data even after putative coding schemas
have been established and revised many times over (Perlman 1973).
This code also represents one of the products of our willingness to engage in wide-ranging discussions about the data even when it was not
immediately apparent that such discussions would lead to productive
understandings.

*Interconnections of victim, witness, and perpetrator.* The three elements or
actors in the so-called trauma triad are inextricably linked; none can exist
without the other two. A thorough understanding of a given case of
trauma rests on grasping the dynamics of the relationships among the
three actors (Staub 1993).

*Victim.* Identifying the victim in the passage of Amendment 2 was a simple task for most respondents. Typically, most referred to themselves individually and/or to the LGB community more generally as the target of the
amendment's victimization. In a few instances, particular subgroups
within the LGB community—LGBs of color or LGB youth—were singled
out as victims.

The central feature of victimization as it was described in the VWP code was the experience of feeling hated by other people. Other codes have focused on issues such as being lied about and feeling betrayed, but it appears that the core of the trauma of Amendment 2 was feeling that one was the object of hatred. A woman in her midforties spoke of being hated and the sense of hopelessness that came from it: *I have a very strong feeling of hopelessness as a result of hatred directed at me as a visible lesbian business woman. I've been "outed" to other members of my profession and potential clients in an attempt to destroy my business and a reference was made by a local man that I would mysteriously "disappear."* This woman's statement makes sense of why feeling hated was central to the trauma experience of many LGBs. If one is viewed as worthy of antipathy, one's very being is called into question at a fundamental level and there is little that one can do to change the situation. What one could bring to bear on matters—namely, oneself—has already been deemed to be bad and unworthy. There is nothing left with which to fight. No wonder hopelessness results, and hopelessness is, of course, central to the experience of trauma (Herman 1992).

A related reason for the emphasis on feeling hated as a feature of victimization in the VWP code may have been the slogan of the campaign against Amendment 2. While other slogans were used for brief periods, the main slogan for the duration of the campaign was the now familiar, "Hate is not a family value." This served as a clever counter to the name of the organization that was promoting the amendment, Colorado for Family Values.

The catch phrase, "Hate is not a family value," undoubtedly reflected the feelings of many Colorado LGBs as the campaign got under way. Gay people viewed the amendment as an expression of homophobia and heterosexism, and it was not a long jump from those construals of bias against LGBs to the notion of hatred against them. In addition, frequent exposure to the "Hate is not . . ." motto may have brought home the understanding that the amendment represented a form of hatred. The repetition of that message during the campaign may have influenced LGBs' understanding of the amendment as a form of hatred. This is not to say that CFV's campaign was not, in and of itself, a clear statement of antagonism toward LGBs; in many of its forms, it certainly was. It is to say that, when LGBs saw the hatred in CFV's message and labeled it as such, they may also have reified that particular understanding of the amendment. The more the amendment was understood in those terms, the more LGBs experienced it as a campaign of hatred.

*Witness.* The role of the witness is all too often ignored in analyses of different types of trauma. In the most negative circumstances, the silence of witnesses has profoundly dangerous implications for the victims of trauma. Staub (1993) has suggested that the silence of witnesses reduces empathy for victims and decreases the likelihood that the perpetrators' actions will be challenged. The net result is that silence is construed as assent and the perpetrators are encouraged in their victimization of others. From a practical and political perspective, then, the role of the witness in traumatic circumstances is a critical, if often neglected, one.[4]

In their comments, LGB respondents not only referred to witnesses; they seemed to be almost obsessed with the witness role. In some cases, this was because they actually knew friends, family members, and colleagues who had failed to witness for LGBs by voting for Amendment 2. This often evoked a great deal of sadness and/or frustration. The 37-year-old homosexual man's comment below illustrates a situation in which family members did not provide witnessing of the sort he needed: *It's especially difficult for me and my family. Everyone is a fundamentalist Christian and I start to think they really do hate me.*

Even when respondents were referring to people they did not know, they tended to give potential witnesses enormous power. In part, this power was based on the effect witnesses sometimes had on an environment that LGBs perceived as dangerous or hostile in the aftermath of the election. Both elements—the perception of a changed environment and the potential power of witnesses to mitigate that change—are evident in this comment by a lesbian: *It is shocking to me, and I continue to be appalled that my community and my state are much more hostile environments than I used to think. It's hard to maintain an optimistic outlook on life. On the other hand, I am encouraged by straight colleagues, government officials, other heterosexuals, other minorities who are speaking out and taking stands against Amendment 2.* The presence of witnesses who spoke out seemed to change her experience of the election for the better.

Speaking out, of course, is relative. A number of LGBs expressed frustration with heterosexuals—that is, with potential witnesses—who were generally supportive but were seen to have done too little. Sometimes, this frustration extended to a wish to exact vengeance on them. In the case of a 28-year-old lesbian, the would-be vengeance took the form of calling them names: *Re: boycott—when the heterosexual population complains about being labeled as bigots, I like to point out (1) what did they do to educate their less enlightened friends, and (2) now they know how the g/l/b community feels [when they are] labeled "deviants."*

As we have seen, most of the references to witnessing in the VWP code focused on respondents' desire to have others witness for them. An occasional comment carried the inverse message: respondents were themselves witnessing for others. Some expressed particular concern about the election's effect on LGB youth. As we saw in the ISMS code, a small number of white respondents used their encounter with Amendment 2 as a basis for increasing their understanding of racism. An even smaller number of respondents said they intended to take an active stand against—that is, witness against—racism.

Some respondents implicitly saw themselves as witnessing for themselves—and by extension for other LGBs—by coming out. In other instances, respondents explicitly spoke of their desire to stand for and be strong for the gay community. These issues are explored in greater depth in the next section of codes.

Two other witness themes warrant mention here, although both will be developed in greater depth later. Both were seen to reflect a witness function by a considerable number of respondents. First, many viewed the judicial challenge to the constitutionality of Amendment 2 in hopeful terms. They were relieved that the effort to enjoin the amendment had been successful, and they trusted that the amendment would eventually be deemed unconstitutional. This perspective led many LGBs to see the judicial branch of government as a witness that had fulfilled part of its potential and, quite possibly, would live up to its full potential ultimately. Second, as we shall see in the summary of the THANKS code, many respondents also viewed this research as providing a witnessing function.

*Perpetrator.* At first glance, identifying the perpetrator of the Amendment 2 trauma would not seem to be a difficult task. However, as we read the VWP-coded comments, it became evident that there was no consensus among respondents as to the identity of the perpetrator.

Some LGBs left the question open; the agent of perpetration was variously labeled *a formless threat, the opposition we seem to face,* or—simply—*the enemy.* Sometimes the presence of a perpetrator was quietly implied rather than addressed directly, as in this comment by a Colorado Springs gay man: *Prejudice is taught, not learned!* At first we were unable to link any of our codes to his statement, but then it occurred to us that he did seem to be referring implicitly to a perpetrator, namely, the person or entity who teaches prejudice.

Some respondents saw the perpetrator in specific individuals they knew. One 20-year-old lesbian referred to having a landlord whose rental company openly supported Amendment 2. Her sense of the danger posed by the landlord was compounded by being *afraid to talk about [Amendment 2] in my own home because my landlord lives upstairs.*

A number of other respondents identified groups of people as the perpetrator. Four particular groups were named. In increasing order of their prevalence in the comments, these were heterosexuals, voters, the religious right, and CFV. The VWP-coded comments often portrayed these groups who had brought about the election in monolithic terms, and as virtually omnipotent. This quality can be found in the words of a 25-year-old lesbian from a Denver suburb: *The biggest sense of helplessness/hopelessness I have is in relation to those (CFV) who would assume they know me—sexually and otherwise and with no respect to me, assume that I have chosen deviance to purposely "eat away" at the family institution.* In many VWP comments, identification of the perpetrator was coupled with statements of fear. A 17-year-old woman was direct in saying, *I'm scared of the power the religious right has.*

Some respondents' had such negative views of the LGB community or of subgroups within the community that they seemed to be suggesting that gay people were responsible for Amendment 2. We explore these statements below in the discussion of codes expressing respondents' relationships to other LGBs. Taking the opposite approach, some VWP-coded statements implicated homophobia and heterosexism as the underlying cause of the amendment. Very few respondents identified homonegativity in this fashion. One who did was a 21-year-old lesbian from Colorado Springs who wrote: *This year is the first year I have come out. Amendment 2 has made me see the necessity of it. When the Amendment first passed I responded with shock, anger, disbelief, and intense work on the issue. I felt the world crash. Since then I have been losing the energy to fight this thing. The larger issue is homophobia and it's looming ever larger.*

The identification of homonegativity as a causal agent in the election offered the advantage of focusing on political analysis and a political problem rather than on group(s) or individuals as the perpetrators. This is also consistent with Staub's observation that in given situations victims—or scapegoats—have often been "preselected" on account of a history of cultural devaluation (Staub 1993:315). Viewed from this perspective, CFV's ideology drew on preexisting divisions in the population. Locating the source of the victimization in homonegativity pointed toward a political solution rather than toward escalating tensions with particular group(s) or individuals.

*VWP and risk, resilience, and recovery.* Focusing attention on a particular group as the perpetrator raises problems. For one, it is sometimes difficult to know just who is—or is not—a member of the group. Some LGBs had expended considerable energy trying to figure out just who belonged to the offending group(s). A 27-year-old woman from Grand Junction described her dilemma in this regard as follows: *Amendment 2 has made me suspicious of organized religion—I am also having a very difficult time not becoming cynical about organized religion and Born-again Christians and Pat Robertson and his gang. I am very angry overall about society in general, at times. I find myself walking through malls or down the street and looking at people, wondering how they voted.*

A 38-year-old homosexual man from Boulder offered the following analysis of the impact of putting considerable energy into an effort to categorize individuals as perpetrators or not: *Though I'm very out, I noticed the subtle way Amendment 2 pushed me back into the closet. I didn't enjoy being outside my home or in public as much as I had. This was due to a preoccupation with wanting to know who I was with who voted yes on 2. Since I couldn't determine who voted yes, I was not being nice to anyone. This made being out in public less enjoyable and being in my home, where I knew how everyone voted, more enjoyable, since I could be nice there. Home was becoming my closet again.*

While these respondents invested energy in identifying individual perpetrators, other respondents wove fantasies of vengeance centered on actions such as burning down churches and attacking perpetrators of hate crimes against LGBs. While the merits and drawbacks of vengeful fantasies are arguable in general, such a strategy is probably seriously limited as a means of dealing with trauma.

Again in general terms, people can begin to move out of the helplessness associated with trauma to the degree that they can adopt an action orientation and/or find and use support from others (Cohen and Wills 1985; Ganellen and Blaney 1984; Hobfoll and Freedy 1990; Moos and Schaefer 1986; Shinn, Lehmann, and Wong 1984; Solomon, Smith, Robins, and Fischbach 1987). Respondents reported taking a variety of countermeasures against helplessness. Some of their actions were intrapersonal in nature. A 37-year-old homosexual man, for example, recounted his cognitive struggle against internalizing CFV's special rights message: *I have sometimes found myself thinking that I don't deserve to be treated special. Then I realize that I do deserve to be protected and I deserve to have others respect my homosexuality.*

Other participants' active coping strategies were more interpersonal in nature. One homosexual man in his forties made it a point to mail literature about Amendment 2 to friends across the country. A lesbian, also in her forties, made an intentional effort to articulate LGB concerns to strangers—something she had previously felt comfortable doing only with friends and acquaintances. These actions represented efforts to increase positive witnessing of Colorado LGBS by others. Many participants chose to come out, an action that, while typically interpersonal in an immediate sense, frequently had political implications as well. Still other LGBs adopted overtly political means, some for the first time in their lives.

The use of active coping strategies allowed LGBs to move out of helplessness and experience a greater sense of empowerment. The consequences of such approaches are illustrated in a 29-year-old lesbian's statement: *Mostly I am determined to be the catalyst for education and change in my circle of friends, family, and workplace. Being out is the most solid foundation I have, and the best defense against feelings of anxiety and rage.* When respondents were unable to identify sources of support or possibilities for action in the face of Amendment 2, their comments often ended on a note of helplessness, hopelessness, and demoralization. In this state of mind the only action they could contemplate was to be more closeted (ISOLATE, OUTL) and/or to leave the state (LEAVE), reactions which we consider below.

## Codes Representing Respondents' Relationships with Other LGBs: Disrupted LGB Identity

As we pursued the phenomenology of what was, for many LGBs, a trauma and their meaning making about that trauma in the previous two codes, we came upon a number of references to the way respondents felt about and behaved toward other gay people. When a victimizing experience involves an identifiable group of people rather than a single individual, certain complexities emerge. One of these is how the victimized group members feel about themselves individually; another facet involves how group members feel about one another. The four codes addressed in the balance of this chapter concern the relationships between and among LGBs played out in the shadow of the campaign for and the passage of Amendment 2: AQ (anger against other LGBs), BARRIERS (perceived barriers to unity within the LGB community), IHE (internalized homophobia—explicit), and IHI (internalized homophobia—inferred).

This set of codes was among the most instructive in the data. In her narrative about the coding experience, Sylvie said that the single code from which she learned the most was IHI. This set of codes was also among the most difficult to code and analyze. It was distressing to read the pain of LGBs who felt victimized by Amendment 2; it was even more distressing to see how often and how intensely that pain was used against other members of the victimized gay community. In his narrative regarding the research team, Sean put the IHI code into perspective: *I had the feeling that the community had really been trampled and that recovery was uncertain. I suspect I wondered if the blow had been too much for everyone and thought that it would set us back many years. At times, I felt very hopeful and thankful that Amendment 2 had brought us together so nicely and that we were only stronger for it. There were also times when I was disgusted, disappointed, and annoyed by the IHI responses. At those times, I felt there was only little hope.*

Sean's statement serves as an important reminder as we review the comments in these four codes. As a group, the comments are harsh and unsettling. They reveal enormous hostility between and among members of a community under siege. It would have been easy for us as a coding team to criticize those who statements fit into any of these four codes. All had been victimized by Amendment 2. When we lost touch with the underlying trauma that had fueled their hostile statements, we lost our empathy for them as well. We also lost the only information that could help us make sense of these or of any of the rest of the codes. Without recognizing the fundamental role of homonegativity underlying their comments, we were in danger of blaming the victims for their responses to Amendment 2.

Realizing this risk, we found it useful to track how easily we moved into victim-blaming. Doing so increased our ability to understand cognitively and to hear empathically the ease with which so many respondents had blamed other LGBs or internalized CFV's negative messages. In essence, our coding team's process in this regard mirrored aspects of our respondents' reactions in the aftermath of Amendment 2. The value of working in a team context was particularly clear in this phase of data analysis. Other members of the team could remind the rest of us when we lost sight of the homonegativity at the root of LGB respondents' anger toward other gay people. The team as a group protected the respondents from an individual member's occasional lapse into victim-blaming. It might be said that as a team we protected each other from such lapses as well.

The relationships between respondents and the LGB community have implications at both the personal and community levels. What follows begins at the community level and moves toward the personal, exploring the codes in this order: AQ, BARRIERS, IHE, and IHI. It warrants noting that, in fact, the sentiments expressed in these comments did not follow in such a clear sequence.

## AQ

The AQ (anger at "queers" or at other LGBs) code had much in common with the other anger codes addressed above (ACFV, ACHRIST, AHET, AMEDIA, APROC, and ASTATE), especially the impulse to strike out with anger in the face of an oppressive assault. However, AQ differed from them in that the target of the anger was not the perpetrators of or even the witnesses to Amendment 2, but other LGBs. It is because AQ described important dimensions of respondents' relationships with other gay people that we discuss it in this section rather than in the anger codes section of the data in chapter 5.

The nature of the anger expressed by participants toward other LGBs varied considerably (though less so than in the BARRIERS, IHE, and IHI codes). Fewer comments fell into the AQ code than into each of the other codes; respondents' criticisms of other LGBs usually came in forms other than direct statements of anger of the sort that were coded AQ.

When participants did express their anger at other gay people directly, typically they were quite explicit in stating their reasons. One theme to emerge was that gay people had allegedly dealt with their oppression in inappropriate or even destructive ways. A white lesbian in her midthirties accused LGBs of a litany of offenses. Interestingly, at the bottom of her list were apolitical heterosexuals and, presumably, members of the religious right: *Fuck them all! It will be a horrible decade. I've never seen so many disempowered "diseased" people in my life: passive queers, internally hostile queers, "nice" queers, apolitical straights, sick and damaged Bible nazis. And to watch people resist dealing with their disempowerment (fucked-upness) gives me a sense of hopelessness that people don't care because they don't see how oppression affects them.*

Other AQ criticisms were both less vitriolic and more focused. In general, respondents seemed to take their own level of political activism as a baseline and to criticize LGBs whose activism fell below that line. A bisexual Eurasian man's comment was illustrative: *Although I am not openly active in the gay, lesbian, and bisexual communities, it angers me to no end that I know more people than I care to count that are gay that didn't even vote. How can these same people and many others complain about how the straight world is so unfair when they don't even use the power to vote for their own community? Emphasizing that there really is a very low sense of community even within the gay people themselves—that both scares and angers me.*

Other prominent themes that emerged in the AQ comments were: anger at closeted LGBs, anger at LGBs who were seen as spokespeople for the community, and anger at members of the community who had failed to represent LGBs in ways deemed acceptable by the respondents.

## BARRIERS

The BARRIERS code reflected barriers to unity within the LGB community. Such divisions are hardly unique to the postelection situation in Colorado; indeed, the diversity of the LGB community has been cited as one impediment to LGBs acquiring a sense of community identity (Garnets and Kimmel 1991). Sometimes community divisions were discussed in hostile terms and sounded like expressions of internalized oppression and/or horizontal hostility. It seemed to our team that, taken collectively, BARRIERS statements represented respondents' efforts to maintain their connection with a community that was under siege and disliked, while also trying to make that community more acceptable to society at large.

The BARRIERS code included a great many statements and reflected considerable variety. However, they fell into two broad groups: some—though relatively few—comments merely observed community divisions without actively participating in them, while others actively participated in such divisions in the process of writing their statements. A 29-year-old Anglo lesbian expressed her reaction to community divisions in very emotional terms: *I have been heartbroken and distressed about how the community (L-G-B) is divided since the election, and how we are sniping at each other. Why aren't we kinder to one another?* Even fewer respondents acknowledged their role in problems related to community divisions. This comment by a Boulder lesbian was exceptional in that regard: *I'm tired of all the infighting around reorganizing after the election (even though I participate in it!).*

In contrast to these comments, the more typical statement went beyond observing divisions and actively engaged in their generation. The following analysis of the election by a 35-year-old homosexual man from Durango explicitly held some LGBs accountable for its outcome: *Part of the problem which helped 2 pass was misinformation and some of the "in your face" tactics/attitudes of some gays and organizations.* A gay white man from Pueblo implied that the community was divided, in the midst of observations about the broader problems of homophobia and heterosexism: *Tired of defending myself and my people! Tired of AIDS discrimination and fear association! Tired of bigotry! Tired of apathy in gay community! Tired of uneducated community.*

A Denver homosexual man expressed his view of divisions within the community more critically, even in the context of a statement ostensibly focused on the media: *I'm tired of the term "Special rights" as Channel 7 commonly refers to it—when showing groups of gays, lesbians, etc., on TV, it would be nice to see "ordinary appearances" rather than "extremists," i.e., skinheads, drag queens, etc. The community is trying to express, through the media that we aren't different, yet the usual medium always shows an extreme. What about professionals, mothers, fathers, etc.?*

*One view or many?* Underlying many comments coded BARRIERS was the assumption that the LGB community had to come together and present a fully unified front to the world. This assumption was seldom made explicit; rather, it was an unspoken—and therefore largely unquestioned—belief in many BARRIERS statements.[5] Some respondents argued for ideological unity, as in the following comment by a 27-year-old lesbian: *Amendment 2 has definitely had its drawbacks and its good points. On the one hand, I feel that it is forcing the gay community to come together to fight this, but our diversity may be our downfall. Everyone is going in 1 million directions. It's almost impossible to really come together and try to fight this with one ideology, or one mind set.* Others focused on the need for unity in more pragmatic terms. A 23-year-old Latino homosexual man reflected on the goal behind unity, even in the face of postelection proposals for compromise amendments: *Amendment 2 has been very difficult on all of my friends in one way or another. The lack of ability to come together, and anger on the newer issues surrounding the new possible amendments, is also frustrating. I hope the gay community can come to a consensus on the issues so we can overturn this amendment.*

Respondents seldom questioned the presumed need for unity. The following comment by a 31-year-old gay man in Fort Collins was unusual: *I'm tired of hearing people (gay and straight) say the "gay community" needs to get its act together—politically, socially, or whatever. Face it, the "gay community" is a microcosm of the larger society, and when has the general American society ever had a consensus on anything?!* Although he did not offer any suggestions about how the LGB community should proceed in light of its diversity, he did raise an important question about a matter most respondents took for granted.

*Disagreements about tactics.* A number of the issues in the BARRIERS code could be subsumed under the question: What kinds of political tactics would the LGB community find most appropriate or promising? By far the most frequent response to this question argued for what has been referred to as an assimilationist position.[6] Respondents did not typically use the language of assimilation and accommodation; rather, they usually wrote about the need for tactics that did not alienate heterosexuals. Queer or separatist positions were referred to indirectly and usually in negative language. Various statements, for example, eschewed *extreme tactics, inflammatory confrontation, "loud mouth" gay people,* and *"in your face" tactics/attitudes of some gays and organizations.* The sole exception to this trend was a comment by a gay man in his twenties who followed a list of threats and harassment that he and his LGB friends had received with this statement: *I feel more committed to queer politics and less connected to assimilationist/mainstream responses to politics.*

*The response of heterosexuals.* The assimilationist position emphasizes full integration of LGBs into mainstream society. Given the locus of power in mainstream society, such a position privileges heterosexuals' viewpoints. Thus it was not surprising that many of the BARRIERS statements, rooted as they were in an assimilationist stance, focused on how heterosexuals would respond to LGBs' political actions. This perspective was called into question only rarely in the data. One of the few to do so was a 44-year-old lesbian who wrote: *The prevailing attitude is, "if we are nice enough, we will change the opinion of those who disapprove of us." I disagree.*

Far more frequently, participants in the study seemed to accept the premise that political activism on behalf of LGB rights should take heterosexuals' reactions into account. Respondents did not usually endorse this perspective explicitly. Instead, it was taken for granted, seamlessly folded into their comments. Only occasionally did respondents offer a rationale for their position in this regard. One who did was a 21-year-old Caucasian/Puerto Rican gay man who wrote: *I resent some gays and lesbians,* and then went on to name particular activists and their actions with which he did not agree. This gay man ended by saying: *I'm not happy about [Amendment 2] but I'm not going to estrange the few resources I have.*

*Other divisive issues.* While tactical questions accounted for many of the disagreements within the community, a number of other issues were also viewed as barriers to a cohesive community. Differences between out and closeted LGBs was one such issue. The two contrasting efforts made to come to terms with acts of disclosure in the face of homonegativity were exemplified in the following two statements. The first was penned by a 35-year-old gay man: *I feel there is a big difference between being "closeted" and showing discretion. Trying to shove our views and values down heterosexuals' throats is going to cause more problems than good.* A 39-year-old lesbian came down on the other side of the conflict: *I became increasingly intolerant of my closeted friends—that distanced me from some people.*

Many LGBs of color in the sample expressed their concerns about being caught between the homonegativity of the broader community and the racism of white LGBs who mirrored that in society at large. In the BARRIERS code, statements by LGBs of color often reflected these tensions. A Latina gay woman explained her feelings in the aftermath of the election: *As a woman of color, now I feel more vulnerable because I will no longer know whether people are discriminating against me for being Latino or because I am gay.* A black homosexual man wrote: *I don't like Colorado anymore and plan to move away. I can't tolerate the ignorance, especially white gays against black gays.*

Other divisive issues raised within the BARRIERS theme included the boycott (see the BA and BF codes discussed below), and the role of EPO-Colorado (see the CCRIT, CCOMP, and the codes—REPOC, RINFO, RLIES, and RMIS—explored above). In addition, a few respondents were concerned about the role of cliques in the LGB community, the rural-urban split in the state, and conflicts with resource distribution. The latter focused especially on how the battle against Amendment 2 had siphoned off resources that might otherwise have been used for HIV/AIDS prevention and treatment.

## IHE

The IHE code contained responses in which internalized homophobia (IH) was referenced explicitly. There were two distinct kinds of references to IH in this code—those in which respondents spoke of other LGBs' problems with IH, and those in which they spoke of their own IH. Distinctly different tones characterized the two types of comments. The tone of the former was sometimes hostile and often critical, with IH viewed as a negative quality in other LGBs. One 50-year-old lesbian, who said she was *stunned and appalled at cannibalism in G/L community,* suggested: *Someone should research internalized oppression as it relates to political action of a minority community.*

Self-observations of IH, on the other hand, occurred most typically in the context of statements describing self-discovery and growth. These comments were also noteworthy for their frequent use of first-person statements that suggested that the respondents making them were able both to acknowledge their own feelings and to tolerate contradictory feelings and situations. Reading IHE statements of this type was a balm to the coding team after our prolonged exposure to so many negative comments about LGBs. For many respondents who made explicit references to internalized homophobia, the campaign and election represented an opportunity for self-exploration. These LGBs were in a variety of positions with respect to their personal experiences with sexual orientation. One 42-year-old lesbian wrote: *I've been a lesbian for 25 years. Before Amendment 2, I felt pretty accepting of myself—sexual orientation. Since #2, I've had to reexamine on a deeper level my own internalized homophobia and shame.* A 50-year-old lesbian with a very different coming-out trajectory offered the following perspective: *I wasn't able to acknowledge being lesbian until I was in my forties. Just as I was starting to feel comfortable with myself, the election happened. It certainly has made me more aware of my own feelings, my own hang-ups, my own anger.*

For some respondents, Amendment 2 represented an opportunity to confront the stigma associated with being LGB (see, for example, Coleman 1986; Crocker and Lutsky 1986; de Monteflores 1986). A 49-year-old gay schoolteacher wrote about changes he had made in the aftermath of the election: *I've come out to more people since the passage of #2—like my neighbor of 18 years and his family. . . . I used to be embarrassed to hear the word gay or queer but the more it is used, the more desensitized I become.* A 37-year-old gay man described how he had used the Amendment 2 experience as a basis for self-discovery: *Amendment 2 has helped me solidify my identity as a gay person. It has drawn me closer to gay people in general and has helped me work through my own internal homophobia.*

Some bisexuals in the sample reported a somewhat different twist on the issue of internalized homophobia—or, more precisely, internalized biphobia. The tension around biphobia often took the form of conflicts about whether to be openly bisexual or not. A bisexual woman described her conflict in terms that illustrate the willingness, so prominent in the IHE code, to handle conflicting views: *I feel more and more obligation to come out when I don't feel comfortable doing so. With so much debate among coworkers and acquaintances, I've found myself in the undesired position of feeling compelled to reveal my sexuality to those who wouldn't need to know otherwise. Also, I identified myself as exclusively lesbian until a couple of years ago; now with Amendment 2 I feel like I'm "copping out" when I admit to bisexuality. I feel very torn between the desire for activism and the need for privacy (and to spend time on other concerns, i.e., career).*

The IHE comments sometimes left issues unresolved; respondents asked difficult questions of themselves and did not always have satisfactory answers. What distinguished the statements coded IHE—at least those written from the first-person perspective—was an openness to self-discovery and change. Taken collectively, the self-referential IHE statements represented an effort to respond to Amendment 2 as an opportunity for change. They differed dramatically from comments in the next code.

## IHI

The IHI code was unique among all the codes on account of the manner in which our team employed it. Our general approach was to use a code only if we could argue that any reasonable person could easily grasp the relationship between the code as we had defined it, and the specific content of the comment. We denied ourselves any legitimate basis for "reading into" the comments anything that was not explicitly there. Occasionally, in the process of coding, a team member would argue for using a code on the basis of something he or she had inferred from the data. One of the functions of the team at such times was to argue against such inferences and to keep the coding process faithful to the statements made by respondents.

Our handling of the IHI code was in marked contrast to this general approach; its very name—Internalized Homophobia Inferred—indicates as much. Here, team members were invited to make inferences about the statements rather than to read them in the relatively straightforward way in which we read other comments. Discussing comments that might warrant an IHI code was therefore a time-consuming and wide-ranging enterprise. Not only were we negotiating what comments constituted the IHI code, but we were also developing a model of internalized homophobia as we went along. In the process, we drew on a broad range of literature on stigma and internalized oppression. Just as importantly, all the members of the team drew on the personal work related to internalized oppression that each of us had carried out.[7]

*The breadth of the IHI code.* This code was designed to flag comments that indicated an internalization of homophobic/heterosexist messages. We knew that IH could manifest itself in a variety of ways.[8] Further, we expected most respondents not to refer to their internalized homophobia directly. (Such direct references warranted the IHE code.) Rather, we expected that hints of IH might be woven into comments on virtually any topic of discussion. The IH construct was more ambiguous than many of the constructs on which other codes were based. This ambiguity, in combination with our broad definition of IHI, required extensive negotiations about the applicability of this code to given comments. It was not surprising that Sylvie singled out the IHI code for two reasons: She worried that we were using it too loosely, and she learned more from it than from any other code. Among other things, Sylvie's discomfort reflected the observation that, in a given case, the inclusion of a particular member (comment) in a class (code) could be questionable because it was more difficult to specify the details of each case than to recognize a "family resemblance" between many members of the class (Kuhn 1970). Given the ambiguity and breadth of our definition of IHI, the code covered a large group of comments, large both in number and variety, which shared a loosely defined family resemblance.

*LGB identity as negative.* IHI comments ranged from blatant to subtle. In a few instances, respondents were overt in describing their sexual orientations in negative terms, as when a woman (whose comment we have seen before) noted: *I am more depressed about being bisexual—I don't understand all the hate, and I don't like being an object of hate.*

As we read these and similar statements, our team was careful to acknowledge that we were making inferences and that, in the absence of further information about the respondents, we were not prepared to make any absolute assertions as to the presence (or absence) of IH. Moreover, we continually reminded ourselves that, to a large degree, being depressed about nonheterosexual identity (for example) or wanting to change one's orientation made sense in the hostile environment that Colorado appeared to have become as a result of Amendment 2. The question of whether a given participant was in fact expressing IH or not could not be determined on the basis of a single comment. But such comments certainly made us want to explore the issue further with these respondents.

*Use of CFV's language.* Some of the comments coded IHI seemed explicitly to borrow language used by Colorado for Family Values. While it was not unusual for responses to contain CFV's language, in most cases respondents bracketed that language, sometimes through the use of quotation marks and at other times by the context, which made it clear that they knew they were using words that had become CFV's code language. Implied in such bracketing was a critical and qualified use of CFV language. This was in contrast to IHI-coded comments, in which CFV's words seemed to be employed without criticism or reservation. When our team encountered language of this latter sort, we sometimes spoke of the respondent having internalized not just homophobia but the very language of homophobia as well.

The internalization of CFV's position was evident in this statement by a 25-year-old gay man: *I feel as if I, as a human being, have been invalidated.* A 24-year-old lesbian's comment contained an interesting linguistic contradiction that seemed to indicate that she had accepted the notion that being a lesbian was something she had to "admit" to—rather than, say, acknowledge: *I hope to feel more secure in the heterosexual community by admitting my orientation and feeling proud of who I am as a person, not solely based on my preferences.* A 38-year-old gay man's comment also suggested that he had internalized the notion that he/LGBs did not deserve protection against discrimination: *During the first week [after the election], I was devastated, as were all of us, that we are not deserving of protection from discrimination.*

Statements of this sort did not "prove" that their authors had internalized the homonegative messages of the campaign. However, they were in striking contrast to statements that expressed serious reservations and qualifications about campaign messages. Consider, for example, the difference in connotation between the last statement and a hypothetical one which would express the writer's qualifications about some homonegative message, as in: "During the first week [after the election], I was devastated, as were all of us, that the majority of voters see us as not deserving of protection from discrimination."

*LGB orientations as a master status.* The concept of master status is used to refer to a stigma that becomes so central in others' view of particular people that it takes on defining properties. The stigma effectively "eclipses all other aspects of stigmatized persons, their talents and abilities" (Ainlay, Coleman, and Becker 1986:6). Nonheterosexual orientation generally operates as a master status in American society. It would seem that, in circumstances where anti-gay efforts are heightened, the intensity with which sexual orientation acts as a master status increases.

The concept of master status was helpful in our team's efforts to understand the IH effects of Amendment 2. It helped us make sense of a number of phenomena that suggested that respondents were struggling with the issue of internalizing negative messages from the campaign. Manifestations of respondents' acceptance of and subjugation to the master status included personalization of the master status, homogenization of LGBs, struggles to be normal, push to assimilation, granting power to heterosexuals, and tokenism within the LGB community.

*Personalization of the master status.* In reference to LGBs, the concept of master status means that gay people are intrinsically and fundamentally defined at the social level by their sexual orientations. If LGB persons accept and act out of that belief, they have personalized the master status. Acceptance of that status is an especially easy move in a climate in which individuals with one characteristic—and, often, no other discernible qualities in common—have been singled out for social and legal mistreatment. Under the circumstances of the Amendment 2 campaign and election, LGBs often saw themselves as primarily or as solely gay people. As their sexual orientations became foregrounded in the social realm, they often accepted this focus. Indeed, to some degree, their political survival depended on their doing so.

In the following statement by a 39-year-old gay man, the personalization of his sexual orientation is quite explicit: *During the hearing on the preliminary injunction, I couldn't help but feel I was on trial, as a gay man. I know Amendment 2 was aimed at homosexuals in general, but there are times I feel Colorado rejected me. I got over these feelings; they don't dominate me but they are there.*

The personalization of her orientation as a master status is more subtle in this 40-year-old gay woman's statement: *Very saddened and appalled by these tallied results brought on by ignorance, misrepresented concepts, self-righteous bigoted attitudes—left oppressed, discounted and judged, legally voted to be reflected as a less than accepted human being, even if a human being.* The author of this statement never strayed far from seeing the election as the basis for her feelings.

As we read such statements, we grew to believe that keeping the external homonegative event or situation in mind had insulated some respondents against the most negative and intrusive effects of IH. We see this process at work in the following two statements, in which the respondents showed signs of personalizing their sexualities as a master status but resisted buying into the personalization completely by keeping the external homonegativity explicit. The first is by a 24-year-old homosexual man from Fort Collins, a city where years earlier a referendum had rejected a proposal to protect LGBs against discrimination: *I am so tired of fighting. I'm tired of having to justify my existence to the electorate every couple years.* In the second statement, a 50-year-old lesbian from Durango demonstrated that she had internalized a view of herself as being besieged but understood the source of this feeling to lie outside—rather than within—herself: *I feel "family values" have become code words for prejudice, conformity, hatred, intolerance, and injustice; and I am totally and completely tired of the issue, the debate, the protest and the position of challenge, protest and defense that is expected [of me] as a lesbian. I really would prefer not to have it in my face most every day, I would die for my rights but I don't want to live each day as a warrior over them.*

These personalizing statements indicate that LGBs can simultaneously accept and reject their own experiences of sexuality as a socially imposed master status. It is unlikely that anyone who belongs to a targeted group can completely avoid personalizing the master status. As we saw in the GRASP code, any attempt to understand the sociopolitical factors that impinge on one's life necessarily entails viewing oneself as a lesbian, gay, or bisexual person who is a member of a marginalized group—a group defined socially on the basis of a single characteristic.

*Homogenization of LGBs.* One of the consequences of being defined by a master status—that is, on the basis of sexual orientation alone—is that one's individuality risks being seen as secondary to one's status as a gay person. In such circumstances, LGBs are viewed as a homogeneous group of people whose sexual orientations are defining and whose individualizing qualities are lost. The master status is thus more significant in defining members of the LGB group than the individual characteristics of an LGB person. Individuality, in effect, is lost to membership in the group.

Many respondents' statements suggested that they had internalized the idea that LGBs exist as a homogeneous group. In some instances, this led to the assumption that all LGBs felt or reacted the same way to external situations. Earlier in this chapter, we read the comment by a gay man in his late thirties: *Amendment 2 was like a communal punch in the stomach. During the first week, I was devastated—as were all of us—that we are not deserving of protection from discrimination.* While it is likely that some LGBs were "devastated" by the election, it would be surprising if that were the experience of "all" LGBs in Colorado. The respondent's assumption of the universality of LGB reactions to the election was underscored by his reference to the "communal punch in the stomach." At one level, the homonegativity underlying the election did collectivize all LGBs in Colorado. However, not all LGBs experienced that homonegative event in the same fashion. Many respondents' assumption that unity was necessary (see the BARRIERS code) may have reflected their subtle acceptance of the homogenization of LGBs.

The acceptance of the homogeneity of LGBs was also manifested in references to the LGB community as a monolithic entity with no reference to individuals or to individuality. This view was most forcefully expressed in a comment in which one lesbian referred to the *Gay and Lesbian Community* with capital letters, suggesting it was an entity unto itself. When a group of people are singled out for discrimination, they are thereby defined in these very terms, as a community; when LGBs are willing to counter that discrimination through collective political action, they reinforce, for themselves and for others, the notion that they exist as a community.

*The struggle for normality.* Members of stigmatized groups often become highly sensitive to or even preoccupied with issues of normality (Coleman 1986; Gibbons 1986; Goffman 1963). In an effort to counter the subtle and overt accusations promulgated by CFV's campaign that gays are "abnormal," many LGBs strove to make themselves look as "normal" as possible, often doing so without any critique either of the concept of normality or of CFV's campaign of misinformation. In the absence of such critique, gay people were in danger of implicitly buying into the idea that normality was definable and positive and that CFV's definition was accurate.

A 39-year-old Greek American lesbian's comment made the equation between normality and positivity quite explicit: *Personally, I think [Amendment 2] is making us more visible, but we need to keep it positive. I'm normal and people need to know we are normal.* A 41-year-old lesbian from a Denver suburb made the connection between being normal and being acceptable to "people," presumably heterosexuals: *But, throughout the course of the campaign, and since the election outcome, I am convinced I must do the work that has the greatest chance for education, and that is to "come out" as often as it is physically safe. People must know I am an average, normal member of society.*

Our coding team noticed two variations on this theme among some of our respondents. One was the notion that the most effective means of countering the charge of abnormality was to be better than everyone else—again, presumably, to be as good as or better than heterosexuals. This strategy for dealing with homonegativity has been described in a variety of contexts (e.g., Russell, Bohan, and Lilly, in press), and may impose enormous performance pressures for LGBs who adopt it. A 46-year-old white lesbian from Colorado Springs offered this description of the strategy along with hints of the pressures associated with it: *I am furious at the stereotypes painted by CFV in their literature. I am publicly out now because I am trying to counter the stereotypes, but I feel like I must be the "perfect" lesbian—responsible, dignified, etc.*

Some members of our coding team recognized this strategy in our respondents because of personal familiarity with its use. The strategy has distinct appeal in that it promotes achievement and success (as usually defined). On the other hand, it often imposes pressures to perform that may not be consistent with a person's other goals or personal abilities. In addition, in the absence of a personal critique of the homophobic basis for this strategy, the homonegativity from which it derives is typically not directly challenged. As a result, LGBs may be operating on the basis of homonegativity without acknowledging that that is so. In such cases homonegativity is invested with a great deal of unexamined power.

The other variation in the push for normality has to do with an apparently unwitting endorsement of classist assumptions. Not surprisingly, one avenue from abnormality to respectability is seen in the acquisition and/or assertion of middle-class privilege. This class-based appeal was quite subtle in some comments, as when a 38-year-old white Grand Junction lesbian wrote: *I was comfortable being a law-abiding, working, tax-paying, home-owning citizen until #2 attacked me.* At other times, the appeal to class as a counter to abnormality was more obvious, as in a comment by a 32-year-old white/Spanish lesbian: *I don't know why people think they are supreme over gay or lesbian people. I personally know lots of professional gay and lesbian people.*

*Push toward assimilation.* Another strategy for dealing with oppressive forces is to move toward assimilation, a position in which members of a stigmatized group emphasize their similarities to the people in power.[9] Assimilationist strategies are a means of saying that LGBs are similar to heterosexuals. Many comments made this assertion. The following, for example, was written by a 39-year-old white homosexual man: *Concerned that current media bits create militant image that is ultimately unfavorable . . . no place for just ordinariness.* A 32-year-old gay woman's comment described her postelection self as more empowered and trying to be normal and similar to heterosexuals: *The passage has made me feel stronger about being open about my sexuality. I feel stronger about standing up for myself and the fact that I'm gay and normal and boring like heterosexuals.*

One very subtle variation on the assimilation theme was the effort by a handful of respondents both to minimize differences based on sexual orientation and to argue that sexual orientation was a matter of privacy. This position seemed to suggest that LGBs were *mostly* like heterosexuals and, where that was not the case, things could be kept quiet.[10] This argument is illustrated in the next comment: *I've found I have to explain or defend myself more often since passage of #2. I believe my orientation (sexual) is immaterial in everyday events and should not be an issue. Who I am and what I am is my business and should not become an issue of public debate.*

The assimilationist strategy made sense in that it countered homonegative assertions about the presumed abnormality of LGBs by emphasizing that LGBs are similar to heterosexuals. In doing so, the strategy takes advantage of the commonalities among all people. But it ignores the political implications of homophobia and heterosexism in the lives of LGBs.

*Granting power to heterosexuals.* LGBs' efforts to be "normal" and to minimize their differences from heterosexuals inevitably privilege heterosexuality. Heterosexuals become the model for normality, for that which is good and acceptable. Moreover, heterosexuals are imbued with the power to judge how well LGBs measure up to their standards of normality. Heterosexuals' power to judge was revealed in this comment by a 34-year-old white gay man: *I think the "gay" community has to be careful because the straight people don't want their kids to be shown homosexual relationships—sometimes gay people are too "loud mouth" and piss off other people. People should be more quiet.* A 40-year-old gay man offered concrete advice to LGBs about how to win heterosexuals' approval: *I really get repulsed by the extreme stereotype people who stand up for gays. Women—wear a dress, put on some makeup, wash your hair and mainstream. Men—get rid of the leather, blue jeans, pierced objects, strange haircuts, wear a grey flannel suit with a white shirt and tie—mainstream. If we want respect, show that we know how to play the game. Stop coming off as "activists."*

Giving power to heterosexuals has the (potential) adaptive value of winning elections along with approval. As a strategy, it implicitly acknowledges and tries to take advantage of the uneven distribution of power in society. However, the disadvantages of relying on this strategy are considerable. It can reinforce heterosexual privilege while ignoring the existence of that privilege. It can also reinforce the heterosexist idea that LGB orientations are inherently inferior to a heterosexual one and that LGBs must therefore mimic heterosexuality in order to be "acceptable." Finally, as the last comment particularly suggests, granting power to heterosexuals can result in LGBs' establishing and maintaining internal hierarchies based on the (presumed) acceptability (similarity) of LGBs to heterosexuals.

*The role of tokens in the LGB community.* The last comment has foreshadowed a final dimension of the enactment of LGB orientations as a master status. The writer of this comment expressed particular concern about LGB *people who stand up for gays.* When a group is stigmatized and seen as homogeneous, the role of spokesperson carries a significant importance and burden. Conversely, when members of nonstigmatized groups speak it is not assumed that they are doing so as representatives of their entire group. Only in rare and circumscribed situations, for example, are heterosexuals presumed to be speaking for all heterosexual people, or whites for all white people. Only when a group is perceived as homogeneous because of a master status may a member may be perceived to be speaking for all members.

Some LGB respondents clearly accepted the notion that visible gay people had become their spokespersons and felt a need to disassociate themselves from them. One way of disassociating oneself from a would-be spokesperson would be to say: that person does not speak for me. However, LGBs often felt (and sometimes were) too vulnerable to use such a straightforward technique. In the midst of a hostile environment, some LGBs feared that their predicament could get worse if LGB spokespeople acted in ways that further antagonized (some) heterosexuals. There was a reality to their perception in that heterosexuals generally saw LGBs as a group and treated a spokesperson as a representative of the group. Therefore, the spokesperson's behavior was something for which any and all members of the group could be held accountable.

The frustration with LGB spokespersons was evident in this comment: *So full of anger, mostly at the media, then homophobes, then gay political activists, the ones who are the self-appointed leaders of our so-called community. Why can't any of them ever treat me as simply an individual, not a member of some group?* This person seemed to be making an effort to resist being a member of a group that was homogenized by virtue of a master status. While some of his frustration was directed at entities that homogenize LGBs—the media and "homophobes"—it was also directed at other LGBs who made homogenizing assumptions. It is not a far step from this man's frustration with "self-appointed leaders" to the general experience of many LGB leaders who perceive considerable hostility from members of their own community (e.g., Osborn 1996).

*Denial of homophobia and heterosexism.* Related to the preceding dimensions of stigma associated with the LGB master status is the denial of homonegativity. Some of the most stunning comments in the data set were those in which respondents seemed to deny the influence of homonegativity on their lives. These comments—which we informally dubbed ANTIGRASP—were especially striking because they occurred in the midst of so many other remarks that emphasized and demonstrated a recognition of the negative effects of homophobia and heterosexism.

As our team read and reread the handful of ANTIGRASP comments, we began to understand that they reflected LGBs' efforts to deal with the negative effects of stigma. Certainly, one way of responding to negative conditions is to deny or minimize their presence and to attempt to move on through life as if they were not there. While acknowledging that different LGBs have differential experiences with homonegativity, it is difficult to imagine any gay person whose life has not been affected by homonegativity in one way or another. If this is true, then efforts to deny homonegativity and its effects may produce negative consequences, including faulty perceptions of homonegative situations; an inability to protect oneself from homonegative situations that are avoidable; confusion about emotional responses to homophobic situations; and a limited ability to address homonegativity at the personal, interpersonal, social, or political levels. Given the potential for such consequences, some theories about internalized oppression have suggested that the failure to grasp the social and political implications of one's group membership may itself represent one dimension of internalized oppression (Batts 1989).

A gay man minimized the role of homonegativity in the passage of Amendment 2 when he wrote: *Once AIDS is understood as being an STD* [sexually transmitted disease] *and not just a gay or drug addict disease, the sexual orientation aspect will not carry discriminatory factors.* This respondent's optimism may have been influenced by his age—35 years old in 1993—but it is unlikely that he (and others) would not have encountered homophobia prior to the AIDS epidemic.

The most compelling comments involving the denial of homonegativity were those in which respondents described a homonegative experience even as they denied homonegativity's impact on their lives. A 40-year-old lesbian from a Denver suburb illustrated this contradiction: *My relationship (lesbian) is 4-1/2 years old. It took us at least one full year, probably longer, to admit and use the word lesbian. We have a happy, strong relationship. We talk easily and feel lucky. Some family members and friends are aware and okay. Some, we know not to discuss the issue with. I personally chose not to be active with Amendment 2—I am content, feel unthreatened and have no personal experience with being a "victim."*

This woman had made a laudable effort to avoid feeling like a victim, which can be a demoralizing and disempowering state. At the same time, she wrote that she and her partner resisted so much as using the word "lesbian" in reference to their own relationship and concealed the nature of the relationship from some family members and friends. Surely, the basis for such decisions was homonegativity and she had been negatively affected by it. One does not have to feel like a victim even in the face of one's own victimization. Indeed, it is a cause for celebration when people who have been victimized do not feel like victims. Nonetheless, this respondent's comment suggested that she had labored under a homophobic burden without quite acknowledging what she had been doing and without taking proper credit for managing to have a "happy, strong relationship" with her partner *in spite of* the homonegative influences around them. It is no surprise that she chose not to work against Amendment 2. Her analysis of herself and her relationship rendered the amendment largely irrelevant.

*Relationship with other LGBs and risk, resilience, and recovery.* The comments that fell within these four codes—AQ, BARRIERS, IHE, and IHI—were some of the most complex in the data. The value of coding in a team context was especially apparent as we dealt with codes that covered a great deal of territory; that ranged from the very subtle to the painfully obvious; and that carried implications for the individual, social, and political spheres. While the themes that have been raised in these codes have implications for LGBs confronting specific anti-gay situations, these themes may also be relevant to gay people's ongoing and inevitable encounters with homophobia and heterosexism more generally. The exposition of each code has touched on risk, resilience, and recovery factors. At this juncture, I underscore a few familiar issues and raise a few others.

If we step back from the codes, we see the value of LGBs' maintaining a balance between an internal and external focus where homonegativity and internalized oppression are concerned.[11] The importance of this sort of balance has been raised by others writing from a variety of perspectives (for example, Batts 1989; Beardslee 1989; Jones 1993; Pheterson 1986). If LGB people fail to acknowledge homonegativity and its role in their lives, they may make poor appraisals of their world and their place in it. Among the potential consequences of this failure are victim-blaming and limitations to problem solving. On the other hand, focusing exclusively on external homophobia and heterosexism may leave LGBs feeling overwhelmed and powerless. Gay people need to know that homonegativity exists; they also need to know that they need not be immobilized by it. They can take action at all levels—intrapersonal, interpersonal, social, political, and cultural. While they cannot eradicate homonegativity, they can limit its influence in small and large ways.

In circumstances such as Amendment 2, working on their own internalized homophobia may be the most direct and effective action that LGBs could take. Attending to one's own IH also seems to increase the potential for accepting the support of heterosexual allies. We repeatedly saw that IHE statements were followed by other statements indicating that respondents had recognized and made use of support from heterosexuals. While initially surprising, the IHE-support connection made sense: if LGBs feel very negative about themselves, they will find it more difficult to consider and recognize that heterosexuals do not see them in a similarly negative light. Here, we are not talking about LGBs courting heterosexual approval as an assimilationist strategy but about LGBs and heterosexuals working together as equal partners in an effort to reduce homonegativity for everyone's benefit.

*The importance of safety.* Although we argue for the desirability of maintaining an internal-external balance, maintaining that balance is not always possible. Dangers posed by external homonegativity almost inevitably pull LGBs' attention away from considerations of internalized homophobia. The trauma literature has long emphasized that traumatized people can scarcely undertake effective psychotherapeutic work while they are still in external danger (Herman 1992). Similarly, it is difficult for LGBs to deal with IH issues when their environments are exceptionally oppressive.

7

■ ■ ■ ■ ■ ■ ■ ■

# The Relationship between Qualitative and Quantitative Data

*A Process Illustration*

AT THE CLOSE of the last chapter, we noted the importance of recognizing external homonegativity as well as internalized homophobia in order to understand LGBs' responses to anti-gay actions. Our exploration of this notion provides an excellent opportunity to step aside from the content of the codes for a moment. We turn now to a process dimension within this project that has implications for the interplay between qualitative and quantitative data.

## The Relationship between Qualitative and Quantitative Data

Generally speaking, there is no reason to include a discussion of quantitative research in a book using qualitative methods. The two types of data stand alone, grounded as they are in different epistemological frameworks—in different approaches to the question of what qualifies as knowledge.[1] However, one illustration of the uses to which the qualitative data from the Amendment 2 study have been put involves the relationship between these data and quantitative data drawn from the same study. Since it serves as an example of the practical implementation of this research project, we will consider it briefly here.

## Qualitative and Quantitative Data from the Same Study

The study discussed here yielded both quantitative and qualitative data regarding the psychological effects of Amendment 2. In general, the qualitative data from the study fulfilled the promise of elucidating quantitative findings in the study (see, for example, Banyard and Miller 1998). In some instances, the qualitative data went further and redirected our attention to quantitative dimensions that had eluded us. A brief illustration of the power of qualitative findings to refocus quantitative analysis follows.

As our team coded comments included in the IHE code, we noted an interesting set of demographic correlates. Only two IHE comments came from Colorado Springs respondents and they were both in the third person (to wit: other LGBs need to deal with their IH). Colorado Springs was the birthplace of Amendment 2 and the home of scores of religious right organizations. Among LGBs in the state, the city was referred to as "Ground Zero" in recognition of its particular role in the anti-gay movement. While LGBs across the state were affected by Amendment 2, gay people in Colorado Springs were in an especially vulnerable position. Under such hostile conditions, it was understandably quite difficult to pay close attention to IH issues, which may well explain the dearth of IHE comments from Colorado Springs respondents. Ironically, of course, attending to IH could be most needed and have the greatest positive impact under such conditions.

## Dose-Response Curve

The infrequency of IH comments was not our only clue that respondents from Colorado Springs had faced a particularly forceful and difficult experience with Amendment 2. A standard construct in the literature on trauma is the dose-response curve, which asserts that in general the closer one is to the epicenter of a traumatic event, the more severe will be the symptomatic consequences. The oft-cited example of a dose-response curve is an earthquake: people who live closest to the earthquake's epicenter are expected to exhibit the most severe post-traumatic symptoms, while symptoms gradually decline in people who live at increasing distances from the epicenter.

When I formulated the survey to study the effects of Amendment 2, I was interested in identifying the dose-response curve associated with the campaign and election. Based on my own experience, I hypothesized that for LGBs in Colorado the biggest "dose" of negative effects from the amendment would derive from a high level of involvement in the campaign. Thus, I expected higher levels of symptoms to be associated with greater numbers of hours of campaign work. Correspondingly, I expected that LGBs who had not participated directly in the campaign would generally evince lower symptom levels. When Sylvie and I ran statistical analyses based on these hypotheses, our results were flat, showing no discernible differences in symptoms as a function of an individual's campaign work.

The dose-response issue lay dormant until our team was well into coding the qualitative data. As mentioned in chapter 3, we initially coded these data with no demographic information about the respondents; despite this, during data coding one member pointed out that comments from Colorado Springs could be told apart from those from other parts of the state. Given that Colorado Springs was the home of CFV and dozens of other groups associated with the religious right, it made sense that gay people there would experience the campaign and election very intensely.

Believing that we had hit upon a dose-response curve in the data, Sylvie and I ran new quantitative analyses, this time looking for differences in symptom levels for three groups of respondents: LGBs in Colorado Springs, in the Denver metropolitan area, and in the rest of the state. The results of these analyses yielded very significant differences, with the highest symptoms found in Colorado Springs LGBs, followed by LGBs in the Denver metropolitan area, and the lowest symptom levels among LGBs in the rest of the state. The qualitative data had pointed the way to an examination of the quantitative data that had eluded us entirely until that point.

Our team was able to verify and expand upon the unique aspects of the responses from Colorado Springs when we included demographic information in the next phase of data analysis. We observed several properties that seemed characteristic of comments from Colorado Springs LGBs: they often used the language of good and evil, expressed a profound sense of danger, and avoided direct expressions of loss. This example illustrates how qualitative findings can be used productively in conjunction with quantitative methods within the context of a larger study.

8

■ ■　■　■　　■　　■　　　■　　　■　　　■

# Support, Strategies, and Actions

IN THIS FINAL CHAPTER focused on the data from the study, we view two major categories of codes. The first section, encompassing eight separate codes, looks at the relationships between LGB respondents and others. The other major category includes fourteen codes, all of which contain information about strategies LGBs considered in responding to the crisis of Amendment 2.

## Codes Representing Gay People's Relationships to Others: Interpersonal and Witnessing Dimensions

The eight codes in this broad category focus on LGB respondents' relationships with others: PRIMARY, KIDS, FAMR, FAMS, SUPPORT, JUD, THANKS, and COMM. They cover a broad range of relationship types, from respondents' relationships with individuals to those with various collectives, and from respondents' relationships with particular people to those with abstract entities. In many respects, these codes represent the specific manifestations of LGBs' relationships with witnesses to their crisis—including in a few instances witnesses who failed, but more frequently those who succeeded in the roles normally seen to fall to witnesses.

The importance of witnesses can hardly be overestimated. In terms of the psychology of the victimized individual, successful witnessing enhances resilience in a variety of ways, many of which will be highlighted in the codes that follow. As mentioned before, at the social level, successful witnessing not only intervenes in the act of victimization but also offers a moral alternative to oppression (Staub 1993). Conversely, the failure of would-be witnesses to act may prolong victimization and inhibit healing.

## PRIMARY

Participants in the study referred to their primary relationships in many ways. For the most part, these references were easily divided into positive and negative groups.

*Positive comments about primary relationships.* The most prominent positive effect of the election on respondents' primary relationships was to increase the shared level of openness about their sexual orientations and the nature of their relationships. Sometimes this development was described as a mutual one between respondents and their partners. For example, a 51-year-old lesbian wrote: *My partner and I are both out to our families now. And many more of our friends are aware of our relationship.* For others, the move toward enhanced openness involved one member of the dyad's taking the lead, as in the case of a 60-year-old man: *I came out nationally and to all friends following the election. I became very much an activist and that has led my boyfriend to come out and be counted.*

Some respondents indicated that the consequences of such openness had not been purely positive in nature. A 26-year-old woman whose words we have read before, portrayed a more ambiguous situation: *Because the issue [of sexual orientation] has taken on a more high profile, I have also become more open about being in a gay relationship. I have found that the openness brings a somewhat more open and deeper understanding on the part of others—it also often makes me feel very vulnerable. But I feel it is necessary to educate folks on who gay/lesbian/bisexual people really are. I do not regret becoming more open and involved—I only hope I do not suffer discriminatory consequences for it.*

A few respondents contributed unique commentaries on their relationships. A 44-year-old white lesbian made an implicitly tender reference to her lover as a source of comfort and safety in the aftermath of the election: *I had a strange personal response to feeling so unsafe after the election. I've always slept nude, but since November, unless I'm with my lover, I started going to bed with my clothes on (no shoes!). I gradually started taking different articles of clothes off, and now sleep as I used to about 50% of the time.*

Similarly, a 19-year-old homosexual man reported that relaxed time with his boyfriend was an antidote to burnout and feeling machinelike: *I feel so burned out after Amendment 2. I have really withdrawn a lot of the work that I used to put in down in Colorado Springs. But I feel good just taking some time to relax and spend time with my boyfriend. I am starting to feel like a person once again—and not like a machine. . . . I still put in my share of work, but over all of this mess I have finally learned to just relax and enjoy any quiet time I have with myself and my boyfriend.*

*Negative comments about primary relationships.* Just as there was a tender quality to some of the positive experiences associated with primary relationships, there were difficult tensions with such relationships as well. In fact, the number of comments indicating that the election had had problematic consequences for relationships considerably outnumbered those suggesting the opposite.

For some respondents, the tension in their primary relationships occurred in the context of the question of how to respond to the campaign and election. As we saw earlier, the campaign and election represented an opportunity to be more out together for some couples; however, they became the focus of disagreement for others. A 30-year-old white Jewish lesbian said she would have liked to have seen the following questions included in the survey: *Have you fought more, are there problems re: differences in how politically active to be (as well as how open), were there problems either giving or receiving support?* This respondent added: *This is where a lot of my distress played out.* In some cases, relationship conflicts were quite specific, as in this 29-year-old homosexual's report of a debate on *whether or not we would put a "no on 2" sign in our yard.* Some conflicts were resolved satisfactorily, as in the debate about the yard sign: *He acquiesced and we did.* Other couples, however, were unable to fashion a mutually agreeable strategy for responding to Amendment 2. A handful reported the demise of their relationship. For example, a 20-year-old woman ended her relationship with a lover of one and a half years *because I was too active for her and she had to be so closeted.*

*Relationships associated with fear.* Relationships that survived Amendment 2 faced a number of other challenges. Because same-sex relationships are typically seen as the outward manifestation of gay and lesbian orientations, they sometimes became the primary focus of fear for respondents. A 40-year-old lesbian, for example, expressed this fear quite simply: *A constant sense of fear that I did not have before, especially when walking with my partner, leaving a women's concert, walking to my car at night.* A 29-year-old gay man wrote of his effort to work against Amendment 2 while maintaining his relationship: *I am involved in trying to stop 2. We've been doing shows and selling bumper stickers to raise money—but I can't get in the limelight because of my lover's job.*

Some LGBs made concrete efforts after the election to live out their gay identities, including their relationships, in accordance with what they perceived to be a changed, more dangerous environment. Although the impact of such changes on her relationship was not clear from this statement by a 23-year-old Greeley lesbian, it is difficult to imagine that the relationship had been improved by the measures she and her partner had taken: *The biggest response I have had to Amendment 2 is the increased fear of being physically attacked. My partner has gone into the closet in the sense that we remain physically and emotionally distant from each other in public situations. My partner has removed gay symbols, such as the pink triangle and the double women signs from her jacket for fear of physical assault. I have also removed such symbols from my car for fear of vandalism or physical attack.*

As the comments thus far exemplify, many respondents were quite clear about the nature of the intrusion on their relationships imposed by the election. But for a 35-year-old lesbian from Durango, it was less clear precisely how the election had affected her relationship with her partner, other than the fact that the effect was decidedly negative: *I feel that Amendment 2 has been fairly detrimental to my relationship with my partner. So much energy and emotion has been focused on the election and outcome that there has been an emotional withdrawal between us. This is very sad for me.*

The following comment was made by a lesbian in her thirties from Glenwood Springs. Her statement may offer a clue as to the subtle ways in which traumatizing events can negatively impact a relationship. Such events produce not only helplessness but also a profound sense of isolation (e.g., Herman 1992). This seems to be reflected in the woman's shift from the use of the first-person plural to the first-person singular as she moves on from a description of her optimistic expectations of the election to the shocking reality of its outcome: *My lover and I sat down to watch the election returns full of hope. We couldn't believe it when 2 started passing and when it was projected to pass. I felt like I had been hit by a Mack truck. The first few days after the election, I varied from shell-shocked to incredible anger. I finally mellowed into hope that it will be found unconstitutional. I hope I'm not just in denial as I was before the election.*

*PRIMARY and risk, resilience, and recovery.* Crises take their toll on primary relationships. Some couples are able to grow together through them, while others are not.[1] For LGBs in same-sex relationships, Amendment 2 produced significant challenges. In principle, the crisis affected both members directly and also vicariously. Two gay men in a relationship, for example, could each be expected to have his own reaction and also to be affected by and concerned about his partner's reactions. This shared experience of crisis may result in mutual understanding and support (Lindy 1985). On the other hand, the joint impact of the crisis on the couple may limit the degree to which they can support each other, resulting in depleted resources within the relationship (Marmar, Foy, Kagan, and Pynoos 1993).

The victimization connected with the crisis was itself tied up with the respondents' sexual orientation, a characteristic typically experienced as intrinsic to one's identity. Thus, for some LGBs, the pain of victimization became specifically associated with sexual orientation (see Garnets, Herek, and Levy 1992). It is but a brief jump from this observation to suggest that the pain of their victimization may have been associated with their primary partners as well. Little wonder, then, that several respondents referred directly to diminished sexual interest in their partners, with specific attributions to Amendment 2 in every case. The difficulties affecting same-sex relationships were in fact less surprising than the fact that some relationships flourished despite the crisis.

## KIDS

The KIDS code, which highlighted any references to children, was smaller than many others in the data. Within this code, there were four significant subthemes. The largest focused on respondents' personal relationships with young people, often their own biological children. In some of these comments, respondents expressed concern about the effects of Amendment 2 on the children in their families. A 26-year-old white/Indian lesbian offered a general admonition followed by an account of her son's reaction: *People need to also take into consideration the children of these gay, lesbian and bisexual couples and people in this state. My son cried at school the day after the election because he was afraid that they would suddenly make his sister and him leave the school because of his moms and the passage of the amendment.*

Most respondents who spoke as parents recognized that it was not entirely possible to protect their offspring from the negative effects of the election. A woman from Pueblo expressed her skepticism about doing so quite simply and unmistakably: *I also have two teenage daughters with whom I'm quite open but want to protect them (ha, ha) from the damaging remarks made by ignorant people.* For many LGB parents, the knowledge that their children would be negatively affected resulted in frustration. A comment by a lesbian in her forties illustrated this reaction in a linguistically straightforward fashion: *Anxiety for high school kid who is "closeted" about lesbian mother and his distress and shame. Anger.*

Difficult though the challenges of Amendment 2 were for the children of LGB parents, there were some potentially positive outcomes as well. The movement toward positive change was evident in the following comment by the 47-year-old lesbian mother of a 17-year-old daughter: *Talk about #2 aggravated the difficult feelings she periodically has about having lesbian parents. Mostly she is happy with our family but she has never "come out"* [that is, disclosed her mothers' relationship] *to any of her friends about us. Now that the furor has died down at school and the injunction has passed, she seems a lot more comfortable with us, and is even becoming more political about the issues of Amendment 2.*

In a handful of instances, respondents described situations in which their children acted as witnesses to their victimization. In one case, a 19-year-old daughter became her respondent-mother's witness: *I have a*

*19-year-old daughter who has known about my lifestyle all her life. This year she was able to vote for the first time so she had studied up on all the amendments. She was absolutely astonished when Amendment 2 passed. For the first time she became aware of what anti-gay discrimination is about and how powerful it can be. It has opened up a lot of discussions between us and her friends so hopefully something good will come of it.*

In another statement without such an optimistic ending, a 44-year-old lesbian described her young daughter's efforts to protect her parents: *My/our 7 year-old daughter just panicked listening to election results— "what are you going to do? You could say you are sisters and one of you was married so you have different names." It broke my heart that a child would even need to consider such things. She has since likened Amendment 2 to Lincoln's struggle with slavery. "It's just wrong, Mom."* Statements such as these demonstrate the pain that anti-gay political actions inflict not only LGBs but on those close to them.

*Respondents who worked with youth.* A small number of participants in the study said they worked professionally in capacities that involved youth. Several felt more vulnerable in their jobs after the election. A 53-year-old gay man who taught in a rural county, for example, wrote of his students' behavior toward him as follows: *Students in my classroom in high school have asked me if I were gay, others accused me of being gay in a negative manner.*

In contrast to the respondents who emphasized the difficulty of working with youth, one 41-year-old lesbian seemed to be moving in the opposite direction: *Perhaps the biggest impact of Amendment 2 on my life now has to do with the fact that I'm working on making a career change. I want to become an educator who specializes in teaching effective parenting.*

*Concerns for gay youth.* A few comments in the KIDS code represented adult respondents' concern about how LGB youth were affected by the election. One bisexual/lesbian in her forties wrote simply: *I feel for the kids.* Several respondents' fears for gay youth were rooted in their memories of their own difficulties with adolescence: *Mostly I'm concerned over the negative message and what will happen to young gays. It was hard enough for me; what will it be like for them if the religious right succeeds, as they are?*

*KIDS and risk, resilience, and recovery.* Worrying about the effects on those they loved and wished to protect complicated the results of Amendment 2 for LGB parents. It seemed to add a whole layer of helplessness to the experience. From a very different direction, LGB professionals who worked with youth also encountered an extra dose of helplessness in their response to Amendment 2. Because of the false accusations in anti-gay rhetoric linking LGB orientations to pedophilia (Herman 1997; Keen and Goldberg 1998), LGB professionals who worked with youth felt especially vulnerable in the wake of the election. Both groups—LGB parents and youth-serving professionals—may well have been at particularly high risk for being affected negatively by the campaign and election.

## *FAMR*

Responses in the FAMR code came from another group of gay people who were probably especially vulnerable to Amendment 2's effects, namely those who experienced some degree of rejection by their families during the time of the amendment. Those who wrote about encounters with failed witnessing by family members were coded FAMR.

Many of the FAMR comments suggested that respondents whose family members had supported Amendment 2 experienced an overlapping set of stresses. One set of stresses came from their confrontation with the homonegativity in the state at large, while another came from the knowledge that their family members were the immediate vehicle by which homonegativity was brought into their lives. Further, when family members voted for Amendment 2 a fundamental belief in the LGB community was challenged, namely, that once heterosexual people get to know gays and lesbians, they will act in less homophobic ways. Many of the FAMR comments indicated that family members knew they had an LGB relative and nonetheless chose to vote for the amendment. Our team's ability to make some sense of FAMR comments was inhibited by the brevity of these remarks. Respondents often wrote brief one-sentence statements about difficult family experiences and moved on to other issues. We return to this comment by a 23-year-old Fort Collins lesbian as an illustration of the limited attention to family issues: *After #2, felt very isolated, some homophobia, and lots of concern for my physical well-being. Burnt out on politics, less understood by parents. Insecure and decreased self-esteem. Was reasonably well-adjusted before all this.* A 30-year-old lesbian from Denver offered this brief commentary: *My immediate family voted "Yes" on 2—lots of feelings of betrayal (my family "can't abide my lifestyle").*

Some respondents tried to make sense of the actions of their family members. This comment by a lesbian in her forties indicates such an effort: *Some of my own family voted for it—they put their fear of quotas above me and then said, "Oh, you can't mean that" when my lover said, "I hope the boycott [of Colorado by some opponents to Amendment 2] brings the state to its knees." People have no concept of what the real issue is.*

A few respondents wrote that they had intentionally avoided confronting family members directly, even when fully informed about family members' actions: *I had been very close to my sister and her family and was supposed to take a trip with them. I didn't go. In fact, I have been avoiding them ever since election day. I think they voted for #2 because they hate job quotas and because they are ignorant.*

Other respondents used Amendment 2 as an opportunity to confront family members. A 33-year-old lesbian related this story: *The parents of my lover of 6 years voted yes. When she discovered it she came out to them. It was tough at first but all seems well on that front now.* For some LGBs, the election and conflicts around it served as a catalyst to major changes. A 38-year-old gay man whose residence was listed as Denver/Cortez, wrote: *I came out openly against Amendment 2—not even mentioning being gay. Yet, my biological family in the same town became very angry. I have finally moved to Denver in order to be honest about my feelings, assist in defeating Amendment 2, and just be myself—which has become very self-liberating and empowering.*

*FAMR and risk, resilience, and recovery.* News reports at the time of the campaign asserted that Amendment 2 had divided the state. In some instances, it divided families as well. LGB respondents who spoke of encounters with family members' homonegativity did so with the poignancy that often accompanies irreconcilable conflicts between people who love each other. There was often a powerless quality to their comments. Our team wondered if powerlessness might account for the brevity of so many of the FAMR statements as well; the topic may have been too painful to elaborate.

In some cases, the election provided a milestone which defied prior avoidance of the conflict between and among family members about equal rights for LGBs. In other families, the conflict had been more open and the amendment was another in a series of issues evoking disagreement. Whatever the situation, LGBs whose family members had homophobic reactions often had to contend with greater than ordinary stresses around Amendment 2. In addition, they were deprived of an important source of social support that some LGB respondents did enjoy.

## FAMS

While Amendment 2 gave rise to conflict between some family members, it also led others to respond to LGBs with new levels of support, a phenomenon reflected in comments coded FAMS (for family support). Some respondents had felt supported by their families prior to the campaign and election. A 38-year-old lesbian wrote: *My family has known (20 years) and became supporters long ago.* Other LGBs indicated that Amendment 2 offered a novel opportunity for family members to make their support felt in concrete ways. A white gay man in his thirties drew this contrast: *Until Amendment 2, I felt more estranged from my family of origin. Since its passage, I have received, for the first time in my life, 100% support from father, step-mother, and siblings.* A 31-year-old homosexual man said the amendment had given him an opportunity to be more open than before, and added: *It's also brought my mom out even more—she's quite the gay activist— I'm so proud. She's now the president of PFLAG!*

Clearly, Amendment 2 was a time of learning and action for the relatives of some participants. In his analysis of how Amendment 2 helped him, a 22-year-old homosexual man made the now familiar parallel between voting no and support: *I came out about being gay to friends and family members shortly before I learned about Amendment 2, but because of Amendment 2, it has been much easier to come out because my friends and family members have been able to do a lot of reading on the subject and choose to oppose the Amendment and support me.*

*FAMS and risk, resilience, and recovery.* Taken as a whole, the FAMS responses suggested that LGBs whose family members voted against the amendment interpreted their action as a clear sign of personal support.

Our team was impressed by the large number of FAMS comments that conveyed a sense of personal safety and of having been witnessed positively.

We saw earlier that many gay people experienced votes for Amendment 2 as a hateful rejection. The presence of familial support seemed to reduce the sense of hatred and rejection for some respondents. A 35-year-old gay woman in Durango had tender words for her family and the support they had given her: *I am thankful for the support my family gives me. When everything was falling apart (election and so forth) I was very emotional. The way I dealt with it was to call my grandmother, just to know someone loved me. Later I called my folks and told them "thank you" for their love and support. I'm very lucky to have a family like mine. I know many others are not as fortunate as I am.*

## *SUPPORT*

The SUPPORT code continued with the theme of relationships between LGB participants and others, reporting the support of heterosexuals who were not members of the respondents' families of origin. Statements in this code alluded to a wide variety of supporters, including respondents' friends, employers, coworkers, and colleagues. Participants also mentioned their unions and other professional associations, as well as various elected officials who had condemned Amendment 2. One gay man wrote that he was *thrilled that 700,000 people sided with gays* in the election.

Receiving the support of heterosexuals appeared to touch respondents deeply. We got the strong impression that such support—especially when it was active and visible—helped gay people hold on to some degree of optimism in an environment that often seemed quite hostile. A Boulder lesbian in her early forties expressed her struggle between optimism and pessimism as follows: *It is shocking to me, and I continue to be appalled that my community and my state are much more hostile environments than I used to think. It's hard to maintain my optimistic outlook on life. On the other hand, I am encouraged by straight colleagues, government officials, other heterosexuals, other minorities who are speaking out and taking strong stands against amendment 2.*

Her statement resembled a number of other SUPPORT comments, which frequently juxtaposed their observations of support with observations about negative manifestations of the amendment. Their statements seemed indicative of the very tolerance for ambiguity necessary to see positive and negative aspects of the election simultaneously.

The support roles of heterosexuals varied in the following five statements, all of which contained such ambiguity. The first came from a 17-year-old woman: *I am more fearful of being discriminated against by random people I meet, but also feel more support from friends and acquaintances.* A 35-year-old Colorado Springs lesbian wrote of these contrasting experiences: *I have been uplifted by the concern and outrage expressed by my heterosexual friends but I am sick to death of being objectified by various media coverages.* A Pueblo man in his forties wrote: *Some feeling of surprise both at the amount of virulent homophobia, as well as surprise at some of the heterosexuals who support gay rights.* A Grand Junction lesbian framed a very public contrast: *I am actually disappointed with the public but very proud of our Governor Romer, Mayor Webb, the city councils of Aspen, Telluride, Vail, Boulder, Glenwood Springs, and any others.*[2] A 24-year-old Grand Junction lesbian told us of her own bottom-line contrast: *It may turn out that I will have no legal recourse if I am discriminated against, but I will have social support and sympathetic friends to talk to.*

*SUPPORT and risk, resilience, and recovery.* The form of many of the statements about heterosexual support suggested that such support served as an important counterpoint to Amendment 2's negative influences. Many LGB respondents took note of heterosexual support and seemed to find it comforting and encouraging. However, some LGBs had a difficult time recognizing and accepting support. This is understandable for a number of reasons. People who have been traumatized initially often have trouble seeing anything positive. In fact, blaming one's supporters is not uncommon (Herman 1992). In addition, as we saw in the TRUST code, it was difficult—and often impossible—for LGBs to know who had supported them in the election and who had not. This was complicated by the fact that preelection polls had strongly indicated that the election would result in the defeat of Amendment 2. The discrepancy between these polls and the election outcome led many people to believe that some voters had lied to pollsters about their intentions at the voting booth. Finally, as many comments suggested, LGBs did not trust nominally supportive heterosexuals who had not been politically active prior to the election. As one woman in her twenties told us: *I've been very heartened by het allies being much more out and visible and vocal [since the election], but a part of me feels bitter, like it's too late.*

For these reasons, many gay people were genuinely confused about which heterosexuals were trustworthy. Sometimes they were unable to recognize support and at other times they recognized it but failed to appreciate it. Even more subtly, there were times when LGBs recognized the support of heterosexuals but responded to it with resentment, as if they were second-class people who had to be grateful for the generosity of superiors—a situation born of oppression and one that breeds unequal relationships and ill will.

Such resentment is very different from the sentiments of a 50-year-old white gay man when he wrote of *co-workers who grieved with me in the days after the vote.* Grieving together typically occurs between and among equals, both or all of whom have had an investment in and a reaction to what has been lost. It was in the context of equal relationships that the best support was given and received.

## *JUD*

The JUD code, which tracked comments related to the judicial case with Amendment 2, was another of those that had not been a part of our initial piloting of codes. Somehow, our coding team kept missing the theme. We finally realized we needed such a code only after we had been reading data for a time.

In retrospect, I think we did not initially grasp the significance of JUD statements because we viewed those comments as belonging to the legal realm, not to the psychological. Even after we had assigned a JUD code, we did not understand the psychological importance of the comments until we read them all together and realized that comments in the JUD code represented the legal witness that could (and did) dismantle Amendment 2 once and for all. That the courts would intervene effectively and successfully was the hope of many respondents, and that was what indeed came to pass. When they were writing their statements, of course, respondents had no way of knowing how the Supreme Court would decide the Amendment 2 case. They were hopeful nonetheless, drawing partly on the court system's legacy of intervening on the side of justice in cases involving other movements for equal rights.

*JUD and meaning making.* The injunction issued by District Judge Jeffrey Bayless on January 15, 1993 meant that Amendment 2 would not go into immediate effect. Subsequent rulings in District Court, the Colorado Supreme Court, and the United States Supreme Court ensured that the amendment would never go into effect. All the judicial decisions on Amendment 2 and especially the final ruling, enacted on May 20, 1996, were testimony to the unfairness of Amendment 2. Collectively, these actions accomplished the two functions of effective witnessing (Staub 1993): reducing the immediate danger and offering a moral alternative. In both respects, gay people viewed the judicial system as their ally.

*Injunction.* LGBs received the initial injunction against Amendment 2 with pleasure and relief. Some LGBs' comments about the injunction were couched in a form we have seen before: the positive observation about the injunction was juxtaposed with an observation about negative reactions to the amendment. Sometimes, respondents expressed unbridled enthusiasm, as in this statement by a 39-year-old Anglo lesbian: *I'm angry that CFV was successful and I was devastated by the election results, elated by the injunction.* In other cases, participants' enthusiasm about the injunction did not seem to match their reactions to the election. A woman in her thirties wrote: *I have been devastated and demoralized by the passage of 2, and only slightly encouraged by the injunction.*

Others saw the injunction as a source of concrete legal protection. A bisexual Native American woman from Boulder was in such a position: *I was scheduled to have my employment terminated Friday of the week of the injunction due to perceived sexual orientation (no one asked or offered any "proof"). My job remains mine solely because of the injunction, and people at work let me know it!*

Still others saw the injunction as a source of psychological safety. That was the quality conveyed by a 27-year-old man who described being *angry, hurt, and fearful for my future* in the aftermath of the election: *I think a major changing point was Judge Bayless' decision. It took so much weight off my shoulders. I could actually feel the tension, stress and anxiety go away.*

Some respondents saw the significance of the injunction in political terms, particularly noting its inhibiting effect on the proliferation of other anti-gay laws. One man wrote thus of the injunction: *It made me feel like we had a chance and the amendment lost its power and couldn't grow or spread to other states.* Other comments seemed to spring from a deeper response. One gay man wrote that the injunction reaffirmed *my belief in the rule of law.* A lesbian viewed it as the source of *hope for potential restoration of righteousness.* The latter two comments seemed to illustrate how much relief successful witnessing could provide to people's disrupted sense of the world as just and predictable. As seen in earlier chapters, such disruption is a part of some people's trauma responses.

*Subsequent judicial rulings.* Data collection for this project occurred after the injunction was issued but before any subsequent court rulings. Respondents nonetheless wrote extensively about Amendment 2's postinjunction judicial journey. Some were certain of an eventual positive outcome, among them the 28-year-old gay man who wrote: *It will be overturned. There is no question in my mind. It specifies a particular group and denies them rights, that is unconstitutional.* Other participants were less certain and expressed their *doubt* and *anxiety* about the eventual outcome. A Mexican American bisexual man expressed his hope and acknowledged the alternative: *I believe that "2" will be overturned. If it isn't, I personally will have a great emotional setback. The injunction is my hope.*

A number of respondents explicitly looked to the U.S. Supreme Court as the site of the *ultimate* decision in the Amendment 2 case. But their expectations for a judicial outcome were not uniformly positive. A 20-year-old gay man from a Denver suburb likened the court case to a war whose venue would change if the Supreme Court decision upheld the amendment: *We will fight this war in court because we are a community of logical people and don't have a history of over-reacting when we are threatened. They are threatening now, but if we lose this war in court . . . we will have a war on the streets, because people in America have a heritage of fighting for rights, even [their own].* A 23-year-old Hispanic lesbian outlined her fears for the consequences should the judicial decision prove unfavorable in the following terms: *I pray that the Supreme Court finds it unconstitutional; if not, I feel every other state in the U.S. will also find similar amendments in their state constitutions. We may find ourselves in a sort of Nazi Germany situation.*

Even some participants who were hopeful about the judicial outcome had some concerns. A Pueblo lesbian wrote: *I am hoping the amendment [will be] overturned, but how many people will have to suffer? I think gay-*

*bashing will be at its highest level if it is overturned. . . . I just hope violence will be minimal when it is overturned.* One gay man in his forties referred to the limits of both the judicial and the electoral decisions when he wrote: *I recognize that our ultimate victory will come not at the ballot box, or in the courts, but in the hearts and minds of the other 90% of society.*

*JUD and risk, resilience, and recovery.* For those LGBs who had hoped for judicial witnessing, the outcome was a happy one. The Supreme Court of the United States struck down Amendment 2, saying that it had been motivated by "animus" against gay people and rejecting animus as a legitimate basis for a constitutional amendment (Keen and Goldberg 1998).[3] The judicial branch of the government indeed served as an ultimate witness for LGBs in their struggle against the election. Despite the apparent certainty of some respondents before the decision, the eventual outcome of the judicial case was not a foregone conclusion at any point prior to May 20, 1996. Yet the expectation of a favorable judicial decision ended up being an asset to many LGBs in the study. Had the Supreme Court decision been unfavorable, those expectations could have become liabilities. Sometimes external situations—in this case, in the form of history—are the arbiter of what constitutes an asset and what a liability.

## THANKS

This code, THANKS, consisted of comments wherein respondents expressed gratitude for the research project and for our interest in their experiences of the campaign and election. Of all the codes in this study, this one most surprised and humbled our coding team. In some respects, THANKS was a straightforward witness code. Yet it had a unique quality: it required us to make sense of comments about our own work, a novel task for most of us.[4] The majority of the THANKS comments came at the end of longer statements by respondents. In some cases, the comments consisted of one word, *thanks,* or a few, *thanks for doing this.* It was only when LGBs elaborated on these brief expressions that we were able to make sense of them.

*THANKS and meaning making.* The comments in the THANKS code suggested that different respondents viewed the role of the research in different ways. For some, the survey was an intervention in itself. A number of participants ended their statements with comments such as *Thanks for asking*, and *Thanks for listening*, and *Thanks for caring to ask*. Reading such expressions, we had the impression that they were making statements of closure on an activity that required some sort of ending. One gay woman in her thirties concluded her relatively lengthy statement with: *It has been helpful even filling out this questionnaire—seeing that the questions you're asking are what I've been feeling—so I must not be alone or "crazy." Thanks*. Other respondents used the survey as a means for introspection. An Anglo-American lesbian from Fort Collins wrote: *Thank you, this was a good exercise to closely examine my feelings*. For these and other participants, completing the survey seemed to represent a normalizing activity that allowed them to put their personal experiences into broader context, one that included other gay people. It seemed, thereby, to foster a reduced sense of isolation.

Other respondents seemed to view their work on the survey as an opportunity to use their own voices. A 41-year-old lesbian, for example, wrote: *Thank you for giving a forum to express feelings!* Another lesbian seemed to be expressing a similar sentiment, but for gay people in general rather than specifically for herself: *Good luck with this project. I know from conversations with other gays and lesbians that, clearly, our community has been hit very hard emotionally with the passage of Amendment 2!*

A related, but more focused, understanding of the survey rested in its perceived potential to represent the lived experiences of lesbians, gay men, and bisexuals—a potential that some respondents regarded as a much needed counterpoint to the lies about gay people that were so much a part of the campaign for Amendment 2. It was often in the context of statements emphasizing either the campaign distortions and/or the need for education that respondents added such closing affirmations as: *Thank you for doing this work!* An 18-year-old gay man wrote: *This is not about Amendment 2, but thanks. It is about time somebody wanted to know how Amendment 2 is affecting us. So thanks a lot. I think what you're doing is great!!!!*

For some respondents, filling out the survey seemed to embody the opportunity to take some action in the face of an amendment that many found disempowering and even overwhelming. The THANKS-coded comments from a number of LGBs alluded to their desire to be helpful. One lesbian from a small mountain town expressed this desire in the context of her broader reaction to the election: *I was in shock when it passed and have certainly felt less valued since. Hope this is helpful, good luck.* Another lesbian's wish to experience herself as efficacious was particularly striking in light of the way she viewed the election and her own efforts: *Discrimination based on sexual orientation is mentally and emotionally a form of genocide. I often wish I was in a position to change what is happening here in Colorado Springs. I often feel that my involvement in the gay community is futile. I will continue to contribute positive energy though, wherever and whenever I can. I hope this survey will assist you in your efforts.* A homosexual man ended his statement with: *I hope this survey proves beneficial to any and all.*

A final observation about THANKS comments was also related to the sense of efficacy. In this case, though, it seemed that participants viewed the research as having a potential impact and therefore saw the researchers as efficacious. A homosexual man specified the nature of the potential results of the research: *Thanks for your efforts. I hope they help people feel better about Amendment 2.* A white/Spanish lesbian made this more general affirmation: *Please keep up the good work—it's people like you that will help make a change!* A gay woman from Durango drew an explicit link between the research survey and efforts to reduce discrimination: *I also am thankful for the people who are fighting against discrimination, such as yourself. Thank you.*

*THANKS and risk, resilience, and recovery.* It is helpful for people who have been attacked to find ways—large and small—in which they can act from a sense of power rather than solely from a position of powerlessness. Taken as a whole, statements coded THANKS came from LGBs who were able to transform a request for their time and energy into an opportunity to conduct self-examination, to express their feelings, to voice their experiences, to correct misinformation, to help others, and to act generously toward researchers they did not know. To use the task in this fashion represented a move away from powerlessness and toward efficacy. This sort of transformation includes active coping and a broader perspective—attributes we rightly view as strengths. It is also the kind of transformation that should serve as a reminder for all researchers: our work itself may be an intervention in a variety of ways; the potential for such impact means that we also shoulder significant responsibility.

## COMM

Thus far, our review of codes delineating LGBs' relationships with others has focused on relationships between respondents and their partners, children, members of their families of origin, heterosexual allies, the judicial system, and our research team. This final code focused on the relationship between participants and the LGB community at large. The code included a great many comments that reflected complex perceptions of and levels of engagement with the community.

*Positive effects on LGB community.* Many respondents viewed Amendment 2 as a source of positive change for the LGB community. Most respondents with this perspective seemed to be quite aware of losses associated with the election. A 38-year-old Denver gay man wrote: *Even though we lost the Amendment 2 battle on election day, I feel [that] in many ways this has unified the gay community.* Another gay man from Denver, this one in his forties, echoed that observation and elaborated: *I feel it gives the gay community a tremendous opportunity to pull together, work together on this and other projects. It has given gays the avenue (media) to educate the public on a wide range of issues.* The perceived benefits arising from the LGB community's responses to the election were not limited to LGBs in large metropolitan areas. The following comment was written by a 29-year-old lesbian from Brush, a small town: *I feel that Amendment 2 has put a lot of strength, togetherness and pride in the gay community, or maybe just brought it out.*

Observations about community growth focused on people as well as on the community in the abstract. A Colorado Springs lesbian made a link between changes in people and changes in the LGB community when she wrote: *People are growing and changing before my eyes. Amazing feeling of community.* For some LGBs, activities centered on Amendment 2 became the means for encounters with the gay community at levels they had not experienced before. Indeed, some LGBs' initial contacts with the LGB community occurred as a result of and in the context of Amendment 2. A

19-year-old homosexual man observed: *I have found out much more about the homosexual community and strength because of this amendment and I think so many other people have too.* Young LGBs were not alone in their novel encounters with their community. A Colorado Springs lesbian in her forties wrote: *I have found a strong, beautiful, energetic gay/lesbian community through A2 activities.*

*LGB community as locus for sharing grief and support.* For some respondents, the LGB community became especially important and helpful after the election because it offered a forum for expressing and sharing grief about the campaign and the amendment's passage. As we saw in the TRUST code especially, many gay people felt that they could not look to heterosexual society to understand their grief and support them in it; accordingly most LGBs shared their sense of loss with other gay people. A gay man in his thirties wrote about his feelings of rage and betrayal immediately after the election and then went on to say: *These feelings have lessened since the injunction, but they remain under the surface, combined with a sense that for me, personally, the social fabric is irrevocably torn. As ugly as these thoughts are, I have been surprised, in talking to gay and lesbian colleagues, that they are shared by others.*

As they were experiencing a range of reactions, many LGBs were able to find support within the gay community. One bisexual woman, who found election night deeply traumatic and whose primary relationship was damaged by differing reactions to the election, wrote of the community in these terms: *I sought out other gay people specifically to talk about issues like support for the legal challenge, the boycott, and the broader agenda of the Christian Right and how to fight it.* A bisexual woman in her twenties described her *depression about the whole world* and then went on: *I am fighting this through a group at my school, and that does give me a sense of empowerment.* A Colorado Springs lesbian detailed her postelection depression, the severity of which surprised her. She continued: *The depression was bad until the glb community started to organize so much. So many people came out.*

*LGB community as means to counter internalized homophobia.* As those in the LGB community responded to Amendment 2, they created extensive opportunities for individual LGBs to meet one another. These opportunities, coupled with a variety of empowering activities, gave some gay people the support they needed to work through their internalized homonegativity. A 19-year-old lesbian from rural Colorado described the amendment as the basis for significant positive changes, including those resulting from community contact: *Because of Amendment 2, I was unwillingly outed by a close friend after [the election]. I then chose to step out of the closet with those I'm closest to, so they would hear it from me first. This is my first year away from home and I have become more and more comfortable with myself and my sexual orientation (since meeting more gays/lesbians). Good support group during and after Amendment 2.* A 37-year-old gay man described how the amendment and the community's response to it had affected him: *Amendment 2 has helped me solidify my identity as a gay person. It has drawn me closer to gay people in general and has helped me work through my own internal homophobia.*

A 25-year-old gay man wrote that his contact with the Metropolitan Community Church (MCC), a Christian church with a largely gay membership, was his primary source of help in trying to resolve conflicts about his sexual orientation that were rooted in early religious teachings: *I have feelings of great fear with respect to my sexual orientation and the church because of the lectures I received in church as a child. These are things I deal with every Sunday at MCC. When the "Religious Right" became more involved with my/our civil rights, I became even more closeted and afraid with reference to the church and my sexual orientation.*

*Parallels between coming out at the individual and community levels.* Amendment 2 created a crisis for many LGBs. A significant response to that crisis was the decision, made by many in the community, to come out and be more public about their sexual orientation. We explore coming out in detail later in this chapter. For purposes of the COMM code, it is important to note that respondents frequently drew parallels between their personal decision to come out and the LGB community's visibility, which itself had greatly increased over the course of the campaign, the election, and the resulting statewide and national response. Participants made the point that coming out was occurring at two levels, that of the individual and the community, simultaneously. Their descriptions pointed to a synergistic quality between the two.

A 21-year-old Fort Collins lesbian described the relationship between the two in these words: *The way Amendment 2 has brought the gay, lesbian, bisexual community together is amazing. It's made me feel like coming out too. My parents will be less difficult because of the incredible strength of the community.* A Grand Junction lesbian 24 years of age made similar observations: *It brought this gay community together, and I found myself being more "out" than I would have imagined possible.* A woman in her late thirties from Boulder reported: *I feel stronger about my lesbianism and more comfortable "being out" now than before. It feels like the community is opening up or coming out more.* A similar observation came from Durango: *The amendment issue has brought more people out of the closet, like myself, and brought the homosexual community here in Durango a lot closer.* Finally, a Denver resident drew the parallel between personal and community changes: *A great part of that change was the opportunity to affirm who I am as a gay man and full human being by becoming very involved with the community (gay) generally and the fight against Amendment 2 in particular.*

*Opportunity for LGB community empowerment.* Many respondents viewed the postelection crisis as an opportunity for the LGB community to gain power and effect positive changes. This opportunity was rooted partly in the perception that isolation among LGBs had been significantly reduced. A bisexual student in a small town near Denver wrote: *Within my high school, it has created a group of people who are gay/bisexual (no lesbians though) that can be there for each other. Before the election, I felt isolated in my school and now we can feel good together about who we are!* Speaking in a similar vein, a lesbian in her forties commented briefly: *Sense of "we are not alone and we are not afraid."*

The movement from isolation to *solidarity*—a word mentioned in several COMM comments—was perceived as opening up the possibility for significant social change. Interestingly, lesbians in their fifties and sixties were more likely to express these optimistic possibilities than were other respondents. We have read this statement from an older lesbian residing in Denver earlier: *I feel the results of Amendment 2 have brought us together to fight for ourselves in ways we haven't ever done before. Hopefully, the result of our coming together will be to help present and future generations to be treated in a more humane way. It isn't easy for anyone, but change never is. . . . Viva the Revolution!*

*COMM and risk, resilience, and recovery.* Comments that were coded COMM pointed to a wonderful give and take between LGB individuals and their communities. We know that negative feelings can spread from person to person in a community; here, we saw evidence that support and empowerment can do likewise. Lesbian, gay, and bisexual people witnessed for one another in a variety of ways and toward a variety of positive ends. This was a source of strength and resilience even in the absence of outside sources of support and, as we saw, there were significant nongay support bases for Colorado LGBs.

While acknowledging the strength and promise inherent in gay people supporting one another, it seems important to offer a caveat. Some, though certainly not all, of the positive change in Colorado's LGB communities was rooted in a reactive rather than a proactive mode (Nash 1999). Empowerment that has its roots only in reacting to an external oppressor is vulnerable to all sorts of vicissitudes, including notably the impact of oppressive agents. The best and most reliable empowerment comes from strength and vision internal to the community rather than from reactions to oppression. The practical realities of this assertion were demonstrated by the following statement by a 21-year-old white lesbian who lived in Colorado Springs. In the context of a larger statement, this young woman posed a dilemma: *I feel the need to withdraw from all this political mayhem but still feel the need for a sense of community.* When the majority of the LGB community's activities were associated with reacting to a hostile act such as Amendment 2, the community had too few resources to simultaneously provide support and respite from what this respondent termed political mayhem. In contrast, when the LGB community is activated by its own vision, it makes available community and cultural activities that provide a much needed break from intense political work and exposure to oppressive messages.[5]

## Strategies

This final category, encompassing fourteen codes, focuses on comments in which LGBs considered various strategies for responding to Amendment 2, including both the personal and the political. Several are fairly brief; we chose to code a given strategy only if a number of participants mentioned it or if its presence made sense contextually. The first two codes, for exam-

ple, deal with respondents' opinions about the boycott of Colorado following the election. A fair number of respondents were against the boycott (BA), expressing concerns about its wisdom. On the other hand, very
few participants were in favor of the boycott (BF). Were it not for the sheer
number of antiboycott responses which seemed to demand a BA code, we
might not have included the proboycott (BF) code in our analysis.

## BA

The BA code focused very much on questions of political strategy with little content of a personal nature. This code was used for comments in
which respondents expressed their disagreement with the boycott of Colorado that had been organized by activists within and outside the state in
an effort to protest Amendment 2. In some cases, participants voiced their
opposition to the boycott without elaboration. A 25-year-old gay man, for
example, had this opinion of Boycott Colorado, the instate group that organized the boycott: *I am a deaf graduate student who happens to be
against Boycott Colorado. I don't discuss my political thinking because I usually am outvoted, but I'm proud of my views.*

Other respondents gave specific reasons for rejecting the boycott.
Some LGBs viewed the boycott as likely to cause a backlash against gay
people. A 31-year-old lesbian from Denver voiced this opinion: *Unfortunately, this negative energy from the boycott is causing more animosity
toward homosexuals.* A gay man, also in his thirties, echoed that opinion:
*I do not support the boycott. I think it is too general and offers a framework
for backlash.* A 25-year-old lesbian was concerned about the image of
LGBs fostered by the boycott and by the effects of the boycott on her
personally: *"Boycott Colorado" is hurting our cause nationally—we're
being seen as spoiled, whining brats. And it hurts personally—I have
friends who won't come to Colorado to visit me. (I feel like I have become
part of the problem—like I am being boycotted.)*

A few respondents suggested alternatives to the boycott. One lesbian in
her forties wrote: *I am also strongly against responding to hate and bigotry
with more hate and bigotry and would like to see more emphasis for adopting
peaceful, educational programs and promotion of understanding rather
than boycott and inflammatory confrontation.* Another lesbian also supported more educationally oriented responses and, in closing, made a

provocative suggestion: *I don't agree with the boycott. I don't believe it's ed-ucating anyone or gaining the support of any of the people we need. I would prefer to see gays, lesbians and bisexuals come to Colorado—especially Col-orado Springs—in droves.*

## BF

As with the BA code, respondents who expressed approval of the boycott did so as a strategic issue. Most of the limited number of participants who wrote in favor of the boycott emphasized its role in maintaining media in-terest in Amendment 2. A 41-year-old gay man, for example, observed: *Boycott only serves to keep issue in media; but through such awareness, silent majority is partially educated.* A lesbian in her twenties had a similar opin-ion: *We need to really focus on education and not so much the boycott, for ex-ample. Although I think the boycott is good and is the only thing keeping Amendment 2 in the news and in people's faces.*

*BA, BF, and risk, resilience, and recovery.* As our team coded the BA and BF responses, we were struck by the absence of any sense that the boycott was a form of witnessing. In some other cases, boycotts have been seen as clear expressions of moral outrage on behalf of people in oppressive cir-cumstances. However, such moral outrage was virtually absent in the com-ments about this boycott. Instead, participants discussed it as a political strategy. Moral outrage of a kind was evident in one lesbian's statement about the boycott; however, her position led her to see the boycott as a means of vengeance rather than an expression of witnessing: *I want the boycott to be successful and to financially cripple Colorado.*

## NTE

The NTE (need to educate) code focused on another sociopolitical strat-egy in the aftermath of the campaign and election—the importance of ed-ucating people about LGBs and their concerns. Our coding team added NTE after we were well into piloting our original set of codes. As with the JUD code, we initially viewed NTE comments as strategic and political in nature and did not immediately comprehend the psychological nature of LGBs' statements about the need to educate heterosexuals. The more we read such comments, the more we understood that respondents were stressing educational strategies in an environment that they now viewed as more homonegative than before. By reading the NTE statements within a witness-perpetrator framework, we were able to construct a different sense of them.

Several respondents viewed education as a means of fostering effective witnessing in the face of further homonegative action in the state. An Hispanic/Swedish lesbian in her thirties, for example, wrote: *Worried that good people can buy into the fear perpetuated by causes/groups such as CFV. Concerned that instead of addressing the fear, we escalate tension. We need to teach gently, firmly and lovingly.* A White/Spanish lesbian from a small town explicated the promise of education for effective witnessing: *Maybe by educating people, in the future we can live a safe and respected life and the people who are trying to get rid of us will be shut up by law and majority of people.*

A number of statements with NTE codes also carried the ISMS code (see chapter 5), signifying that the authors were making some connections between homonegativity and other forms of oppression. A white/Hispanic lesbian's single-sentence statement included both NTE and ISMS assertions: *I believe education is the most important thing to be inclusive of all people.* A white gay man wrote: *Has given me a stronger sense of the need to educate others about gay, lesbian and bisexual people. Has made me feel more comfortable being "open." I'm much more militant in my response to discrimination of any kind.*

This last statement provided an example of another frequent characteristic of NTE comments: they often included references to the need for LGBs to be more open about their sexual orientations. In some cases, the references were personal in nature, as in the gay man's comment above. In other cases, the reference to being out was less about the respondents themselves than about LGBs in general. A 23-year-old Hispanic lesbian's statement closed with this exhortation: *I encourage my gay brothers and sisters to keep visible and keep educating!*

*NTE and risk, resilience, and recovery.* As a group, the NTE-coded comments represented an effort to fashion a sound strategy for changing the environment in the state. These comments implicitly—and sometimes explicitly—acknowledged the role of homophobia and heterosexism in

Amendment 2's passage. Again, taken collectively, the NTE comments expressed both an orientation toward active coping and some sense of hopefulness that education could change difficult realities.

Our team was struck by the number of LGBs of color whose statements included NTE themes. We wondered if LGBs of color were generally more likely to be aware of and acknowledge the election's underlying homonegativity and the role of oppression, and therefore emphasized strategies designed to challenge them.

## *MOVE and NOMOVE*

The MOVE and NOMOVE codes are not strategies per se but rather ways that LGBs made sense of the campaign and election. Specifically, the MOVE code represented a perspective on Amendment 2 that viewed the election as one element in a broader movement for equal rights for bisexuals, lesbians, and gay men. In constructing and using the MOVE perspective, LGBs were able to see Amendment 2 not only as a loss and a crisis but as a part of an ongoing movement that included LGBs and allies in other states and even nations, as well as across historical eras. Judging from the sheer number of MOVE-coded comments, many participants in the study had adopted this perspective. The NOMOVE code was what one might expect from the name. Far fewer in number than MOVE comments, NOMOVE responses asserted that nothing good had come of Amendment 2.

*Backdrop of invisibility.* Respondents who included MOVE-coded statements in their comments were generally not speaking from a place of denial or naïveté. They commonly made note of negative aspects of the campaign and election at some point in their comments. Many of the MOVE statements were predicated on the belief that, whatever else it did, Amendment 2 had allowed LGB issues to become very visible. Sometimes explicitly and more often implicitly, respondents argued that breaking the silence around LGB orientation would be one of the positive outcomes of the amendment, at least in the long run. The very debate—painful as it was for many—was a necessary opening.

For example, a lesbian who began by saying she had been angry and devastated by the election went on to write: *I feel that the increased media attention to "gay and lesbian issues" of all kinds . . . indicates a breakthrough—the taboo about talking about gayness is being challenged, which can only create more awareness in the long run.* Another lesbian made a similar observation: *I feel that the Amendment 2 controversy has had many positive effects—bringing the sexual orientation issue out into the open as a valid topic of discussion and exploration.* A gay man noted that, in the aftermath of the election, Amendment 2 had moved from the state to the national stage: *I am glad to see the debate and reaction to the issues on a National level.*

Most of the MOVE statements were premised on the assumption that increased visibility of LGB issues was always positive in effect. In many comments, this assumption was cast in a familiar form: if heterosexuals knew LGBs, they would be more likely to reject anti-gay actions. A 24-year-old white man from Boulder made this assumption in a very straight-forward fashion: *I think it has turned being gay from being a "dirty little secret" to being out in the open and recognized. People in general will become more comfortable with knowing gay people.*

*The individual and the community.* Many of the MOVE comments combined attention to the individual realm with thoughts about the sociopolitical sphere. For instance, a 51-year-old white lesbian from Denver wrote: *I have felt a "joining together" of the community. I do think that the election has put our situation before the nation at large and given us a chance to accomplish much more than we even thought about originally. Also, my partner and I are both out to our families now. And many more of our friends are aware of our relationship.* A 48-year-old gay woman's comment reflected a similar balanced focus between individual and community domains: *Empowered me to be more completely "out" and honest, not to sell myself short. Received support from many. This vote has enabled Colorado to be an important mirror to reflect issues needing change.*

The following comment by a 60-year-old lesbian illustrated the intermixing of individual and community changes: *Because of the passage of Amendment 2, I decided to come out to my nieces and nephews—all 16 of them. I had been out to my brothers and sisters before Amendment 2 was even in the works. I went to the rally at the Capitol after Amendment 2 passed. I have been to only one other rally in my life. I decided to go to the March on Washington this year. I have been out to myself and others for only five years.*

*I feel Colorado is in a position to educate not only our state, but the nation. We have the opportunity to ensure the rights of gays and lesbians for the whole country. I feel Colorado gays and lesbians are very special people.*

The recognition of an interplay of positive changes at the individual and community levels was a very promising phenomenon in the data. There is a reciprocal relationship between changes at the two levels; change can start at either level and have an impact on the other. When LGBs, even those who have been affected negatively by an anti-gay action, can tap into positive pockets of the LGB community, they can draw strength from these relationships. Conversely, LGBs who are healing can infuse their communities with greater strength as well (Dworkin and Kaufer 1995; Paul, Hays, and Coates 1995).

The positive interplay of personal and political changes was evident in a great many of the MOVE comments. The sole exception was a statement by a Denver lesbian; it was striking because her observations about the personal and political dimensions did not proceed in parallel directions (an observation that reminded us that differences in the data alert us to similarities and vice versa):[6] *The discriminating effects of the passage of Amendment 2 brought up personal feelings of anger and surprise at the number of Colorado voters who have no tolerance for my lifestyle. Its passage internalized my homophobia and made me want to hide my sexual orientation even more than before. However, I feel the long-term effects of this amendment will be positive because more people will become aware of the positive influence of the homosexual community on the world.*

### NOMOVE

The NOMOVE code yielded far fewer comments than did MOVE. Comments in this code often had a lonely quality. They also tended to coincide with AQ (anger with other LGBs) and BARRIERS (to unity in the community) codes. Two major themes emerged from our analysis of NOMOVE. The first was a straightforward judgment about Amendment 2 as unhelpful in every way. Illustrative of this theme was the following 22-year-old lesbian's statement: *I thought that many things were moving forward in terms of rights but now feel that we have taken a giant step backwards. I was shocked to find that so many people could be so hateful and also so misinformed.*

The other major NOMOVE theme viewed Amendment 2 as a waste of scarce resources. A few people maintained that the needs associated with the HIV/AIDS epidemic were particularly endangered as a result of the resources spent on Amendment 2. In the words of a 34-year-old homosexual man: *I was appalled that we had to drain so many resources from our community to defend our very basic right. Those resources are especially needed now to fight AIDS but they were virtually wasted.*

*MOVE, NOMOVE, and risk, resilience, and recovery.* It seems self-evident that a MOVE perspective offered promise and optimism while a NOMOVE stance was likely to be isolating and without promise. That said, we must consider some additional aspects of the two codes. Comments associated with the MOVE perspective may be taken at their positive face value only if rooted in a realistic appraisal of circumstances. For the most part—and in contrast to some comments in the HOPE code which we explore later in this chapter—the MOVE statements generally seemed to be rooted in solid ground. They were not isolated positive statements but usually occurred in the context of some acknowledgment of the negative aspects of the election. Moreover, they often seemed inextricably connected to the respondents' own personal growth and changes. It seemed that, when respondents could see the positive changes in their own lives, they could also see the possibility of their community's changing in a positive direction. The converse is probably just as true; some LGB individuals saw positive changes at the community level and drew on them as inspiration and support for personal change. (It is worth noting that, in either case, this linear language does not do justice to the complexity of the dynamic relationships between LGBs and their community.)

A more significant concern about at least a few of the MOVE comments was related to the unspoken assumption that increased visibility of LGB issues inevitably leads to positive changes. Our coding team wondered whether this assumption might not be a variation on the now familiar belief that, once people get to know LGBs, they will support equal rights. While we agreed that visibility is generally—perhaps almost always—desirable, we were less certain that visibility would always produce a particular desired outcome. We have seen this belief directly challenged by the experience of LGBs whose own families, friends, and colleagues voted for Amendment 2. While this concern arose in response to a handful of

MOVE-coded statements, one statement especially helped us to elucidate the limits of visibility. It was written by a 47-year-old gay man who lived in a rural part of the state. He wrote: *On the positive side, I think all of the people in rural Colorado where I live—are being made more aware, if only because of all the publicity. If we had had more statewide publicity, i.e., TV/radio, etc.) before the election, we would not have lost.*

It is debatable whether increased publicity would have influenced the election outcome. In any case, this comment seemed to reduce the entire election outcome to one factor, namely, publicity or visibility. It is doubtful that any amount of money, talent, and time devoted to publicity could have single-handedly defeated the deep-seated homophobia and heterosexism that garnered so many voters' endorsement of Amendment 2. This is not to suggest that visibility is unimportant. Indeed, it is vital to the struggle for equal rights for gay people. It is only to say that a MOVE perspective or campaign strategy rooted in reductionistic beliefs about visibility may well encounter unanticipated difficulties.

Our final observation is that comments that viewed Amendment 2 as a total waste of resources tended to be rooted in a progressive change assumption. In this perspective, change is seen to occur in a linear fashion and there is no place—and no explanation—for setbacks and backlashes. Holding the progressive change assumption does not allow for anything other than a negative, disappointed response to and explanation for the losses that randomly alternate with positive social change. History, like everything else, may be read in a limitless number of ways. If read as a story of the vicissitudes in progress on a given issue (however one defines progress on that particular issue), then all sorts of responses to and explanations for apparent setbacks become possible. Having access to a variety of responses and explanations for setbacks would seem to offer greater possibilities for thinking and acting constructively.

## *ISOLATE*

The ISOLATE code dealt with explicit statements indicating a strategy of isolation, estrangement, or alienation from the LGB community and/or from society at large in response to Amendment 2. Two major kinds of isolation were described. In the first, respondents reported feeling detached and estranged from others—again, a reaction sometimes focused on the LGB community and sometimes on society in general. They spoke of themselves in relatively passive terms and saw their estrangement as something that had happened to them as a result of the campaign and election. The other major kind of isolation occurred in a more active context, being a strategic decision taken by LGBs in an effort to deal with Amendment 2.

The language of alienation in the ISOLATE statements is striking. At one point during our team's reading of comments in the ISOLATE code, Sylvie made an astute observation: this is how people who have been traumatized talk when they are not thinking specifically of trauma; they are simply reporting their phenomenological reality. The language in this code was peppered with the sense of being different: *alien, alone, alienated, unwelcome, less like I belong, like a second-class citizen, not fitting in.* In many cases, our team read ISOLATE comments as reflecting the way LGBs felt because they had internalized negative messages about themselves.

*Alienation from LGB community.* On the whole, comments that described respondents' feelings of alienation from the gay community were rooted in the implicit belief that LGBs whose views differed from those of the (presumed) majority in the gay community were not tolerated. Disagreement often centered on the appropriate response to the Amendment 2 crisis. A 30-year-old gay man told of his experience: *This amendment has caused me some personal distress for many reasons, and including the fact that I have felt alienated from many of my gay friends over the "proper" way to go about protesting No. 2. All along I've felt that the gay response has been just as hurtful and, in some ways, as base as the proponents of the amendment have. I'm at a loss as to how to proceed at this point.* A similar experience was reported by a 25-year-old lesbian: *I also feel very displaced from the Colorado Gay and Lesbian Community as many of these people's action have set us back, not thrust us forward. We cannot command respect as long as we cannot give it.*

As the above two examples suggest, the ISOLATE comments that focused on the LGB community were frequently coded BARRIERS and occasionally AQ as well. As the following statement by a 19-year-old gay man illustrates, ISOLATE was also associated with the FEAR code in a number of instances: *I feel very scared and pushed into the closet. I feel isolated from gays, lesbians, and bisexuals especially in my age group. I also feel that I must fight for gay rights in my everyday reactions and discussions but [I am] afraid to do so.*

*Alienation from broader society.* Some participants felt alienated from society in general. The same young woman who, in the COMM code, spoke of her simultaneous need for a sense of community and for a break from the political mayhem, wrote: *Because of Amendment 2, I feel hate and fear directed against me personally. I feel very out of synch with the mainstream.* A bisexual woman in her thirties wrote of her mistrust of heterosexuals in general and concluded: *Bottom line: I feel hurt. I feel less like I belong.*

Although most ISOLATE comments referred to alienation either from the community or from society as a whole, occasionally respondents expressed a more widespread sense of estrangement. A 31-year-old white woman highlighted the intersection of homonegativity with other forms of oppression in her life: *As a Jew and a lesbian, I felt totally unsafe in the world. Before the election, I felt I would always be "safe" with my family (biological) and with the world of Jews. I felt rejected by the Jewish community, and felt I had no one. As a Jew, I never feel totally safe in the Queer community, and I now experienced hate from my other community.*

*Isolation as a strategy.* The tone of the comments in which isolation represented a strategic decision was different from that of comments where isolation was simply a response to the election. Participants in the strategic group were actively and intentionally choosing some degree of isolation. Being chosen, their response was an active one; they were not simply passively allowing the election to have such an effect on themselves.

The degree to which respondents chose to isolate themselves varied. We have already encountered the response of the 38-year-old white gay man who took steps to withdraw from the media after the election: *Have stopped taking the paper, have stopped watching the news on TV, have stopped listening to radio (NPR). Also have "unsubscribed" from computer bbs (Internet).*

Another gay man, this one from a rural area, described the steps he took to ensure his safety in the aftermath of the election: *(1) I am more cautious when going to a gay bar—day or night . . . (3) I believe I would hesitate more, since the passage of Amendment Two, to "come out" to someone even though I may have known this person for some time; (4) To be seen in public with a gay male "screamer" would cause me more concern now than before the amendment was passed.* The decisions made by this rural high school-teacher made sense in view of his need to protect himself from the possibility of being assaulted and/or fired. He was apparently responding to a perception that his environment was significantly more dangerous than it had been before and/or that it was more dangerous than he had previously understood it to be. In either case, his decisions isolated him from the LGB community, keeping him away from gathering places and particular individuals, and from LGBs and others with whom he might have been more open before Amendment 2. His decisions, while sensible in terms of self-protection, may have resulted from his internalization of homonegative attitudes as well.

While the gay man in the preceding instance withdrew from some specific arenas in a move toward greater safety, the 38-year-old white homosexual woman below was describing a decision she might make in the future if homonegativity could not be reduced: *I want gays to be better organized and get our message across more loudly than theirs. I feel I need to get very actively involved in this effort and convince my friends to do so also. I fear if we fail, I'll want to disassociate myself from society, i.e., move to another country more friendly to gays or buy a lot of land and cut off contact with the rest of society.*

A Chicana lesbian, also aged 38 years, had formulated an alternative to the homonegative environment as well: *It brings to my mind what to me separatism—or Sonia Johnson—talks about—pulling away our emotional self from the system. Learn how system (government, patriarchy) functions and how to function in it. Then to invest our energy in healing, loving, enjoying life, fun, caring for ourselves and others. I'm learning more about inner strength.*

*ISOLATE and risk, resilience, and recovery.* The positions described in the ISOLATE comments could have a number of implications, depending on the following factors: the locus of the withdrawal (from the LGB community or from society), the nature of the withdrawal (reactive or strategic), the time frame (temporary or permanent), whether it represents running from something or to something, the level of control felt by the individual, and the degree to which the decision represents a choice or the internalization of homophobic messages. Isolating oneself from the LGB community may be a temporary strategy with some merit, if used as a means of taking a break either from the experience of victimization or from intense political activity. In addition, temporary withdrawals from the gay community may enable LGBs to explore and exercise nongay aspects of themselves.

However, while we acknowledge the potential value of withdrawing from the LGB community, integration into the gay community has been shown in general to be associated with various indices of mental health for LGB individuals (Adam 1992; Crocker and Major 1989; Dworkin and Kaufer 1995; Kurdek 1988; Paul, Hays, and Coates 1995). The benefits of integration have also been demonstrated by many LGBs in the present study; the COMM code, in particular, details the variety of ways in which contact with the LGB community can be helpful. LGBs who withdraw from the gay community are in danger of forfeiting all those advantages.

Such isolation may be especially problematic when it reflects the internalization of homonegative attitudes and beliefs, a phenomenon not always easy to discern from withdrawal behaviors alone. To the degree that it does reflect such attitudes, withdrawing from the community, especially as a long-term response, may exacerbate an individual's problems in two ways. First, as noted, it may cause isolation and loss of the advantages of contact with the community. Second, it may increase internalized homophobia and decrease potential support.

In a slightly different vein, withdrawal based on the fear of holding unpopular opinions may have negative consequences for the community as well as for individual LGBs. As we saw in chapter 6, the belief that all LGBs have to hold identical views and philosophies may reflect homonegative assumptions about the homogeneity of members of a marginalized group. This is intrinsically problematic, again both for the community and for LGB individuals. It robs the community of a diversity of perspectives that can enhance the quality of its vision and its success in solving problems; and it robs individual LGBs of a sense of home.

As in withdrawing from the LGB community, isolating oneself from society more broadly may be advantageous on a temporary basis but is likely to be problematic over the long run. Time-limited respites may offer LGBs a sense of psychological as well as physical safety and an opportunity to relax and rejuvenate themselves. Such respites may also allow gay people to immerse themselves in the positive aspects of the LGB community that were described in the discussion of the COMM code.

The critical question is whether withdrawal from society at large represents, to paraphrase Valerie Batts, a pro-LGB position or an anti-heterosexual avoidance of contact (Batts 1989). The latter, withdrawal to avoid heterosexuals, is likely to be problematic in that it is largely reactive to others rather than predicated on one's own strengths and vision. LGBs who take this course of action may be making major life decisions based on what heterosexuals do or expect; they may thereby be handing over enormous amounts of power to the very people they want to avoid. Clearly, it is sometimes necessary and prudent to make decisions in response to heterosexist expectations—for example, to keep a job or have custody of children. In such cases, gay persons must understand not only the homophobia fueling their decisions but the (sometimes inevitable) power that they are giving to heterosexuals and to heterosexist institutions.[7]

One final note about withdrawal from society at large seems warranted. While several respondents made an effort to identify alternatives to withdrawal, the task of escaping from heterosexist and homophobic circumstances is daunting, if not impossible. Most of this society (and, indeed, most societies) is characterized by extensive homonegativity. Cultural differences notwithstanding, it is difficult to know where one goes to create a situation devoid of homonegativity. This assertion, of course, is based on the understanding that homonegativity was at the root of the passage of Amendment 2. If one relies on a different explanation, different implications emerge. Some LGB respondents viewed the fundamental problem not as homonegativity in general but as characteristics of the state of Colorado in particular. For some of these LGBs, there was an obvious solution: leaving the state.

## LEAVE

The LEAVE code, which referred to the desire to leave Colorado, was one of the more painful ones in the data set. It conveyed the sense of psychological homelessness as thoroughly as any code. LEAVE comments seemed to be the outcome of a line of meaning making that identified Colorado as the cause for the psychological distress associated with Amendment 2. In very few cases did respondents' contemplated departures from the state seem to be instant reactions to the election. Instead, they were the culmination of an extended effort to solve the problem of how to deal with the disruption created by the amendment.

In a few exceptional instances, the impulse to leave the state came immediately after the election. A 46-year-old woman wrote: *My instinct is to flee Colorado.* A 32-year-old gay man, who expected the election outcome to be different, described his reaction thus: *My 32 year love affair with Colorado died that night—a loss I'll never regain. The beauty of this state (which I often gain spiritual strength from) is smeared black by naked hate and bigotry. I wanted to run, leave, yet I knew I would never find that place I could come "home" outside the state.*

Many participants with plans to leave had significant practical ties to the state. However, their postelection sense of betrayal by Colorado outweighed these ties. A 32-year-old gay man explained: *My partner of 8-1/2 years and I had just bought a house in 1991 [just a year earlier]. We both have good jobs. But now I despise Colorado. The people are bigots and liars (I remember what the polls said). I want to move away from this repulsive place.* Other respondents emphasized the change in their sense of psychological connectedness as a result of the election. A 43-year-old white lesbian wrote: *I think Colorado is a horrible place to live. It went from being beautiful to a sordid trash heap in my mind. I'm still thinking of moving away.* A homosexual woman in her twenties wrote of her analysis of the election results and decision to leave: *People knew exactly what they were voting for. I don't believe for a minute that people were "confused over the issue." At first I vowed to fight, but now as time passes, I see that I won't change people's attitudes toward us. The court might overturn #2, but people's homophobia, bias, and hatred will remain. This is the most depressing thought of all. I'm looking forward to moving out of state this summer.*

This last comment illustrated the powerlessness underlying many of the reports by those leaving—or contemplating leaving—Colorado. A handful of participants said that their impulse to depart the state was conditional; if Amendment 2 were overturned, they would be more likely to stay. An example was this statement by a 28-year-old gay man: *I am a tenure-track faculty member and the possible effects of #2 on my tenure decision sometimes worry me. I'm tired of the whole thing—I'm waiting to see whether it is over-*

*turned in the courts. If not, we'll start looking for a new place to live (i.e., new state).*

*LEAVE and risk, resilience, and recovery.* Most of the respondents who made LEAVE comments felt that their options were limited after the passage of Amendment 2. The analysis underlying LEAVE statements placed the onus for the amendment on Colorado and its people. This reading of the situation allowed respondents to hope that other states might be safer. Leaving Colorado might well have offered in relief from some of the more acute expressions of homonegativity that thrived in the state before and after the election. However, leaving would not have provided complete relief from the homonegativity that is a basic phenomenon of life anywhere in the United States.

## INSIGHT

The INSIGHT code was designed for statements in which respondents described the process of learning something at a personal level. We used this code sparingly, wanting to reserve it for participants' comments about the experience of self-analysis and self-discovery. The INSIGHT comments were active ones, framed in first-person terms, and often containing clearly articulated feelings.

*INSIGHT and GRASP.* A number of the statements coded INSIGHT focused on respondents' changing understanding of the pervasiveness of homophobia and heterosexism in the world and were therefore also coded GRASP. The INSIGHT code was employed only when the statements clearly showed that respondents had been personally affected by their changing perceptions about homonegativity. In a sense, they were working to undo denial at a personal level as they grasped the homophobia in the external world.

A few respondents used Amendment 2 as the basis for a retrospective analysis of their prior denial or complacency. We return to the statement by a Glenwood Springs lesbian who described her complacent, almost numbed acceptance of homonegativity: *Amendment 2 concerns me—but it is not affecting my life a whole lot. I have always been concerned about discrimination—I have lost a job in the past in Iowa—and know that this*

*Amendment is a real threat. Is it possible I have gotten used to this life? Yes, I believe so.*

A 40-year-old gay woman, in the next comment, described her experience of challenging long-standing denial at a deeply personal level. The challenge left her with a mix of strong feelings and confusion about how to proceed: *I have felt incredible rage, frustration, sadness, fear—I am so appalled at the hatred directed at gay people—it seems so senseless, inexplicable. I feel, despite my volunteer work, helpless against it. I believe that "we" are right, but I am so anguished by the cost, the suffering, that will be the payment for this struggle, this resistance. I am afraid of my anger. I wish I could quit my job and be a full time activist/educator. I'm shocked, finally, after deflecting the hatred and indifference all these years by what it feels like to let it hit me, full force. In short, a lot of responses, confused and contradictory ones. I felt guilt for not having done more before the election. I never thought it would pass.*

Some respondents seemed to be less confused by their insight into homonegativity. A gay Hispanic man in his thirties articulated considerable meaning making about the nature of the homonegativity he had come to recognize. He also described a significant change in himself: *I do not believe that "special rights" is a correct phrase. All people want equal rights under the law. I think that groups like CFV are afraid of what they don't know. I think that there are a lot more people out there that do not understand or like homosexuals than I believed previously. I am more awake and sensitive about being homosexual. I wish that individuality rather than sexual orientation was more important to heterosexuals. At times I wish that sexual orientation was a switch I could flip.*

The 36-year-old lesbian quoted below was able to translate what she learned from her shock about the election outcome into the ability to consider that denial sometimes masqueraded as hopefulness: *I was so hopeful before the election; the worse George Bush did, the happier I was. I never dreamed Amendment 2 had any chance of passing. I just didn't think it was possible. My lover and I sat down to watch the election returns full of hope. We couldn't believe it when 2 started passing and when it was projected to pass. I felt like I had been hit by a Mack truck. The first few days after the election, I varied from shell shocked to incredible anger. I finally mellowed into hope that it will be found [to be] unconstitutional. I hope I'm not just in denial as I was before the election.*

*INSIGHT about internalized homophobia.* While a number of respondents gained personal insight through their new understanding of homonegativity in the external world, an even greater number described experiences of self-discovery rooted in a deeper understanding of their own internalized homophobia and its effects on them. We also saw examples of this kind of discovery in the IHE code, some of which were cross-coded with INSIGHT. A white lesbian in her early forties wrote: *(1) I've been a lesbian for 25 years. Before Amendment 2, I felt pretty accepting of myself—sexual orientation. Since #2, I've had to reexamine on a deeper level my own internalized homophobia and shame; (2) I've never been one to feel or express much anger. Since #2, I get angry often and spend a lot of mental time writing letters to the editor in my head, holding imaginary debates, etc. I also get more angry about things not related to #2; (3) It is shocking to me and I continue to be appalled that my community and my state are much more hostile environments than I used to think. It's hard to maintain my optimistic outlook on life. On the other hand, I am encouraged by straight colleagues, government officials, other heterosexuals, other minorities who are speaking out and taking strong stands against Amendment 2.*

The following 37-year-old homosexual man described his efforts to work with the homophobic messages he had internalized from CFV's campaign. In the last part of his comment, he may have offered a clue as to one of the avenues by which homonegative campaign messages had reached him: *I have sometimes found myself thinking that I don't deserve to be treated special. Then I realize that I do deserve to be protected and I deserve to have others respect my homosexuality. It's especially difficult for me and my family. Everyone is fundamentalist Christian and I start to think they really do hate me.*

*Anger and INSIGHT.* As several of the INSIGHT statements thus far have illustrated, new awareness about homonegativity—in the world and in oneself—is often accompanied by some degree of anger. This is not surprising when we consider that change in a more positive position is often predicated on rejecting a previous position, sometimes through recognition, for the first time, of what was problematic about it.

In the following two statements, respondents reported having to contend with anger in the face of new understandings about internalized homophobia. Both challenged themselves to see that their gratitude to heterosexuals had been shrouded in implicit beliefs about heterosexual superiority. The first statement was by a 31-year-old lesbian: *The injunction felt great on one hand; yet on the other, I still felt like shit because here were all these people having to work so hard so some straight white man could "grant" us an injunction. I'm angry because I'm supposed to be "happy" and "hopeful" from a crumb.* A 27-year-old bisexual woman wrote as follows about her insight, tinged with anger: *Often my response to info re: Amendment 2, the boycott, the legal challenge is to get teary. My response to having my basic rights protected by some is gratitude. Kind of like a starving dog being thrown a bone. And then I get mad—why should I feel gratitude toward those who believe I'm a person who deserves to have these rights?*

Dealing with anger at a time of emerging insight can be doubly challenging. The frequency of reports of anger in the statements coded IN-SIGHT would suggest that anger sometimes accompanied LGBs' personal growth in response to Amendment 2—especially where it seemed to further the insight rather than be an end in itself. Although not all anger is empowering, it is certainly part of an empowering process at times (Herman 1992). Indeed, one lesbian respondent reported using in another context what she had learned through her anger about Amendment 2; the other situation involved victimization in the past: *The therapy I am currently doing is primarily concerned with relationship and incest issues; however, we have spent some time dealing with the Amendment 2 nonsense. The one area of reaction your questionnaire didn't really deal with is the positive aspects of being forced further "out." My family has known almost as long as I have—but I have never before confronted my born-again Christian sister with her homophobia. Painful, yes! Ultimately honest and freeing, yes! My response to Amendment 2 of anger and rage has in some odd ways helped me face and deal with my incest experience and my own internalized homophobia.*

In some cases, by reading statements from start to finish our team saw another value to anger, namely, as a means of accepting the support of heterosexual allies. A 37-year-old gay man wrote: *Initially, latent pain. Discovery of internalized homophobia. Lots of anger toward heterosexual friends for "getting it" too late. Finally, acceptance of their support.* As we saw in the SUPPORT code, acknowledging and accepting support from allies can both reflect a gay person's strength and also give him or her strength in return. However (as we saw in the two statements at the beginning of this section on anger and INSIGHT), when LGBs viewed heterosexuals as more powerful than themselves sometimes they did so because they had internalized messages of heterosexual superiority. The initial anger at heterosexuals of the gay man quoted above may have reflected his ability (finally) to deal with them as equals which, in turn, put him in a better position to accept their support. While this suggestion is, of course, speculative, it does offer an explanation for the conjunction of anger and insight in the aftermath of Amendment 2.

As a whole, the statements coded INSIGHT stood out as clear demonstrations that LGBs could learn, change, and grow even in a climate rife with homophobia and heterosexism. The ability of some gay people to respond to such a vitriolic anti-gay incursion with such resilience is admirable but not unique. Consider our earlier discussion (in relation to the TRAUMA code in chapter 6) of the increasing attention by scholars to the processes and circumstances by which individuals who have been traumatized evidence positive outcomes. As we saw, a positive outcome sometimes occurs even in individuals who have had significant symptoms associated with trauma (Burt and Katz 1987; Lyons 1991; Tedeschi and Calhoun 1995; Tedeschi, Park, and Calhoun 1998). In fact, there appears to be an independent relationship between trauma symptoms and positive outcomes: a given individual's experience with trauma symptoms is in no way predictive of her or his subsequent growth through trauma.

Certainly, we have seen the apparently paradoxical phenomenon of trauma and transformation many times in this data set. Lesbians, bisexuals, and gay men expressed a great deal of pain and distress, but they also spoke of how much they had gained from the Amendment 2 experience. Sometimes the positive gains were new connections, courage, and skills. In some instances, the positive outcome was the simplest and most profound of insights, as in the following statement by a 31-year-old white gay man in Fort Collins: *Well, I don't know if you could tell from my responses [to the quantitative items] or not, but Amendment 2 was partly to largely responsible for my coming out. (Wouldn't Will Perkins [of Colorado for Family Values] be thrilled to hear that?) The thing I probably remember the most from election night was thinking, "Why has this been done to me? I'm a good person, dammit." That was actually kind of a breakthrough for me. I had never really thought of myself as "a good person who just happens to be gay."*

Even where INSIGHT comments were less overtly joyful than this one, there were seeds of hope. Reaching a new understanding of oneself and/or the world typically holds out the hope for new possibilities.

## HOPE

The HOPE code, as its name suggests, dealt with respondents' statements of hope for the future. We used HOPE only for comments written from a first-person perspective and with an explicit orientation to the future; hence, this was not an extensive code. The comments coded HOPE were (perhaps surprisingly) not uniformly inspiring.

Some HOPE comments seemed to be attempts at meaning making in light of the negative aspects of the election, as the following one by an 18-year-old white gay man: *I am 100% opposed to Amendment 2 (like I really need to say that) but I think that it's doing good for the gay/lesbian/bisexual community in the long run. People are now being forced to deal with something they'd rather ignore. They're being educated and taught that there is more to homosexuality than "perverted" sex. This will eventually be seen as the catalyst for the successful civil rights movement of the '90's!*

Occasionally, our team was confused about how the authors arrived at the hopeful part of their statements. We sometimes even wondered if hopeful endings had been tagged onto distressed statements, perhaps in respondents' efforts to cope with their own distress. The authors of a few statements made it clear that their hopefulness in relation to Amendment 2 was part of a broader approach to their lives in general. A 23-year-old black gay man, for example, conveyed his hopefulness in this fashion: *I'm not a political human being. I look at it as a way of life. The more things change, the more they stay the same. Think Diana Ross' song, "Reach out and touch somebody's hand, make this world a better place if you can," and you'll see how optimistic I am.*

As a team, we found it easier to trust HOPE statements that were rooted in personal commitments and/or concrete observations about the LGB community than those in which hopefulness seemed to be a tagged-on ending. Personal commitments of this sort often coincided with the PERSONAL code, as in the following 34-year-old lesbian's statement: *I understand where this could have gone, if it wasn't addressed as aggressively as it was. I fully intend to see this through to the end and am hopeful that the decision will be in our favor.* A 29-year-old lesbian began her comment with: *Mostly I am determined to be the catalyst for education and change in my circle of friends, family and workplace.* Later in her statement, she observed: *I feel that cohesion within our community and between communities is likely to take place in the wake of this Amendment.* The hopefulness in both of these statements seemed at least partly grounded in the respondents' own ability to be active in their commitment to pursue change. They were reminiscent of the existentialist psychologists' emphasis on absolute engagement, in contrast to nebulous hopefulness and baseless expectations (see, e.g., Kast 1994; Snyder 1994). In similar vein, hopeful comments that sprang from the kinds of concrete observations made above (*cohesion within our community . . . this Amendment*) seemed to have a basis in the world that rendered them more solid and credible to us.

In some cases, we saw respondents' increasingly familiar ability to make apparently conflicting observations and/or have contradictory feelings simultaneously, allowing them to express hopefulness even as they acknowledged difficulties associated with the election. A lesbian in her forties observed: *At the same time I think that the passage of Amendment 2 will open the closet door for lots of us and that the debate is necessary in order to effect change. That doesn't mean that I'm not discouraged and angered by the amount of opposition we seem to face, AND, at the same time I am hopeful that we will finally win the simplest of rights.*

*Content of HOPE statements.* The content of comments coded HOPE clustered around several specific issues. First, a number of respondents expressed hope in the context of a MOVE perspective; both MOVE and HOPE perspectives were generally characterized by orientations that went beyond the immediate present. Both were apparent in the following comment by a 22-year-old white gay man: *In a sense, I am glad about it, in that it is forcing people to really think about their beliefs. I think that the passage of Amendment 2 may be a blessing in disguise, because I think the attention will bring progress.*

A related connection was the coincidence of HOPE with discussions about the visibility of the LGB community, a connection clearly articulated in the statement above by the 22-year-old who regarded Amendment 2 as a *blessing in disguise.* Finally, the HOPE code was prominent in relation to observations about successful witnessing. A 47-year-old Pueblo man explicitly associated his increased hopefulness to the presence of support (as well as, implicitly, to his own engagement in the issue): *It has allowed me more openly to discuss Amendment 2/gay issues with heterosexual friends and in support groups (mixed) in which I participate. I feel more positive because there is a large pool of voters who do support gay/human rights and they're not ashamed to admit it. There is more support all around.*

As we saw in the JUD code, some respondents also connected hopefulness with the judicial treatment of the amendment. The following statement by a 32-year-old homosexual man was representative of this HOPE-JUD connection: *I am glad to see that Jeffrey Bayless has suggested Amendment 2 would be unconstitutional. It is comforting to live in a great nation where the rights given under the U.S. Constitution prevail over a majority vote of the people. Hopefully, higher courts will uphold the U.S. Constitution and stamp out discrimination.*

The HOPE code offered a mix of optimism related to the long-term effects of Amendment 2. Some comments seemed more grounded than others; some made connections that were more accessible to our team than others; all seemed to bespeak participants' efforts to recover from the negative consequences of the campaign and election.

## RECOVER

From the beginning, the members of our team were interested in understanding which factors respondents identified as helpful to their efforts to rebound from the campaign and election. The RECOVER code was designed for comments in which the writers made specific references to their ability to recover from negative consequences of the election. We used the RECOVER code only when respondents made three specific references: to some negative consequence of the election, to feeling better in some way, and to a particular factor that had contributed to their feeling better.

In reviewing some of the important dimensions of the RECOVER domain, we will see a number of comments repeated—largely because earlier codes inevitably corresponded to the factors identified by participants as instrumental in their recovery. Here, selecting the best exemplars of observations about recovery seems more important to us than avoiding repetition of comments quoted earlier.[8]

*Taking an active stance.* The literature on recovering from traumatizing experiences emphasizes the importance of moving from the reactive stance that is virtually inevitable in times of crises to one characterized by self-control and choice (see, for example, Herman 1992). Assertions of the value of assuming an active role occurred with great frequency in the RECOVER statements. Some participants seemed to suggest that by taking action they were reversing an earlier passive stance and perhaps even trying to compensate for that earlier attitude. This statement is illustrative: *I felt shocked at the passage. Guilty that I wasn't more "out" and have since been more vocal at work and feel better about that.* Other respondents limited their commentary to the postelection period. A 42-year-old Anglo homo from Denver made the following statement (in its entirety): *I've been involved every day since the election and am energized by my involvement.*

Several LGBs attributed personal recovery to their participation in support groups or individual or group psychotherapy. None of their statements offered further details as to precisely how such experiences were helpful. The opportunity to make sense of the election and to give and receive support immediately come to mind as potentially relevant factors. Some may also have benefited by coming to understand the adaptive as well as the problematic nature of their own responses. People who have encountered significant crises in their lives frequently question their own responses and need to make peace with them. Sharing the experience of a given crisis in a group may be helpful in that process.

On the other hand, no matter what has been shared, people need to find the route to recovery that fits their own personalities and lifestyles. This issue was raised in the RECOVER statement written by a 54-year-old lesbian: *Immediately after the election and for about a week thereafter, I froze, then experienced extreme anger. Finally found the best way to become active which best suited my talents and personality, and since then, although frequently tired from doing so much, [I] am better able to handle the effects of Amendment 2.*

Some respondents attributed their recovery to internal self-examination, while others focused on external actions. Occasionally, RECOVER statements covered both dimensions. A bisexual woman in her early thirties, for example, gave her attention to internal and external change throughout her comment: *Since the amendment passed I've had more in-depth conversations with heterosexuals to help them understand homophobia in all its forms. I've also had to examine the last remnants of my own inter-nalized homophobia. In all, I feel this has been a really intense opportunity to continue to heal on many levels, personally and societally.* A lesbian in her early fifties also conveyed her ability to act on the internal and external levels simultaneously: *As a lesbian therapist, I was devastated by the passage of Amendment 2 for both myself and my patients. I was surprised at the inten-sity of my reaction and at the guilt I felt and the personal responsibility I felt because I did not actively work on the campaign. I am currently working to change that, beginning with my own internalized homophobia. Becoming ac-tive has had a healing effect on me.*

For many respondents, the external action taken consisted of coming out (that is, of disclosing their sexual orientation). Decisions to be more out are explored in the final section of the data (OUTM, OUTL). One re-spondent addressed the relationship between increased outness and RE-COVER in the following comment, parts of which we have already seen: *The day after the election, I was definitely depressed. I felt as if I'd awakened to Nazi Germany. In the next few weeks, I experienced some fear but eventu-ally I did begin to feel a sense of empowerment. I decided, as others have, that the best way to fight Amendment 2 is to be more open and to come out to more people—and I have.* An active stance, as illustrated in these statements, helped LGBs move from a sense of helplessness and victimization to one of empowerment. The relationship between RECOVER and taking per-sonal action seemed both straightforward and commonsensical. In con-trast, a more complex relationship was suggested when LGBs responded to Amendment 2 by withdrawing.

*Withdrawal and RECOVER.* A number of participants attributed their re-covery to having withdrawn in the aftermath of the election. Differences in the descriptions of this behavior alerted us to the possibility that we might be reading about withdrawal behavior in some cases and about avoidance behavior in others. One way—an active way— of taking control in the aftermath of this crisis was to create a safe space in which to recover; some comments conveyed that quality. As an example, we return to this statement by a 19-year-old homosexual man: *I feel so burned out about Amendment 2. I have really withdrawn a lot of the work that I used to put in down in Colorado Springs. But I feel good just taking some time to relax and spend time with my boyfriend. I am starting to feel like a person once again—and not like a machine. The injunction was great news! I still put in my share of work, but over all of this mess, I have finally learned to just relax and enjoy any quiet time I have with myself and my boyfriend.* This young man's description indicated that his activity had been so intense that he had ended up feeling like a *machine*. By temporarily and purposefully moving back from such intense activity, he was apparently trying to decrease burnout, feel more in control, regain a sense of balance in his life, and enjoy his primary relationship. By continuing to put in his share of the work, he was avoiding total withdrawal and presumably maintaining a sense of himself as efficacious.

A similarly active decision to withdraw on a temporary basis as a means of recovering was evident in the following statement by a 26-year-old Fort Collins man. However, his withdrawal after intensive work on the campaign seemed more extensive and the reengagement more tentative: *In mid-December, I checked out and crashed at friends in the mountains to detox: no newspapers, no media appearances, no meetings. We banned A2 talk and conversation! By mid-January, I was starting to feel alive again. I still fatigue politically fairly quickly, and am cautious of both the media and "well-meaning" liberal straights; I'm willing to slowly reengage in the process!* This respondent's statement also reflected an intentional withdrawal from campaign activity that had left him feeling less than alive. His reengagement was slow and deliberate, perhaps even fragile.

*TRAUMA and RECOVER.* As our team read such comments, we wondered about the ambiguity of the line between purposeful withdrawal and the withdrawal characteristic of the constricted phase of trauma responses (Herman 1992). Obviously, the two have very different implications for recovery. Withdrawal can precede taking active control and restoring both calm and energy, but it can also be a reaction to trauma in which people feel and act disconnected from their worlds.

The following entry by a white bisexual woman strongly suggested that her withdrawal was related to the constriction phase and the anhedonia (that is, loss of pleasure in activities that typically give pleasure) that often accompanies this phase: *For me, the problems didn't end with [the injunction]. I think the military debate was a double whammy. I'm just now beginning to recover—mostly by shutting all media out of my life and doing a lot of psychic protection exercises. During January, I lost interest in work, play, everything. Thank you for caring to ask.* This woman's withdrawal sounded less deliberate and more like a reaction to the overstimulation of the national debate on gays in the military that quickly followed the passage of Amendment 2. While her withdrawal may have helped her, it may also have been associated with the constriction phase of a trauma response. At the very least, she was having to use considerable energy to avoid all media.

Reading statements of such limited length and breadth, we had no way of knowing when a respondent had crossed the line between adaptive withdrawal and avoidance of a more problematic nature. Nonetheless, such differences in the data have significant implications for recovery.

*Other factors in RECOVER.* A number of respondents raised three other specific issues as helpful to recovery. The first of these has been described in the section on the TRAUMA code: some respondents used personal experiences with other traumas or other forms of social oppression as a basis for dealing with Amendment 2. A second helpful factor was contact with other gay people; the nature of such contacts was explored in the COMM code. Finally, a number of respondents attributed their recovery to experiences in which they felt witnessed by others. Prominent in this category were cases of witnessing by heterosexuals (SUPPORT) and the injunction against Amendment 2 (JUD).

More generally, RECOVER statements frequently included descriptions of well-differentiated feelings, an action orientation, and some explicit meaning making around Amendment 2. More often than not, comments in the RECOVER code also contained references to issues broader than the individual—to other LGBs, to witnesses, and to the movement for equal rights. For some, the path to recovery was through a personal commitment to action in response to Amendment 2.

## PERSONAL

This code referred to statements in which respondents took personal responsibility for undertaking some action in the aftermath of the Amendment 2 election. We used the PERSONAL code only when respondents' explicitly articulated their intention to undertake personal action.

*The timing of the PERSONAL commitment.* Participants' PERSONAL comments suggested that their commitment to act was a direct result of the election itself, rather than of the campaign. A 44-year-old gay man, for example, made it quite clear that he had been changed by the election: *I strongly believe that I was placed on this earth—at this time, in this place—to fight for gay rights. Amendment 2 woke me up!*

Other respondents indicated that their personal commitment to action had been in place during the campaign prior to the election. A 37-year-old white lesbian described her activism and some of the thinking underlying it as follows: *I had no money to give to the campaign; therefore, I attended rallies, wore buttons, put on bumper stickers, signs in window, in yard. Talked to a lot of people, known and strangers, about amendment 2. Mostly, the ig-norance about amendment 2 confirms my feeling that most people are passive about something until it directly affects them. It simply adds more fuel to my anger at any social injustice, racial, sexual, or civil. Fear and silence are what keep people in chains. My work on my incest issues has helped me to more effectively channel anger over these social injustices, such as amendment 2.* In a few instances, respondents had been activists earlier in their lives and re-newed their activism after the amendment. Among them was a 52-year-old gay man who worked with Ground Zero, a Colorado Springs organization that sprang up around the time of the election: *I am strongly committed to the overturn of 2. In the late sixties, I was instrumental in establishing sev-eral gay rights groups. Since the mid-70's, I have been content to go my way. Amendment 2 has re-empowered me and I work daily for Ground Zero to re-verse misperceptions of homosexuals and to fight the right.*

*Focus of PERSONAL statements.* One of the issues that interested our team in the statements of personal commitment was whether the respondent's focus of attention was internal or external. In a previous section we read the following statement by a homosexual woman of 38 whose personal ac-tivism was focused outside herself and specifically on those she hoped to educate: *I've been very angry that the religious right is powerful enough to bring out people's worst side. I want gays to be better organized and get our message across more loudly than theirs. I feel I need to get very actively involved in this effort and convince my friends to do so also. I fear if we fail, I'll want to disassociate myself from society, i.e., move to another country more friendly to gays or buy a lot of land and cut off contact with the rest of society.* When this respondent mentioned other gay people, she emphasized their ability to get their message across to nongays. While she undeniably saw educating heterosexuals as important, the way her statement was framed showed that she assigned heterosexuals the power, including the power to determine whether she would leave.

A similar picture—with differing focus and framing—was evident in this 36-year-old lesbian's comment: *Yes, I'm pissed, but I'm active and not silent. At times it seems ludicrous to defend my personhood; at other times, I'm glad for this opportunity to educate others. This has increased my sense of personal strength, my attachment to our community. I do fear for the more vulnerable of us, and hold a personal vow to fight this nonsense in every aspect of my life. I also feel great sadness and despair for the CFVers and other assorted right-wingers but this is secondary. I do not fear them, though. I dream of when they'll channel their energy into something helpful and constructive, not hateful and hurtful. It's hard to share the world with them.* Despite her extensive focus on CFV, this woman regarded that focus as secondary. She also emphasized her strength and her connection to the LGB community, thereby tacitly acknowledging that the power rested there.

Some respondents' PERSONAL statements were characterized by a very obviously internal focus. This was clearly the case for this gay man in his forties: *I will not give up the fight. Human rights are battles always worth fighting for and never ending. Amendment 2 may be undone by the courts but it will be a long battle. Never stop fighting.* This participant departed from a first-person focus, only to remind the reader of the value of a long-term perspective and to keep fighting. He paid no attention at all to those who opposed the struggle for equal rights for gay men, bisexuals, and lesbians.

In a handful of cases, respondents' PERSONAL statements described the way their focus of attention had changed over the course of the Amendment 2 crisis. A bisexual woman in her midthirties wrote that her preelection focus had been on CFV and the voters and her postelection focus on herself: *I felt unbelievably naïve after the election. I never participated in the campaign—it seemed much ado about nothing in the sense that*

*Amendment 2 supporters were hate-filled and dishonest. Like Jews before the war, I trusted the society to stop the reactionary CFV. I became intensely involved in gay-lesbian rights after the November 3 horror.* A similar type of transition was described by a 28-year-old lesbian who wrote: *I tend to be more vocal when I hear people discuss Amendment 2. There was a time when I defended the amendment with a "them" attitude. Now it's more of a personal attack and I defend it with an "us" attitude.*

*Nature of PERSONAL commitments.* The two actions to which respondents committed themselves most frequently were: educating heterosexuals and being more open about their own sexual orientation. The emphasis on education has been explicated in the NTE code, where participants perceived that education was essential to changing attitudes and ultimately to changing the environment for gay people.

Related to education was participants' decision to be more open as lesbian, bisexual, or gay persons. In fact, many respondents believed that by being out they could educate heterosexuals about LGB people and issues. The decision to be more out had an important advantage over some other types of commitment: it had a decidedly internal focus and it was something that LGBs could accomplish, no matter what others did or how they responded. In that sense, it seemed to be a powerful option. In the upcoming final section on data exposition, we explore the complexities of LGBs' personal decisions about how out to be both prior to and after the election.

## Codes Related to Coming Out

Even the most perfunctory reading of the data set indicated that Amendment 2 had had a profound effect on the way gay, bisexual, and lesbian respondents thought about the issue of being open about their sexual orientation. The sheer number of comments in which LGBs wrote of their decision to be more out as gay people was striking in itself. One of the earliest codes we defined, therefore, was OUTM, in which participants reported being more out. Although far less frequent than OUTM comments, those coded OUTL (for "out less") also caught our attention early on. The OUT code, another that we added to our coding schema after piloting, contained references to being out that were neither out more nor out less. In contrast to OUTM and OUTL (where we could anticipate the themes), we had no idea what to expect from the OUT code.

## *OUT*

OUT comments covered a good deal of territory, in part because of the multiple meanings of the word "out." Most OUT comments centered on the issue of LGBs being open about their sexual orientation. One sub-theme in the code had to do with respondents' attempts to assess how out they were—that is, whether heterosexuals knew or suspected that they were bisexual, lesbian, or gay. A Colorado Springs lesbian wrote: *Though I'm "out" to very few colleagues, I believe many of them know. I'm in the library business, and (I believe) the majority of my colleagues are adamantly opposed to #2 for numerous reasons.* A gay man from a small town near Colorado Springs also discussed the ambiguity of colleagues' knowledge about his sexual orientation, although his view of his own prospects were more pessimistic:[9] *I am really afraid I will be fired the day Amendment 2 becomes law. I have been at my job 7 years, I love my job and would not know what to do if I was fired. No one at my job knows about me but comments have been made. This really worries me.*

For some respondents, the election forced the question of how out they should or could be. One participant wrote: *I find myself being much more aware of other people—I try sizing them up to determine whether I should hide my buttons (anti-Amendment 2). I feel very torn between coming out further and with pride, and protecting my person from possible physical and verbal abuse.* A 33-year-old gay woman who declined to indicate her city or town of residence described her fear of being out and the way her thinking had been challenged by the election: *I have always been very fearful of people knowing that I was gay. The passage of Amendment 2, however, has made me start to re-think the way that I handle my life as far as being gay. I feel as though there are days that I really want to tell my family and hope their response is ok; however, I also have days when I don't want to change the way things are.*

The passage of Amendment 2 represented an environmental change that led many LGBs to reevaluate their degree of outness. A Denver lesbian in her thirties explained her conflict: *I do feel very guilty for not being willing to be out at work. I was a lesbian activist in the 70's and I'm very hard on myself about not doing my part now by being out at work. I feel very alienated from younger activists. . . . I didn't feel guilty about being closeted at work before Amendment 2 (before last summer when the campaign heated up), but I feel very guilty now. I don't speak my mind or share my personal story at work, and I give myself a very hard time about that.*

Outness is a relative phenomenon. In his comment, a 27-year-old gay man described how the changes brought about by Amendment 2 had challenged him and given him the opportunity to be out at new levels: *I was not used to talking about being gay to others, defending myself verbally or just saying that's not how I act. I did feel powerless and had other feelings of anxiety since I now had to figure out how to verbally defend myself without fear and overwhelming emotions. I never had to defend myself like this before. It takes time and practice. I know more now because of Amendment 2.*

Some LGBs took note of the changed environment but did not anticipate significant changes in their own levels of disclosure as gay people. Among these were two lesbians, both white and both about 40 years of age. One wrote: *Work for a large Fortune 500 company. Though I have fantasies of "coming out" at work, I doubt I ever will. My dream is to be able to work in an environment where I can be out.* The other wrote that Amendment 2 was yet another manifestation of an ongoing homonegative environment: *I am aware that I will not put bumper stickers or signs due to fear of assault of some kind. I already did with years of paranoia due to being gay. The inherent nature of having to keep a secret, not really being able to be "out" in the world, accepted—lots of internalized homophobia even though I'm out with friends, family and in my work. Now that I'm 40 (came out at age 18) I look back and see how hard it has been.*

Other respondents gave the impression that they were determined not to let the election change their levels of being out, despite their heightened fear. A 26-year-old Jewish lesbian made the following assessment: *The primary thing that has changed for me is the feeling that I was relatively safe as a lesbian. I am out to everyone in my life and have never been discriminated against, and do not become involved with homophobic people; therefore, they can't hurt me on an emotional level. But the election—and the fascist propaganda preceding it—often makes me feel like the world is not so safe.*[10] A 27-year-old Grand Junction lesbian made a similar statement, both in form and content: *Being a very attractive woman working in a male-dominated work force, I get tired of them saying I'm a waste to mankind. I feel anger with this. But I always fight back and am very open. I also feel fear that the Amendment 2 will not [be overturned], then they would have a right to fire me, but I doubt they would.*[11] Another Grand Junction lesbian's also wrote of being committed to being out despite her fear: *I have always been openly homosexual in my community. With the passage of Amendment 2, I am fearful of being discriminated against and/or physically assaulted. Should this happen, I would have no legal recourse. For this reason, I am extremely fearful of what the future may hold.*

*Particular impediments to being out.* In exploring the OUT code, our team was struck by the presence of several subthemes in which LGBs described particular barriers to being open about their sexual orientation. Several respondents referred to the way a professional job status inhibited them from being out. Such references were especially strong among professional educators. A Colorado Springs lesbian in her thirties told of her conflict: *Struggle greatly with urge to be open lesbian acknowledged by people, not needing to hide and used to protect[ing] myself as a person and professional (education) who is lesbian.* A school counselor, a lesbian in her forties, described her efforts to be out where possible and her frustration when she could not be out: *My biggest frustration is working in a public school setting and sensing a great deal of homophobia around me. I feel support from my professional organization of Colorado School Counselors (CSCA) and have written articles concerning human rights and Amendment 2. Will also be presenting "Gay and Lesbian Youth Issues" at our spring conference. The conflict comes from "choosing" to remain silent in my own schools and district.*

Another group of LGBs described conflicts between being out and their relationship status. A 56-year-old white lesbian outlined her dilemma thus: *I am celibate so it's easier to "pass" but I'm increasingly open to identifying with gay issues. I've only been out to self/others since September, 1986 and increasingly feel good about myself as I don't need energy to sit on feelings. Problems such as #2 challenge me to activism, yet I feel happy and peaceful personally.* A 39-year-old Boulder lesbian asserted that her willingness to be open as a lesbian would change if she were in a relationship: *I'm just scared to make a general announcement and I'm not in a relationship but the major people in my life know about me. If I had a partner, then everyone would know.*

Some respondents experienced conflicts about being out because they were in relationships with partners of the other sex and were therefore taken to be heterosexual. While most such respondents identified themselves as bisexual, it was a lesbian-identified woman who wrote: *I am also married and so I have a good "cover" even though I have a pink triangle and 2 "Undo 2" bumper stickers on my car. I'm afraid to drive my car to Denver or even to wear my "Undo 2" pin in Denver (and sometimes I get afraid and take it off my coat in Boulder, too) because I'm very afraid of being physically attacked. . . . She who fights and runs away, lives to fight another day.*

*Benefits of being out.* Even though the OUT comments were neutral (as distinct from OUTM and OUTL), they did contain references to privileges and benefits associated with openness about one's sexual orientation. We revisit a comment by a 29-year-old lesbian from a Denver suburb who spoke very personally about the benefits of being out: *Being out is the most solid foundation I have, and the best defense against feelings of anxiety and rage.* A lesbian from the same suburban town noted that, despite owning her own home and business, she felt *threatened* by the election. She went on: *If I'm feeling threatened (and I'm really out) how do people who are closeted feel?* (As we shall see in OUTL, many LGBs who were less out associated being out with fear. Both the women quoted here appeared to argue that, on the contrary, being more out reduced fear and anxiety.)

*Comments by newly out LGBs.* In our exposition of the OUT code so far, we have used the term "out" to refer to the degree to which gay people disclosed their sexual orientation to others. Another important meaning of the term "out" is intrapersonal rather than interpersonal in nature. The notion of coming out to oneself refers to a person's awareness of and acknowledgment to her/himself of a lesbian, gay, or bisexual orientation. Several respondents used coming out in this sense.

Being a bisexual, gay, or lesbian person in Colorado during Amendment 2 was both exceptionally challenging and exceptionally rewarding; the same could be said for coming out in that context. Some LGBs who came out during the Amendment 2 era wrote about the challenges of the situation. A 22-year-old gay man from a rural area, for instance, said: *I came out right before the passing of 2, and it really made me wonder what I was doing in this state.* A 21-year-old homosexual man from Alamosa recognized the stresses associated with the election but came to a different conclusion: *Amendment Two came along as I was coming out. It made me immediately aware of the situation and the predicament I could be in. When Two passed, I felt afraid of what might happen. Since then, I have learned to realize we may still have a large struggle ahead of us. Now though, I am more confident and happy with myself and my orientation than ever before.*

A recently out lesbian approaching her thirtieth birthday had this to say: *I have only "come out" over the past 1-1/2 years and my answers reflect that breakthrough along with the growth I have acquired through the aid of psychotherapy. Having "come out," I feel much freer and [more] confident in myself and, regardless of the outcome of Amendment 2, I am a much stronger, more vital person.*

The variety of comments in the OUT code illustrated the value of adding codes beyond the piloting stage and the benefits of being patient with a code that, at first glance, appeared to be less interesting and complex than many others. The comments coded OUT described the experiences of some LGBs during Amendment 2 in unique ways.

## OUTL

The comments coded OUTL expressed the decision to be less open about one's sexual orientation or, at the least, a strong ambivalence about being out. OUTL comments were few in number and were, for the most part, straightforward. OUTL coincided with FEAR much of the time; it also coincided with three other codes—BARRIERS, TRAUMA, and VWP—although less frequently so.

For a few participants, the decision to be less out was based on decidedly negative encounters with being out. A lesbian in her thirties, for example, reported: *I was physically assaulted since the election and demeaned so now I do fear much more, frightened and closeted.* Hers was a rather classic example of how institutionalized heterosexism renders LGBs less visible and punishes those who are more visible (Herek 1994), thus effectively silencing them (Garnets, Herek, and Levy 1992).

Anti-gay violence was not the only reason why some respondents chose to be less out. In some cases, the mere threat of such violence was sufficient to influence LGBs to be less visible. A 20-year-old Greeley lesbian explained: *I have a severely increased fear of other people's reactions to my sexuality (verbal abuse, threats, physical abuse, etc.) than I have ever had before and I have lived in the same town my entire life. I took the pink triangle and double women's signs off my jacket for fear of being beaten up. I am much more tense about being out in public now. I am afraid to talk about it in my own house—because my landlord lives upstairs and his rental company openly supported a Yes on 2 vote.*

Even among the small number of OUTL statements, the decision to be less out was not unequivocal. A woman who described herself as bisexual-identified-as-lesbian wrote as follows of the ambiguities of her decision to be less out: *I decided to come out more prior to the election to normalize my life, but then felt very vulnerable after the election (and scared). I kept low for a while for stress reasons. Then I joined some anti-2 groups, then dropped out, feeling more empowered in my normal life. I'm Jewish and amendment 2 has a special horror for me—anti-semitism, Holocaust.* A Fort Collins lesbian in her twenties had adopted a situational approach to being out: *I've noticed more tolerance to gay issues from peers and coworkers in urban Colorado. Rural Colorado scares me to death, I continue to jump back in my closet when confronted by bigots—or totally avoid them.*

For many respondents who made OUT and OUTL comments, Amendment 2 inspired fear about being open about their sexual orientation. As we saw in the OUT code, the sense of increased danger did not necessarily result in a decision to be less open. Indeed, as we see in the next code, far more respondents used the campaign and election as a springboard for greater visibility as gay, bisexual, and lesbian people.

## OUTM

The OUTM code gathered comments in which LGBs described their decision to be more open about their sexual orientation in the aftermath of the passage of Amendment 2. The code emerged very early in our team's discussion of the data set, and it was clear that OUTM would be frequently used. As we began to read all the data organized under each code, we made an intentional effort to vary the codes we read, alternating between those with more negative content and those that were more positive. As a group, we looked forward to OUTM, expecting that it would be filled with positive, empowered statements. But we soon realized that it was far more complex than we had anticipated. Even though we had read every OUTM comment at least twice during the earlier phases of coding, we had failed to grasp the multifaceted nature of LGBs' decisions to respond to Amendment 2 by being more open about their sexual orientation. Only when we approached the OUTM statements from a detailed "microscopic" perspective were we able to appreciate that the same behavior—in this case, coming out—could represent many underlying psychological processes.[12] The act of coming out would never again look the same or as simple to any of us again.[13]

*Different motivations for coming out.* Amendment 2 was the backdrop for many LGBs' decision to come out. It is perhaps paradoxical that a campaign characterized by so much fear, threat, and oppressiveness ended up being the basis for so many LGBs' deciding to be more open about their sexual orientation. OUTM decisions sprang from different considerations for different respondents. In particular, many wrestled with their own fears as they made the decision to be more out.

*The role of fear in OUTM.* As we saw in the FEAR code, LGBs' struggles over how out to be in the aftermath of Amendment 2 were often accompanied by a good deal of uncertainty and fear. A close reading of the OUTM code gave our team another opportunity to explore the role played by fear in LGBs' decisions to be out. It also served as a reminder that fear, while powerful, does not have to be the determining factor in important life choices.

For participants who came out more, fear and the response to it took many forms. A 60-year-old gay man from a small town in the mountains came out widely after the election. He noticed: *For the first time in 18 years I keep my doors locked at home.* A Latino gay man of 22 years came out to important people prior to the election. He wrote: *Now I am more comfortable being out and vocal about the amendment; but I am more worried and tend to be more careful than before.*

In some instances, LGBs pinpointed the precise nature of their fears regarding being more out. In addition to threats to jobs and housing, LGBs also had less concrete fears related to their outness. A 49-year-old homosexual woman's comment—especially the final sentence—reminded our team how much consequences of this sort can matter: *I feel less need to hide who I am and I am much less able to be with people who object to my (closeted) lifestyle. I am also unable to use the denial I always did about the intolerance around gay issues by society in general. Thus, I feel more solid about my identity and less trusting about the risks involved in being who I am. By that, I mean more a fear of rejection than any tangible risk.*

Our team was also struck by the paradoxical quality of many of the OUTM statements, several of which suggested that their authors were weighing the fear of being out against the positive prospects of doing so. A 30-year-old Anglo woman from Grand Junction presented the dialectic in a very straightforward way: *Oddly enough, though I am more afraid of being assaulted or discriminated against, I am more willing to be open about my sexual orientation.* A 22-year-old white man from Boulder referred to the dialectic between fear and being out in various ways throughout his comment: *I came "out" in January of '92. Up to the election, I talked to my straight friends about #2 and a few people at work. I never had a whole lot of fear about people in general or how they would react to my being gay. After the election, I did start to become fearful of people's reaction, but the election caused me to come out even more than I had. I'm more fearful today than before the election, but I'll be damned if I'm going back to the closet!*

*OUTM as an expression of nothing to lose.* In the aftermath of the election, some LGBs felt that their losses had been severe indeed; some even felt that they had nothing left to lose. One 30-year-old queer woman expressed this sense in very poignant terms: *More a feeling of nothing to lose; people have publicly voted that they believe it is okay to be bigoted about lesbians and gays. My reaction is to be more out and less patient with homophobia. I feel a personal responsibility to let people around me know that their bigotry affects someone around them—me. I believe it reinforces the knowledge that they have that being anti-lesbian is hateful, period. It is also yet another of life's burdens.* A similar sentiment was echoed by a 31-year-old lesbian: *Absolute disbelief that it passed, then a feeling that if I'm already condemned, I might as well be out and live as I wish. Started coming out to previously "unsafe" people. Now a sort of complacent acceptance.* The sense of having nothing to lose as a basis for coming out had both a plaintive and a passive quality. Such people expressed the decision to be out as a reaction against Amendment 2, and gave no indication that their decision had fostered any useful response either in themselves or in the broader world.

*OUTM as an expression of anger.* The identification of anger and outrage as the basis for the decision to come out carried a very active tone. Anger is a far more energized position than is the sense of having nothing to lose and is typically associated with some expectation of an outcome, even if that outcome is no more than the angry person's feeling of relief that his or her angry message has been heard.

The following comment, by a lesbian in her thirties, referred to both outness and anger without elaborating the connection between them: *Anger! Angry at straight colleagues who said "it will never pass." Angry with straight people saying "I'm sorry," or making no response. I feel a need to be more out in straight crowds.* A 20-year-old gay man was clear about his anger and his increased outness: *The election results have pissed me off to such an extent that I'm "outing" myself to people left and right and am actively seeking participation in gay and lesbian groups and organizations. . . . Ironically the election has provided me with the gumption to stand up and shout: "I'm proud to be gay!"*

The mix of anger and the decision to be out also showed up in this comment by a 48-year-old lesbian: *Made me want to be more open, more out, made discrimination issues much more clear, feel offended and mobilized.* A 31-year-old homosexual woman from a small town wrote: *Some animosity toward heterosexuals. Strong negative reaction toward fundamentalist religions. Actually more determined to be out. Strained/loss of a friendship with a straight co-worker who voted Yes.* Another lesbian described her coming out directly in terms of her fury: *My biggest reaction to Amendment 2 came the day after the election. I was furious and took it to work with me. Came out to a couple of people in my fury. I've become more "out" ever since in small ways. I stamp all of my checks: "LESBIAN" and had several made as gifts for friends. So I am out to most of the people that I regularly do business with.*

*OUTM as an expression of personhood.* Some LGBs who came out more in the context of Amendment 2 reported doing so because of transformations that they had made within themselves. They used Amendment 2 as an opportunity for an encounter with themselves, and they changed as a result.

A 44-year-old Irish-American lesbian wrote the story below with what must have been a wide grin on her face: *To a great extent, I think my decision to quit my job of 11-1/2 years as a systems analyst at [a large aerospace company] had to do with the reactions and opinions of the people I worked with over Amendment 2. I was closeted at work and these people thought they didn't know anyone gay. I feel that Amendment 2 has propelled many people out of the closet and that overall it has had a positive effect on the gay, lesbian, and bisexual community. I quit last Friday and wore my "Nobody knows I'm a lesbian" T-shirt. I was pleasantly surprised at the reactions. It was fun!*

The playfulness in this lesbian's coming out was matched by the joy in the comment made by a homosexual man who came out in a two-part story on a local television news show with his lover: *I don't think I could be more "out" than proclaiming it on TV—it's a wonderful feeling!* A 43-year-old gay man from Greeley told the following story of coming out and the sense of personal change that accompanied it: *I was asked by EPOC [the anti-Amendment 2 campaign organization] to speak to the local press on election night. By allowing myself to be identified as a gay member of the community in a newspaper, I came out in a pretty bold way. . . . Coming out completely was the greatest thing that ever happened to me except for falling in love. It has been a sea-change.*

*OUTM as an expression of activism.* Coming out as an expression of personhood was sometimes related to coming out as an expression of activism as well. Those who connected their decision to come out with considerations of personhood tended to state its impact in personal terms. But where coming out was associated with activist inclinations, the desired goal was more political in nature. Despite these distinctions, however, it would be inappropriate to ignore the overlap of the personal and the political in either set of statements about increased outness.

For some participants, the campaign alone did not provide sufficient incentive for being more open; only the election was able to do that. For example, a 39-year-old Anglo lesbian, for example, wrote: *I personally have come out to more people because of the passage of amendment 2, in order to impact people that I know. Didn't have as much courage before it passed, sadly enough.* A gay man in his midtwenties described how his involvement in the campaign clarified for him not only the importance of being out but the very experience of being out as well: *My involvement was integral to my coming out process. By speaking to strangers about the amendment, as part of the campaign and as a presumed homosexual, I started to realize that people would deal with me as another human being*

*and not as a stereotype. I also started to understand the power and impor-
tance and critical need of being out.*

For the 31-year-old gay man from Pueblo quoted below, Amendment
2 was the occasion for his appreciating being out and politically involved
and recognizing the relevance of the LGB equal rights movement to his
life: *This is the first election I have been politically involved in—due to
Amendment 2 and support for the Democratic platform and Bill Clinton's
stance. The election has changed my life from one of political observer to political activist. The Gay Rights Movement wasn't something that affected me
(I thought), now I realize how important and critical it is to come out, be out
and speak up.*

*Codes related to coming out and risk, resilience, and recovery.* The OUT,
OUTL, and OUTM codes offered us a great deal of insight into the nature of gay people's decisions about when, to whom, and under what circumstances to disclose their sexual orientations. Most LGBs in this country are in the position of making such decisions on an ongoing basis.
Amendment 2 presented LGBs in Colorado with an unwelcome but valuable opportunity to look at and explore the costs and benefits of being out
and of being in the closet. Lesbians, gay men, and bisexuals in Colorado
were able to question coming out decisions in an environment where anti-
gay activity had rendered homonegativity more visible, more pointed, and,
to all appearances, more acceptable. It was also an environment where the
advantages and drawbacks of being out could be seen in clearer relief.

These three codes—OUT, OUTL, and OUTM—demonstrated the
complexity of what is often mistaken as a unidimensional phenomenon—
namely, the process of coming out. Coming out is more than the decision
to disclose one's sexual orientation in one situation, on one occasion, at
one historical moment. It is an ongoing individual decision that encompasses personal, interpersonal, and political consideration. The same overt
coming out behavior in two people can represent substantially different
underlying processes.

*Fear and coming out.* Fear appeared to accompany many LGBs' coming
out decisions, references to fear appearing frequently in statements coded
OUT, OUTL, and OUTM. Our team was struck by how often we were

unable to identify what in particular the respondents feared, given the vagueness of the references. We recognized that it would be more difficult to know how to act when the fears were vague and ill-defined than when they had been clearly articulated.

This vague-versus-defined dimension interacted with another axis for understanding fear, namely, that of material versus psychological fears. Both material and psychological fears can be vague or specific. For example, the young man who expressed his *fear of what might happen* was dealing with a vague fear in the material world, while the middle-aged lesbian who identified her fear as that of *rejection* was dealing with a very specific fear in the psychological world.

It warrants repeating here, as our team members often repeated to one another, that psychological fears are just as real and powerful as are material ones. It is all too easy to make objective assessments of what a gay person who comes out has to lose in the material sphere and to make premature judgments about such decisions. As the variety of motivations associated with disclosure decisions suggests, coming out does not represent a singular pathway, nor can it be reduced to a few simple factors. This complexity was illustrated by several LGBs who expressed particular reticence about coming out. Our team took note of the number of LGB professionals who had so much to lose that they were reluctant to come out. Similarly, we noted the number of bisexuals (and others) who acknowledged that the comfort of their relationships with partners of the other sex inhibited the likelihood of their coming out.

Coming out, then, was the culmination of multiple pathways involving many factors—some unexpected, some unique to a given individual. Fear was sometimes one of these factors, but how it fit into or affected a given person's coming out decision was quite varied. The data suggested that there was no strong correlation between fear and OUTL or between fear and OUTM. Some people seemed immobilized by fear while others were energized by it. It seemed to us that the ability to be ambivalent was useful for LGBs trying to make a decision about coming out. Many respondents seemed to be quite aware of their fears about coming out even as they were coming out.[14] Indeed, many articulated their fears and, in the very next sentence, described the empowerment they felt as a result of their decision to come out.

*Losses associated with coming out.* Mirroring many respondents' lack of precision about their fears in coming out was their vagueness about the losses associated with this decision. We were able to identify specific losses in the data, but such identifications occurred in the DISC code and were not directly related to decisions about being out. A physician in private practice noted that being open about her lesbianism had cost her business income. Several LGBs described how their decisions to be more open had had a negative impact on their primary relationships. But even here, they attributed their relational problems more to partners' conflicts about how out to be than to being out *per se*.

For the most part, respondents spoke of the losses associated with being out in the same general terms as their description of fears about being out. They spoke vaguely of *burdens* and *expecting the worst*. A handful of participants did identify an internal conflict between the desire for privacy and relaxation on the one hand, and the impulse to be more out on the other. As a whole, though, LGB comments coded as OUT, OUTL, and OUTM suggested that these people's coming out decisions occurred in the context of unclear fears and unfocused expectations of losses. It appears to be far easier to make good decisions under exactly the opposite conditions, that is, when people know what they fear and what they can stand to lose.

The dilemma for LGBs deciding how out to be highlights one of the fundamental conundrums associated with having to manage social oppression: no matter what its form (whether homonegativity or other), it is not predictable. It takes many forms and sometimes comes from unlikely sources and not from likely ones; hence there is no way to prepare for social oppression. This leaves LGBs with the awareness that something bad *might* happen, but without any means to prevent or prepare for the bad event. Perhaps a clear understanding of homonegativity—including its unpredictability—is one of the best cognitive defenses in dealing with it, and therein might lie the importance of the GRASP code discussed in chapter 5.

*Different motivations for coming out.* Respondents' different motivations for coming out gave rise to several questions in our minds. For example, how do LGBs who come out because they perceive they have nothing to lose, maintain their outness over time? When anger significantly motivates the decision to come out, what happens when it abates? How do differences in motivation interact with the choice of political strategy? These questions are important and fascinating and merit the attention of researchers, theorists, and clinicians.

As we studied the data, one question that captured our team's interest was, Who was the focus of a given individual's coming out decision? Some LGBs' experiences of coming out were far more focused on heterosexuals than on LGBs themselves. For example, even when she reported being more out and called on other LGBs to be out, the lesbian quoted below focused more on heterosexuals, and especially on those who supported the amendment, than she did on gay people: *I feel frustrated by the inability of those opposing Amendment 2 to enlighten those in favor of #2!! I am dumbfounded by the ignorance, fear, and hatred of those in favor of #2. And although I was raised in a somewhat religious (Lutheran) home, I am sick of formal religion and its narrow view of normal. I cringe when religion comes up in just about any form, in any conversation. And [I] find that I am now vocalizing my desire for people to keep their religion, and its views, out of my life!!! In the last year, I think I have come to a slow boil, and I don't see things cooling off for me in the near future. My level of activism is increasing and my "outness," although scarier than pre-1992, is increasing as well. We need to be out!! To challenge the belief systems of those supporting Amendment #2!!*

This woman illustrated how easily deeply disturbing events force the attention of those who are victimized away from themselves and onto the victimizers. It is an understandable position, designed as it is to protect against further victimization. However, it may result in giving more power to the perpetrators than to oneself and to other LGBs, even when taking such self-affirming actions as becoming more out.

Some comments detailing OUTM decisions focused on heterosexuals in ways that were more subtle and (possibly) more benign. The following statement was framed in very positive and empowered terms, but still gave a great deal of focus and credit to heterosexuals—in this case, to supportive heterosexuals: *I enclose an article about coming out publicly in Pueblo, which has been favorably received generally. My feelings have involved a great deal of gratitude to my employer for support, especially the union and many, many comments and attitudes of personal support from coworkers. I have experienced empowerment resulting from this positive feedback which overshadows any negative results momentarily. The election has made me strong in my resolve to become visible. I have seen more tolerance because my coworkers admire my courage and now have a face to attach to the issue.*

This statement reflected the author's ability to recognize and use the support of heterosexual allies. As we saw in the SUPPORT and related codes, this was a significant strength for LGBs in the aftermath of Amendment 2. However, our team wondered what might happen if this support were withdrawn. Important as it is to be able to appreciate heterosexuals' support, it is also important to recognize the support of other LGBs and one's personal successes.

*Links between coming out at the individual and community levels.* There were various parallels between the individual and community levels in the data. First, LGBs who chose to be less out seemed to have less access to the gay community. The nature of that association is not clear. It is possible that access to the community helped some LGBs to come out; certainly, many of the COMM statements would support that notion. Respondents frequently reported that community contact gave them information, helped to reduce their internalized homophobia, and gave them support—factors that have been linked to increased coming out activity (D'Augelli and Garnets 1995).

Conversely, the decision to remain (relatively) closeted would probably restrict LGBs' access to the gay community. Among other things, it may result in a loss of access to the kinds of resources described by respondents in the COMM code. Despite the observation that many LGBs in this study used both the act of coming out and access to their communities to deal positively with the crisis of Amendment 2, such acts are not necessary or optimal for all people who identify as bisexual, lesbian, or gay. As D'Augelli (1994) has suggested, there are many and varied pathways for LGBs to lead healthy lives.

Another issue related to this individual-community link is the frequency with which respondents drew (usually implicit) comparisons between their personal decisions to be out and the increasing visibility of the LGB community. In many cases, there seemed to be a synergistic quality between coming out and visibility at the two levels. That synergy is evident in the following comment, quoted before, by a 21-year-old lesbian from Fort Collins: *The way Amendment 2 has brought the gay, lesbian, bisexual community is amazing. It's made me feel like coming out too. My parents will be less difficult because of the incredible strength of the community. I also feel a sense of responsibility in coming out in order to educate people and break the myths of homophobia.* It made sense to our team that the individual and community, acting in dynamic reciprocity, would empower each other. Indeed, this was one of the most promising phenomena in the entire data set.

*Beneficial effects of coming out.* The results of increased outness varied among respondents, depending largely on the motivational basis for being out. There was a dramatic difference between the OUTM statements rooted in the sense of having nothing left to lose and being angry on the one hand, and those motivated by a sense of personhood and activism on the other. In particular, the costs of being out were alluded to more frequently by those whose coming out was rooted in anger and a sense of having nothing left to lose. In contrast, most of the respondents whose coming out was rooted in personhood and activism expressed pleasure, a sense of freedom, the ability to be honest, and a recognition of their own courage. The single word most frequently employed to describe the effects of increased outness was "empowerment." As a psychological construct, empowerment is viewed in a variety of ways (Zimmerman 1995), and while the formal meaning of respondents' use of the word was not clear, it was clear that on the whole they were describing an experience that felt freeing and powerful and good. Many lesbians, gay men, and bisexuals saw Amendment 2 as hurtful, mean-spirited, and oppressive. However, it also became an opportunity for them to mobilize at both the personal and community levels. A majority of voters in Colorado had endorsed an amendment to the state's Constitution that voted gay people *out* of the political process. Those voters (not to mention Colorado for Family Values) would never have anticipated that the same election would vote lesbians, bisexuals, and gay men—in a word—*out*.

9

■ ■ ■ ■ ■ ■ ■ ■ ■

# The Study in Broader Context

*Implications beyond Amendment 2*

THE DATA FROM THIS STUDY, as we have encountered them, tell not one but many stories about how lesbians, gay men, and bisexuals in Colorado responded to Amendment 2. In generating the themes discussed in previous chapters, our coding team was not trying to come up with general principles of behavior. Rather, in keeping with our interpretive approach, we see the themes as reflecting and contributing to an understanding of the variety of experiences of the Amendment 2 campaign and election that gay people had.

While research on real-world issues could be conducted in an effort to generate broad principles, this was never the goal of our project. Instead, our research was predicated on the desire to develop useful understandings of LGBs' reactions to Amendment 2. The usefulness of our understandings is rooted not in abstract principles (although such principles might in fact be helpful), but in the application of our findings about the real world to real-world contexts. To that end, our first step is to recontextualize this study and the data derived from it.

The process of understanding the themes derived from the study in a real-world context is an interpretive effort, as was generating the themes from respondents' statements in the first place. Just as multiple understandings of the data were possible and even expected, so also are multiple understandings of how the data fit into a broader context possible. Judgment and sensitivity are vital to both interpretive efforts.

## Recontextualizing the Data

Given that a particular sociopolitical event formed the immediate context for LGBs' psychological reactions to Amendment 2, recontextualizing the psychological data requires that we return to the sociopolitical sphere with our new understandings, be prepared to ask new and different questions, and look for clarity in new ways. The process of recontextualizing qualitative data is, of necessity, a speculative and creative venture that acknowledges and relies on ambiguity and possibility—in contrast to the statements of probability typically associated with quantitative studies.

### How We Understand Amendment 2

From the data in this study, it is clear that Amendment 2 was far more than an exercise in participatory democracy for Colorado voters. Even though the amendment never became law, its effects were substantial. The results of this study indicate that some LGBs in Colorado were profoundly affected by the amendment. This impact was neither uniformly negative nor purely psychological in nature.

In the first chapter, we approached the amendment from several perspectives. At one level, Amendment 2 was designed to counter gains made by gay men, bisexuals, and lesbians in their efforts to enjoy full rights in American society. At more subtle levels, Amendment 2 reflected processes by which LGBs were objectified and constructed as the "other"—as different, distant, suspect, dangerous, and undeserving. Eastland (1996a) has emphasized the devastating emotional effects of a process she calls conceptual liquidation. Many of these effects have been articulated broadly and passionately by the respondents in this study. Similarly, the responses we have read may easily be understood to correspond with the effects of ethnoviolence (Ehrlich 1992), with the effects of verbal harassment (Garnets, Herek, and Levy 1992), and with the cognitive substrates of traumatic responses (Janoff-Bulman 1992).

Without ever having taken legal effect, Amendment 2 took an enormous psychological toll.

In the Supreme Court's majority opinion in the case, Justice Kennedy referred to the Colorado vote as an effort to "deem a class of persons a stranger" to the state's laws (cited in Keen and Goldberg 1998:251). In finding this vote unconstitutional, the Supreme Court blocked LGBs from becoming strangers to Colorado's laws. However, the Supreme Court decision could not prevent or fully undo the negative effects of the campaign and election. Colorado for Family Values' campaign discourse and its endorsement by voters rendered lesbians, gay men, and bisexuals strangers to their neighbors and even to themselves. The pain, alienation, protest, and despair of such effects are disturbingly clear in the data in this study.

On the other hand, respondents have also given voice to a different kind of reaction to the campaign and election. LGBs were galvanized by Amendment 2. They came together and they came out and became political in the face of what many experienced as a massive and very personal assault. Indices of the community's having been galvanized occurred along a variety of dimensions, from simple increases in the number of participants in pre- and postelection Pride Marches (Stafford 1993; Stevens and Gibney 1993), through the proliferation of gay and ally organizations after the election (Nash 1999) to the postelection presence of a gay statewide political infrastructure (Nash 1999). Regardless of which indices one chooses to examine, it is clear that an anti-gay campaign and election may do as much to politicize LGBs as it does to silence them. In effect, if one is looking for a strategy that maximizes the chances of conceptually liquidating lesbians, gay men, and bisexuals without simultaneously empowering them, one would be well advised to try something other than an anti-gay amendment such as this one.

## Who Is the Target?

As with most political actions, Amendment 2 was enormously complex. One somewhat elusive aspect of the amendment has been its relationship to other issues on the political landscape. Events that are experienced as traumatic often have a tone of singularity; they feel unique in their impact and their importance. Such events and the reactions they generate have discouraged the individuals affected by them from making connections between these specific events and others with which, in fact, they have something in common. The tendency for respondents to view Amendment 2 in such singular terms was evident throughout the data set, but especially in the TRAUMA and VWP codes.

From a political perspective, one problem with the trauma-related tendency toward singularity is its attendant restraint on making political connections. To many LGBs, Amendment 2 felt like the only—or, at least, the worst—time a group of people had been unfairly targeted and had their rights threatened. While the amendment surely was a grossly unfair violation of LGBs, it was not the only, or even the worst, such occasion. The very nature of the violation, however, made it *feel* that way. In the absence of an explicit political analysis, one might be tempted to accept the emotional reality of the singularity of Amendment 2 without further inquiry.

Even LGBs who were able to use Amendment 2 as a springboard for personal and political growth did not transcend the sense that the election was a singularly negative experience. The growth experienced by some LGBs in the aftermath of the election was positive in many respects: people reduced their internalized homophobia and with it their sense of powerlessness, isolation, and frustration. They took personal action and often political action as well. In general, these were positive consequences which testified to the human ability to transform decidedly negative experiences into individual and collective gain.

Much of this gain—again, at both the individual and collective levels—was predicated on an intensification of LGBs' sense of themselves as lesbians, gay men, and bisexuals. This move toward identity politics was essential and adaptive in view of the clearly oppressive circumstances LGBs were facing. At the same time, the intensification of identity politics often has negative consequences, including the sense that one's own group and its oppression are unique. At the political level, immersion in identity politics frequently discourages an understanding of the connections—the similarities as well as the differences—between various forms of social oppression (Russell and Bohan 1999b). Ultimately, extreme immersion in identity politics limits one's ability to work in coalition with other groups targeted for oppression.

In fact, Amendment 2 had much in common with other manifestations of oppression. More concretely, it shared significant commonalities with other political actions taken in Colorado and elsewhere. In a 1993 address, Boulder's City Attorney, Joe de Raismes, pointed out that the amendment's passage occurred not only because of a "backlash to the movement for gay rights" but also due to "a backlash against affirmative action, having nothing to do with gay rights" (de Raismes 1993:4). De Raismes, who served as the attorney for one of the municipalities that was a plaintiff in the case, went on to broaden his assertion (1993:4):

> The language in the Amendment addressing "special rights" reflects an attitude among white males and probably some white females—expressing a feeling of being threatened by other groups who have claimed quota status. These other groups have claimed affirmative action more broadly, but a portion of the majority population feel that homosexuals are another group that can potentially make that claim and that it is time to stop it.

Subsequent commentaries have echoed this theme. Bull and Gallagher (1996) point out that the language of affirmative action and quotas was one scare tactic used in the Amendment 2 campaign. In fact, they consider the amendment to have been a "precursor" (1996:113) to the battle over affirmative action that took center stage several years later.

While it is impossible to determine precisely the relative influences of homophobia on the one hand, and sentiments against affirmative action on the other, it seems clear that the passage of Amendment 2 capitalized on many voters' belief that yet another group of people was getting something that they were not (see also Donovan and Bowler 1997). Without minimizing the pervasiveness of homophobia and heterosexism, this more general sentiment was evident in much of the discourse—formal and informal—surrounding the campaign.

Regardless of the influence of anti–affirmative action attitudes on election behavior, the election outcome certainly had implications for groups other than gay men, bisexuals, and lesbians. The fact that the following commentators speak from very different political positions highlights the common observation made in separate commentaries by Bull and Gallagher, and by Pharr. Bull and Gallagher (1996:278) argue that fencing out one particular group from the political process casts "the durability of every minority's legal standing into doubt." Pharr (1996:79) elaborates on this notion:

> If it can be established that any one group of people in this country does not "deserve" civil rights and therefore can be legally discriminated against, it calls into question whether other groups "deserve" civil rights. If civil rights can be seen as something one group of people can grant or deny to another group, then it follows that these rights can be brought to a popular vote for any other group.

Popular votes on matters of civil rights implicitly erode the general notion of civil rights as accessible to all and, therefore, may be viewed correctly as a legal threat to all.

Just as importantly, as the data from this study suggest, campaigns directed against particular groups of people have social and psychological consequences even when the legal threat is neutralized by judicial intervention. Just as such campaigns allow civil rights to be construed in new and regressive ways, they also allow groups of people to be regarded and discussed in ways that are victimizing and dehumanizing. Such discourse has negative implications for the targeted group, as we have seen in this study. It also has negative implications for society as a whole; it is divisive and mean-spirited and invites human beings to act upon their least noble impulses. Discourse directed against any group of people is likely to breed fear and aggressiveness simultaneously. Ultimately, it serves no one in society.

Although generally viewed as a moderate state, Colorado has seen a variety of campaigns targeting specific groups. Among those that the state's voters have endorsed in recent years have been an English-only measure and another prohibiting the use of state funds for abortions for women with limited incomes. Given our understanding of the psychological effects of Amendment 2, we believe the discourse associated with the campaigns to pass these measures also had consequences apart from those of a legal nature.

In yet another vein, it is perhaps not coincidental that the same election that resulted in the passage of Amendment 2 also saw the endorsement of a tax-limitation initiative in Colorado. Measures to limit taxes weaken the tax base and may force reductions in public funding for a variety of basic services, including education, health, and welfare. Tax measures typically affect the middle and lower classes and benefit members of the upper class (Pharr 1996). Although tax-limitation measures do not ostensibly target particular groups, at least some of the discourse involved in campaigns to limit taxes employs language that is derogatory of those most in need of publicly funded services, such as "welfare queens."

It is not my purpose to suggest that public debates are uniformly negative in either tone or consequence. However, the data from this study led me to have significant reservations about citizen initiatives targeting particular groups of people—whether they be gays and lesbians, poor people, people of color, immigrants, or welfare recipients. Citizen initiatives, often touted as democracy in action, have long generated concerns about their potential for being both antidemocratic and antiminority (Donovan and Bowler 1997). The results of the current study extend these concerns to include considerations of how the initiative process can be psychologically abusive of communities as well as cause the legal erosion of group rights.

## 10

■ ■　■　■　■　■　■　■

# The Coding Team

*A Revisitation*

HAVING REVIEWED THE CODES that our team created for this research project—the content of the study—we now return to the team's process. Specifically, this chapter looks at how the team approached the task of preparing the results of the study for presentation to professional groups. We examine two troublesome points in that process, both of which were instructive, if painful. We then turn to a retrospective description by team members of the effects of participating in this project. The chapter concludes with a brief update on where team members are now.

## Relationships among Team Members
## after Coding Context

By the time the coding and analyses of the data had been completed, Sylvie had left Colorado for her yearlong internship in clinical psychology in Michigan. Lou, Sean, Rob, and I remained in Boulder, although Rob and Sean were making plans to apply for graduate programs in other states. All of us were excited about the project and the richness of the data, and eager to share our findings with both professional and community audiences. In this chapter, we concentrate on formal presentations in professional settings. Our efforts to reach community groups is the focus of chapter 11.

### Efforts to Write Together

I wrote a proposal on behalf of the team (and several other professionals engaged in similar work) to present research on anti-gay referenda at the annual meeting of the American Psychological Association. Team members agreed to a plan whereby I would write a paper describing the study and some of the results from the quantitative analyses, Sylvie and I together would write a second paper detailing the results from more complex quantitative analyses, and the four of us still in Boulder would write about the qualitative part of the study. The first two papers were completed without difficulty.

However, as Rob, Sean, Lou, and I set about to write the qualitative report, we encountered a great deal of difficulty. With Sean taking the lead in the library, we all read additional materials related to our findings. We discussed which codes to present and how to organize our paper. Despite such constructive beginnings, we seemed unable to commit anything to paper. Moreover, we were not able to understand why we were experiencing this collective writer's block.

Facing deadlines, with some sense of desperation I requested a consultation with Judith Dowling, a psychologist with whom I meet for peer consultation on a regular basis. In a lengthy discussion, I explained the positive and productive working relationship that team members had enjoyed throughout the coding phase. I emphasized that, despite differences in credentials and control of the project, we had been able to work as equals—which arrangement had been critical to the success of the project. I then explained our inability to carry out the joint writing project.

At the end of our explorations, Judith offered her analysis of what was inhibiting the team's ability to prepare the papers on the qualitative research. She said I was asking Lou, Sean, and Rob to do something for which they lacked expertise and experience. While it had been possible for us to approach the coding as equals, we could not achieve the same equality in the writing task. I strongly suspected that her analysis was accurate, and although I felt some relief at having a perplexing mystery solved, I also felt tremendous sadness. I was grieving for the end of what had been a truly wonderful working relationship among us. If Judith was right, then Sean, Rob, Lou, and I had to end the effort to write as equal participants and acknowledge that some very satisfying aspects of our work together were over.

I presented Judith's analysis at our next team meeting, which, with Sylvie on her internship, included Rob, Lou, Sean, and me. As I came to the conclusion of my comments, I asked the three if they agreed. The sighs in the room were audible and their agreement with Judith's analysis was unanimous: the three were not able to take an equal part in writing up the qualitative results for a professional audience. They were as disappointed as I was, in part because we all knew that the symmetry of participation in our team enterprise was ending, and, as a team, we spoke of this loss.

### Team Members' Response to Our Writing Efforts

When members of the team generated a list of questions about the research process that they would answer in preparation for this book, our unsuccessful efforts to write together was one of the issues included. Two of the team members discussed their experience during that period. First, Sean offered the following account: *Honestly, that was a very important milestone for the work, and an important event. I think it felt very serious for those of us who had never attended such an event, nor written an article worthy of presenting at such a meeting of psychologists. I think the enormity of the event, i.e., putting on a good presentation, got to the team somewhat. Maybe there is little that one can do to relieve that. One problem that did occur for us, however, was in determining who would do the writing. I recall the initial plan of group-writing and how scary that felt. I recall countless hours of literature review expecting that I might have to weave theory with the data, on my own, and how challenging that would be. I think we were trusting the leader's belief that we could each write a piece of it, or that we could hammer it out during our sessions, and that somehow it would all come together. It was a relief to put it out in the open that this approach was not going to work because it couldn't logistically ("too many cooks") and because the skill level amongst the team members varied as it did. My relief put the burden of writing on the leader's shoulders where I think we all agreed, in the end, was where it belonged.*

Lou also described his perspective on the team's efforts to write together: *The next period of time I felt the power dynamics re-surge was when we reached the point of assembling the information and preparing it for presentation. I relish the opportunity I had to present at the American Psychological Association Convention in New York that year, but getting to that point was extremely difficult. I again started to feel incompetent because I had no knowledge of what it took to put something like this together. I could feel the group strain in an attempt to preserve a balanced power structure; to preserve the magic we experienced in our fairly equal roles during the coding process. But in retrospect, there was no way to avoid the adjustments that had to be made. The magic we experienced was based on the value we held as insightful and disciplined individuals. When we expanded our understanding of competence to the external definitions of power based on resumes, procedures and titles, power dynamics inevitably shifted. We most probably should have acknowledged these external influences more directly and accommodated them accordingly.*

*I attribute the difficulty we experienced during this time in part to the leader's desire to see other "less qualified" team members have their contributions formally acknowledged. Though it led to confusion, I appreciate her desire to see this happen. Yet, she was the team leader, as she well should have been. I think it would have been helpful to acknowledge this role more thoroughly, and set better boundaries around it. There were times when this power dynamic was essential, but there were also times when this dynamic could not have been present for the coding process to work as it did. It would have been better had these different times been more clearly defined.*

Once we had understood our problem with writing together, we divided up the tasks and proceeded. I did the actual writing, although the other team members provided extensive input. For example, we worked together as a team to select the specific comments used to exemplify each code to be presented in our papers. We also rehearsed the delivery of the papers together; these efforts succeeded in that we were able to present a series of papers seamlessly and well despite time limits and a very large cast of presenters. In delivering our work together to a professional audience, we momentarily recaptured a bit of the magic we had experienced as members of a competent and caring team.

## Public Presentations

Another delicate point arose between a single other coder and me. It was handled between the two of us; I include it here because it was an understandable problem and one that I, as the leader, might have been able to prevent. In addition, it raised issues that emerge easily from the team environment we had built together and, therefore, that others working as a team are well advised to consider.

This difficulty involved the question of how to maintain the integrity of research data. Perhaps it was not an accident that a rupture to that integrity occurred after several members of the team had made a joint presentation of our findings to a community group. The fact that the presentation went well may have fostered one team member's sense that he was free to make unilateral decisions about using the data. By the morning after the presentation, I had received word that this team member had given a second presentation of the research to another community group just after leaving the first gathering. He had done so without consulting with me or the rest of the team.

My response to this action included a sense of having been violated and feelings of guilt for having failed to draw clear-cut boundaries around the data and their uses. I met with the team member and belatedly established these boundaries. Our discussion began with some degree of anger and defensiveness, but it ended with an appropriate understanding of boundaries in place.

## What Went Wrong, Lessons Learned

In retrospect, I think that both these difficulties sprang from similar sources. In each case, the team environment that we had cocreated worked very well for coding but disguised the need to set appropriate boundaries around other team activities—specifically, writing together and using the research findings. It would reasonably fall to the team leader to have anticipated problems in both arenas; had I been able to do so, I could probably have prevented these difficulties. By refusing to move out of the very comfortable coding environment when other tasks called me to do so, I put undue pressure on other members of the team and allowed unnecessary mistakes to occur.

On the question of the joint authorship of papers, I should not have assumed that because team members could function as equals in some areas they could do so in all areas. As Sean's account of the writing effort suggests, team members followed my lead in thinking we could write as a group—a task that is difficult even for researchers with similar training and backgrounds (Becker 1986; Ellis, Kiesinger, and Tillmann-Healy 1997; Erickson and Stull 1998; Gow 1991) and even more tricky for colleagues with such varied backgrounds. Lou's assessment of the situation was correct; it was my responsibility to move much sooner into the leadership role and assign a more appropriate division of tasks for writing the research. Had I done so, it would have served the research and the team members well.

As for the unauthorized presentation of the research by a team member, I was similarly accountable. I knew that team leaders are responsible for the way research findings are handled and that our qualitative data represented, for Colorado LGBs, very fragile and volatile responses to Amendment 2. It was absolutely necessary that the task of returning the research to the community be carried out with sensitivity and judgment. I had failed to establish clear boundaries with team members about this issue despite my awareness of an ethical mandate within my profession to do so. Moreover, my failure was compounded by a working relationship that could easily seduce a team member into thinking he was more capable of exercising the requisite sensitivity and judgment than he was. It is no surprise that I felt guilty, as well as angry, when I learned of the transgression.

### Lessons Learned

The central lesson learned is the same in both these cases: to conduct this kind of research, one must create a team environment in which everyone's input is genuinely valued. It is equally important to know and to state clearly the limits of those equal relationships. The boundaries to be set may differ for various team members. As I mentioned earlier, Sylvie took the leadership role in writing one of the papers on quantitative findings from the project; she was more than prepared to do so and she carried out the task with competence and grace. This stands in strong contrast to the authorship of the qualitative findings that I have described above. In short, the noncoding tasks related to the research must be tailored to the skills and experiences of team members, and the desire to prolong very positive experiences as coding equals must be set aside.

## *This Book*

As with so many other experiences, writing this book gave us the opportunity to redo and correct our mistakes. When the idea of a book project was presented to the group, we all knew we wanted to avoid previous unpleasant experiences. At the same time, it seemed important to include the voices of all team members for two reasons: to acknowledge their invaluable contributions, and to try to recapitulate the collective nature of our efforts. We all agreed that we would collectively generate a list of questions about the research and everyone would write individual responses to those questions. I would then write the book drawing on the observations and experiences of all team members. In fact, this has been the process I have followed. It was intellectually and emotionally satisfying to have the input from Sylvie, Sean, Lou, and Rob as I wrote.

## Effects of the Research on Team Members

It was clear to all the members of our team that one of the approaches that had improved our effectiveness as a group was our willingness to look at the way we, as individuals and as a collective, were responding to the research on an ongoing basis. With some exceptions (see, for example, Charmaz and Mitchell 1997; DeVault 1997; Maines 1989, 1993; Mykhalovskiy 1997), neither descriptions of methodologies nor reports of research findings include attention to the way researchers are affected by the process or the findings associated with their research. However, our attention to just such matters was crucial to our work, as we were committed to one aspect of reflexivity—"a continuing mode of self-analysis and political awareness" (Callaway 1992:33)—in relation to our research.

Given this perspective, it was fitting that several of the questions we formulated for team members focused on how team members had been affected by their participation in this research project. As I read each person's responses to these questions, I was struck by how much research accounts miss when they ignore this dimension.

*Lessons for Clinical Work*

Working on this project helped team members on a variety of levels. Sean noted that his participation in the project *has been very important in my professional development.* He continued: *As part of this process I received an education about trauma theory through assigned readings of both books and journal articles. The theory when applied to the raw data served to illuminate it. This was not an experience I'd had before, applying theory to raw data. It was fascinating to see issues discussed in text unfold in the respondents to the survey. In short, I came to appreciate research and to see the connection between theory and application. On a more personal level, after seeing so many responses to Amendment 2, I got a sense for the subtle, idiosyncratic ways that individuals were affected, and that often individuals were conveying a great deal of information even with short statements. I also came to appreciate discovery for client's experiences.* Finally, Sean wrote that *working on the project seemed to have had an impact on my empathic attunement to others. Prior to this work, I had not had significant clinical training, so it helped tune my ability to "hear" others. The experience opened up my sense of intuition and I came to trust it more.*

Sylvie also wrote about acquiring clinically oriented skills from the project: *What surprised me about the data were the variety of responses and the richness of the data. I had no idea that so much clinical information could be obtained from short comments. But the number of the comments and the process of the coding gave me an understanding that would never have been obtained from quantitative research.* Sylvie elaborated on the value of the research to her *thinking as a clinician: The project was an excellent training tool for learning to interpret communications even without context. Actually, I would highly recommend it for any clinician. The ability to listen to a brief statement and identify the issues are among the most beneficial skills for a clinician.*

I strongly endorse Sean's and Sylvie's comments about how coding data in this fashion can enhance what we normally think of as clinical skills. There may be a converse advantage for clinicians who conduct interpretive research: such research encourages an integration of research and clinical skills in an enormously satisfying way. More broadly, it allows clinicians to understand their work as psychotherapists in a systematic and nonpositivist way. This understanding has given me a more appropriate framework for thinking about the therapy I do. In the process, I have become a better therapist.

### Lessons in Challenging One's Own Homonegativity

Both the heterosexually identified team members emphasized the contributions of this work to their efforts to reduce their own homophobic and heterosexist attitudes. Rob wrote: *I was required to work with my own homophobia in the process of doing this research. I was fortunate to have worked with a group where I could challenge the stereotypes and conceptions that I acquired from our culture. I learned a great deal about how oppression plays out. I was able to see the dynamics of external forces at work in the lives of a targeted group.*

Rob elaborated on seeing the experiences of members of the LGB community from his vantage point as a heterosexual: *I really learned to understand the pain (and the joy!) of the LGB community through my work on this research, though my understanding was obviously hindered by the fact that I had no overt experience being the target of homophobia and oppressive legislation. Through my participation in the research I was able to see the effects of Amendment 2 through the LGB community's eyes. What a sight it was! As an outsider to this community, it was strange but also understandable to see the dichotomies: in-fighting and coming together, motivation and hopelessness, fear and bravery, and the pride and self-doubt of the LGBs in Colorado. Amendment 2 had far reaching effects, and the opportunity to discover all of the ways in which people were affected was an invaluable experience for me and for the community.*

Sylvie also remarked on the effect the research had on her homonegativity. She went on to personalize her experience: *I had an epiphany when I was thinking about answering these questions. During that period of time, I became more comfortable with my own sexuality in many ways. I was in therapy and working through my own issues. This clearly enabled me to be more comfortable and experience more pleasure. But also, I came to know the bisexual side of myself and had no difficulty accepting that part of me. I think the coding experience and getting into that culture was partially why I had no difficulty accepting that part of me. It was a natural progression in self-awareness. By the way, my husband also had no difficulty accepting that part of me. He was thrilled that I was becoming more open and self-aware.*

*Influences on Decisions about Work*

All of us have commented on how working on this project has influenced our subsequent work lives. My understanding of myself as a professional changed from that of a psychologist who does psychotherapy and conducts research on the side to that of a psychologist for whom research and psychotherapy are twin loves. With regard to content, doing research on Amendment 2 has led me to stay focused on how lesbians, gay men, and bisexuals manage homonegativity.

Sylvie noted that participation in the project *may have influenced my job choice. I am providing psychological services to HIV-infected children and adolescents, and many of the adolescents are gay males with issues related to the research.* Sean mentioned that the project had been valuable in *showing me how psychologists could influence and help heal their communities in ways I hadn't imagined.*

Rob related his work on the project to his experiences as a graduate student in psychology: *I feel that through my work on this project I have a better ability to provide help for LGBs that I see in my clinical work. Using the coding method as we did, I feel that we operationalized many of the common constructs that LGBs present in treatment. Having done this allows us to better recognize and contextualize the key pieces of the LGB experience. This research has broadened my awareness and provided me with a necessary knowledge of the issues at hand. Being so involved with this type of data exposes you to the whole range of experience in first-person terms. Reading these responses gave me an insider's view of how Amendment 2 was experienced, as well as a common vernacular that is useful for working with the LGB community.*

Lou offered a very different perspective. His work on the project was influential in his decision to change his plans about applying to graduate programs in clinical psychology: *I am the only member of the coding team that has not pursued a career in Clinical Psychology. I feel that to some degree this project contributed to my career decision. I do not see this impact as negative, but as a result of gained insight and self-understanding about what it means for me to be "healthy," and what it takes for me to move in a "healthier" life direction. I have found that the "helping professions" have a tendency to pull me away from focusing on my own personal growth. I think I put this project in that "helping professions" area whether it deserves to be there or not.*

## Lessons about Internalized Homonegativity

When I first read team members' narratives about their experiences with the research, I was struck by the frequency of references to internalized homophobia (IHE and IHI). Rob noted how challenging these codes were for the team: *The internalized homophobia codes (IHI and IHE) were difficult for the group to work with. It was painful to see the effect of Amendment 2 as LGBs turned their anger and hostility upon themselves. The fact that groups like CFV were able to further capitalize on the internalized homophobia already present in the LGB community was sickening. I feel that, as an outsider, I could see the full scope of what was occurring. Being heterosexual, I have been exposed to much of the homophobic sentiment of other heterosexuals. It was fascinating but also very painful to see the sentiments of homophobic straights begin to creep into voices of LGBs.*

For Lou, the IHI and IHE codes presented a personal challenge as well as a challenge to our team: *Of the codes which we developed and worked with as a team, the most difficult, complex and personally rewarding were IHI and IHE. Consider some questions I had to grapple with when considering these codes: What can we as LGB people do with all the negative information we are force-fed (and thus internalize) throughout our lives? How does an event like Amendment 2 influence what we do with that information? How do I, as one person looking in at another LGB person's life, pass judgment about how he or she deals with it? I will precede everything I write with the answer, "I'm still not quite sure." But, I truly feel that I know a great deal more about these questions now than I did before my involvement with this project.*

*Putting homophobia and heterosexism in the context of trauma theory helped with this understanding. Trauma theory addresses the need to find a perpetrator. If I have been injured (which homophobia, heterosexism and more specifically Amendment 2 had done) then upon whom do I place the blame? The most difficult part of this research for me was to see LGBs in Colorado struggling to find their perpetrators. Just as difficult was to sift through all the stories and determine who was dealing with the task effectively and who perhaps was not. Last and maybe most difficult of all, was taking this information and applying it to my own life.*

*Too often we saw people blaming other LGBs for not reacting to homophobia and heterosexism "correctly" (i.e., blaming other gay and bisexual men for being too feminine, or blaming lesbian and bisexual women for being too butch . . . blaming LGBs in general for being too loud, too quiet, too ignorant, too weak, or blaming them for not being good representatives or leaders in the LGB community). We, as a coding team, likened this to blaming the victim. We also saw LGBs blaming entire groups of people such as heterosexuals or Christians. This creates a perpetrator around every corner. Some LGBs blamed no one (i.e., Amendment 2 was all just a big mistake), thus saying there was no perpetration at all. Not surprisingly, I have experienced each of these reactions (and more) at different times in my own life. I now realized that in doing so, I was losing sight of what I have now found to be the most true truth: that homophobia and heterosexism, along with every other "ism," exists within each of us. In other words, every person has the potential to be a perpetrator, and each of us has at one time or another, knowingly or un- knowingly, caused harm to another based on our differences. Likewise, each of us has the potential (and I believe, responsibility) not to perpetrate. One of the most valuable parts of this project for me was to discover this phenomenon more fully, and to do so within the supportive, trusting "community" context of the coding team.*

Sean's observations about the internalized homonegativity codes had become integrated with aspects of his training in a clinical graduate pro- gram: *The IHI and IHE codes were the two most informative codes and were very important for this project. I came to realize in time how important those two codes were, especially in light of their connections to the prevalence of other codes (how often IHI and IHE codes were met with other themes). A careful examination of, first, the differences between the two and, second, the ma- terial itself gave me an understanding of internalized homophobia that I hadn't acquired in years of coming out support work or my own process. What I learned was that internalized homophobia operates differently in people, de- pending on how aware of it one is. For those with good observing egos we saw more IHE; and on the contrary, for those who weren't as in touch with their own internal process, we saw raw homophobia, the IHIs. My thoughts about IH developed with the team's over time, and in the end, I could conceptual- ize a theoretical model of how IH is maintained often as an unhealthy de- fensive process. Looking back, I see now that people often enter therapy and project onto their therapist those elements of themselves that they find intoler- able (splitting off bad objects). This survey, particularly the final open-ended*

*question, served that function for many people, including those who aggres-*
*sively expressed their homophobia. Hopefully, queers of all kinds are finding*
*opportunities to explore their homophobia and re-integrate these split notions*
*about queers.*

Sylvie's comments about the internalized homophobia codes have been foreshadowed in this book. In addition to her struggles with the team's use of the codes, she explained how she was using the knowledge gained from participating in the project in her current professional work: *The IHI and IHE codes were the best learning experience because I had never had any training in that area (surprise, surprise). The LGBs on the project were very patient in explaining what it was and how to spot it. I must admit, I sometimes thought they were over-coding it in places, but that is because it is so prevalent. What helped me get it the most was realiz-ing that internalized homophobia is a form of internalized shame and so many people have internalized shame regardless of background. This un-derstanding has helped me in my clinical work with gay and straight clients. It has helped me working with the adolescent HIV population. Thinking about these questions made me revisit this issue. I realized that not only the gay HIV kids have IHI issues, but there is an internalized shame that comes with being HIV positive—internalized HIV phobia—and the same issues apply.*

I share the enthusiasm for what we learned from the IHE and IHI codes. Respondents' comments in these codes challenged us mightily. They were painful to read and we often wished to distance ourselves from them; we also knew that doing so would mean distancing ourselves from the LGBs whose statements we were exploring. Staying with distressing material and constructing a coherent framework for understanding it was our sole alternative to blaming the LGBs who had indeed been victimized by the campaign and election. I believe we succeeded in that effort. I have continued to develop ideas about internalized homonegativity through a variety of clinical and research contexts since that time, and I look forward to an exposition of those ideas in a future book. When I write that book, I will know two things: Colorado's LGBs were my best teachers about in-ternalized homonegativity, and the other four members of the coding team were my fellow explorers in developing and clarifying an understanding of internal efforts to manage external stigma.

## *Lessons in Appreciating Other Forms of Oppression*

In their narratives, all team members alluded to the value of making connections among different forms of oppression. Part of our recognition of the importance of making these connections was rooted in particular codes, especially in the wisdom of some comments in the MOVE, GRASP, and ISMS codes. When LGBs were able to understand homonegativity as another form of oppression, they seemed to feel less singled out and perhaps even less victimized. They had a broader framework for understanding homonegativity in general and Amendment 2 in particular—a framework that sometimes suggested strategies for countering homonegativity. While every coder made frequent references to the importance of linking the oppressions, each did so by focusing on other issues, thus creating the impression that the lessons of ISMS had become integrated into the way we all viewed and talked about the world.

## *Lessons about the Community*

All team members' narratives about experiences with this research alluded to the value of working in concert with other coders. Many of these allusions have been discussed in the section on team dynamics in chapter 3. Not included there were some of Lou's observations about community that highlight important, if implicit, dimensions of our work together. *I've learned how community, support and belonging are important factors in building resiliency. But in a more general sense, I've learned the importance of how I define my own community and how that definition changes. My community consists of those with whom I feel some sort of connection or familiarity. At times my community can be as large as humankind, and at other times it can be as narrow as gay, white, Jewish, middle-class, temporarily able-bodied men in their mid-twenties . . . which gets kind of small. I began to understand this concept of community when our group discovered that many of the "PERSONAL" and "INSIGHT" codes (more favorable codes in terms of potentially understanding oneself) were coming from women. I remember looking at my community then as gay (probably white, Jewish, etc. . . . .) men, and feeling really down. This was in part my own internalized homophobia, which of course I need to keep working on. And then the idea that my community is flexible occurred to me. If I were to just include lesbians in my com-*

*munity, then my community would grow stronger (which of course is sexist).*
*The problem through this whole thought process, though, was that I was still*
*allowing my sense of community to be externally defined and that was the real*
*discovery. So regarding community, I've come up with a few personal guide-*
*lines: First, community begins with me, and I still have a lot of work to do on*
*myself. Second, my community consists of whomever I choose and that person*
*still has a lot of work to do, too (but that is ultimately that person's responsi-*
*bility). Third, it's inevitable that I'm going to get grouped together with some*
*people in negative ways, but I have choices about what I do with that, and*
*about the ways in which I may do that to others. And last, I still have a lot of*
*work to do on myself, and that answers a lot of my questions.*

## Working through the Amendment 2 Experience

All five members of the coding team lived in Colorado at the time of the
campaign and election, and all of us were affected by them. In fact, our
shared reaction to the amendment constituted one basis for our coming
together as a work group. In one way or another, our work on this research
project represented an attempt to integrate our experiences of Amendment 2. Two members of the team addressed this issue specifically.

Sylvie wrote about an incident in her graduate program; she had told us
this story earlier during the formative stages of our work together: *Dur-*
*ing the campaign, the graduate students in the department met about for-*
*malizing our opinion about Amendment 2. A few students argued that we*
*should not "go public" in any way because psychologists should not publicize*
*"political preferences." I felt outraged and sick to my stomach. I still get a*
*lump in my throat when I tell this story. It seemed just like the stories I heard*
*about Early Nazi Germany—like what they did to the Jews and others was*
*just a matter of political opinion. I had to leave the room. When I did, I re-*
*alized that a few other students did as well. We were all standing in the hall-*
*way, and we realized that every one of us who left was a minority—Jewish*
*Egyptian woman, gay male, and two Latina women. The experience of being*
*a minority in some sense gave us a connection with all ISMS.*

From her current vantage point, Sylvie again made connections between her Jewishness and Amendment 2: *Working on this project absolutely*
*helped me to integrate my reaction to Amendment 2. First, because I was not*
*directly affected by the amendment, my fear is that I would have gone about*

*my life, left Colorado, and forgotten about it. This is the number one fear among Jews—NEVER FORGET. The Holocaust can always happen again, and the passage of Amendment 2 was a reminder of that. Working on the project helped me to get a feel for the total experience and impact of the event.*

Sean also commented on how he had used the research as one means of working through his reactions to the election, which had begun at the postelection gathering of LGBs and supporters at a club called Mammoth Gardens: *The depth to which Amendment 2 affected people was really surprising. I understood after the election that it was devastating for people as I watched friends cry at Mammoth Gardens but it wasn't until I'd read some of the data that I understood what was behind the tears. I was also surprised at the variety of responses, paranoia to empowerment to "I'm leaving Colorado." I was surprised that so many people had so much to say, particularly because my defensive style was to contain some of my despair and quickly assert that it "would never get past the Supreme Court." In many ways, the process allowed for a working through of my own experience of Amendment 2 in a way that I hadn't achieved on my own. Even though we were working with a goal of delivering the data back to the community, we did, in fact, create a safe place for ourselves to work through our experiences of Amendment 2. As we systematically explored the feelings that Amendment 2 generated in others (by their self-report), I was also able to examine my own responses and found that I was not alone in my experience. Of particular importance to me was that it helped me understand my reactions and those of others. In the presence of trusted friends, I found a sense of shared experience that helped relax my defenses to examine how I was feeling in the aftermath of Amendment 2. The process itself gave me a sense that something good would come out of something bad, that people really were mobilized by this event, and that our community would rebound stronger from the experience. It gave me the sense that I could understand such a complex psychological event, and that I was doing something to help others understand their own responses.*

As for me, working on this project clearly provided me a significant means of integrating my experience of the campaign and election. I had worked steadily for a year in a variety of campaign contexts, doing everything from fund-raising to field organizing, from stuffing envelopes to debating representatives from CFV. Even though I fully expected the amendment to pass, I was greatly saddened when it did. As I moved through my grief, I also began work on this research. Someone who knew me well observed that I had found a perfect means of sublimating my reaction to Amendment 2. He was right.

## Where the Team Members Are Now

In anticipation of this section of the book, all members of the team recently wrote a brief description of their current situations. Lou Bardach says: *I have broadened my work in the field of psychology and now bring its applications to high-tech environments. I received a degree for Multimedia in the spring of 1998 from the Colorado Institute of Art. Combining this with my background in psychology, I now run my own business specializing in Graphical User Interface Design, including applications for learning on the Internet. I continue my work around issues of equity and justice, serving on the Steering Council for the Center for Diverse Communities in Boulder.*

Sylvie Naar provides this update: *My current position is Assistant Professor (clinical-educator) at Wayne State University Medical School, Department of Psychiatry and Behavioral Neurosciences. I am a pediatric psychologist, providing services (outpatient clinics, consultation liaison, and some therapy) to children and adolescents with chronic medical conditions. I coordinate mental health services for children and adolescents infected or affected by HIV. As part of working with the adolescents and young adults, I work with gay youth and issues of homophobia and internalized homophobia. Because the kids are primarily inner-city youth, I also deal with racism and internalized racism. Combine that with the stigma of HIV. My research efforts are focusing on improving adherence to medical regimens for HIV and also diabetes. I direct the Play Therapy program where I provide seminars and supervision in Play Therapy to the Psychology Residents. I also have a small private practice (about 5 hours per week).*

Rob Perl sends word of his latest adventures from California: *I received my Masters in Clinical Psychology in 1997 and I am currently completing my doctorate at The Wright Institute in Berkeley, California. Following my training as Chief Intern at California Pacific Medical Center, I will be in private practice in San Francisco conducting psychoanalytic psychotherapy with adults. I will also be working with children in Kentfield, California, doing psychological assessment, and completing my dissertation.*

Sean Riley is also in graduate school at the Wright Institute: *I am now completing my dissertation and internship after finishing my doctoral coursework in the spring of '99. I have spent the last several years gaining experience with individuals of all ages, conducting therapy in a variety of modalities. Although I anticipated feeling uncomfortable conducting couples, family and play therapy, I have learned that I really enjoy these. Nonetheless, I am hoping to return to individual adult work, preferably with gay men. In concert with this interest, I have begun my dissertation focusing on the conscious and unconscious influences that affect HIV-risk sexual behavior in this population. I am uncertain how the dust will settle after completing my doctoral program, and I have even entertained the idea of returning to the information systems arena, especially their application to the delivery of psychological services.*

Personally, while I was writing this book, I continued to live, practice, and conduct research in Boulder and remained politically active. As of July 2000, I am a member of the core faculty in clinical psychology at Antioch New England Graduate School in Keene, New Hampshire. While I have engaged in some quantitative research since the Amendment 2 study, my energies have moved more and more toward qualitative work. My passions as a psychologist—and there are many—include finding optimal ways for returning research results to the people on whose lives those results were based. Broadly speaking, that is the focus of the next (and final) chapter.

## 11

■■  ■  ■  ■  ■  ■  ■  ■

# Community Applications of Research Findings

FOR A VARIETY OF REASONS, some of them accidents of history and politics (Bakan 1977), psychology has not attached much importance to returning the products of research to members of the communities of interest. Certainly, there are exceptions to this observation in the field (for example, Albee 1981, 1990; Caplan and Nelson 1973; Prilleltensky 1989, 1994; Sarason 1981; Unger 1992). However, even when psychologists speak of the value of making use of research results, they have done little to act on these principles (Walsh 1989). Neither the discipline, nor the structure of the academy more generally, has done much to promote the intentional application of research results to real-world issues. In fact, some critiques have insisted that the discipline simply supports the status quo (Caplan and Nelson 1973; Prilleltensky 1989, 1994). Moreover, efforts to make social science research findings available to the public at large have often been met with disinterest or with radical distortion of the findings (see, for example, Conrad 1997).

And yet, many psychologists initially gravitated to the field because of an impulse to be helpful to others (Gergen 1973). Similarly, many research projects—including the one discussed in this book—were born of the desire to do *something* in the face of pain and suffering.

## Using Research: Quantitative Approaches and Their (Usual) Associated Epistemology

To a significant degree, the field of psychology limits its practitioners in their ability to conceptualize and act on research because it is grounded in a modernist conception of science that emphasizes value neutrality, objectivity, and positivist criteria for determining what qualifies as knowledge (Bohan 1992). Each of these assumptions inhibits the application of psychological research to genuine problems.

### Value Neutrality

Working within a positivist paradigm implicitly entails a denial of values. Psychology is viewed as a science and is therefore seen to exist beyond the influence of values. To the degree that researchers view their work as value-free, they limit their consideration of how their results can be applied to real problems in the world, where values influence every definition of a problem and every proposed solution to it. Recent critiques have challenged the assumption of value neutrality directly and forcefully (for example, Buss 1975; Crawford and Marecek 1989; Myrdal 1969; Sampson 1983). While the specifics of these critiques are beyond the scope of this book, suffice it to say that I reject the assumption of a value-free discipline, believing that values infuse every aspect of our work. That being the case, what is called for is not the denial of values in the practice of psychology, but rather close and consistent attentiveness to the way values influence all aspects of the discipline, including every phase of the research project.

### Objectivity

The positivist notion of objectivity maintains that the researcher and the subject of inquiry are wholly separable entities (Morawski 1985). Existing in some sort of virtual isolation from each other, the researcher can go about her work untouched by the subject of her investigations; conversely, the subject matter stands apart from and impervious to the influence of the researcher. If researchers maintain this dictum, their participation in the real world will be limited. They must remain neutral and apart from social questions lest they acknowledge that they, their "subjects," and their research, are not separable and do not exist apart from and outside any mutual sphere of influence.

Notions of objectivity have also been the focus of extensive critiques (Banyard and Miller 1998; Gadlin and Ingle 1975; Koch 1981; Sampson 1978). It should be clear from chapters 1 and 2 that I view objectivity in research as neither possible nor desirable. My intention both in assembling a team of coders and in using an interpretive approach to the data is epistemologically grounded outside the positivist paradigm. In addition, as we saw in the previous chapter, I do not subscribe to the idea that researchers are not touched by their work.

## Criteria for Knowledge

Within the positivist framework, knowledge is understood to be the endpoint of explorations in which a few variables are isolated and manipulated systematically. The results of the manipulations are quantified and subjected to statistical analysis. In the process, the target variables are stripped of their context (Crawford and Marecek 1989; Mishler 1979). One consequence of context-stripping is that research results frequently bear little relationship to the world in which human beings interact, a world characterized by multiple and dynamic variables. In short, it is difficult to know how one might apply to the real world the results of the sort of decontextualized research that the positivist vision of well-controlled research designs produces.

## The Tension between Internal Validity and External Validity

The effort to control all the variables in order to determine precisely the relationships between them is commonly reflected in internal validity—that is, the condition in which the research has measured what it purports to measure and not the effects of other (extraneous) variables. Within the positivist paradigm, internal validity is regarded as essential for understanding the results of research (Campbell and Stanley 1963). The gradual accumulation of internally valid studies is assumed to form the basis for the formulation of general principles or laws of behavior, the ultimate goal of positivist psychological research. External validity, on the other hand, is concerned with how generalizable the results of a study are; it addresses the question of the usefulness of the results of one study to other populations and contexts. "Both types of criteria are obviously important, even though they are frequently at odds in that *features increasing one may jeopardize the other*" (Campbell and Stanley 1963:5; italics added). Thus, it would appear that increased concern with internal validity is likely to jeopardize applicability.

Further, many researchers who work within a positivist framework believe that generalization is never fully justifiable on logical grounds. As Campbell and Stanley have observed:

> Whereas the problems of *internal* validity are solvable within the limits of the logic of probability statistics, the problems of external validity are not logically solvable in any neat, conclusive way. Generalization always turns out to involve extrapolation into a realm not represented in one's sample. Such extrapolation is made by *assuming* one knows the relevant laws. . . . *Logically*, we cannot generalize beyond these limits, i.e., we cannot generalize at all. But we do attempt generalization by guessing at laws and checking out some of these generalizations in other equally specific but different conditions. (Campbell and Stanley 1963:17)

The logical limits to the generalizations of research, along with the tension between internal validity and such generalizations, place a significant barrier on efforts to make use of the results of research. If operating strictly within a positivist framework, one cannot legitimately make use of the results of one well-controlled (i.e., internally valid) study except by running an equally well-controlled study with the specific population of interest (thus generating a new internally valid, though equally ungeneralizable result). Under such conditions, the results of research move slowly and tortuously from one setting or population to the next, and their potential for active use is severely delimited. This is certainly not to say that no research grounded in a positivist epistemology has ever been put to productive use. It is, however, fair to say that adherence to the positivist paradigm places a great many constraints on applying research results to real-world questions—and even to asking questions relevant to the real world in the first place.

## Using Research: An Interpretive Approach and Its Related Epistemology

Researchers using an interpretive approach—and qualitative research more generally—draw on nonpositivist epistemological considerations. These so-called postmodern approaches reject traditional notions of value neutrality, objectivity, and positivist criteria for what qualifies as knowledge (Altheide and Johnson 1994; Denzin 1994). The qualitative data described in this book originated in a survey in which all items but one were quantifiable. For all intents and purposes, the quantitative section of the survey was developed and used within a positivist framework. However, the single question that gave rise to these qualitative data was rooted in a postmodern framework. Underlying that item were several ideas (all of which depart from modernist assumptions): that LGBs could describe important elements of their own experience of Amendment 2, that these descriptions would be informative although non-quantified, and that the descriptions might be useful in some fashion that could not be hypothesized in advance. Once LGBs had responded to the item and I had gathered a team to use an interpretive approach, we had moved well beyond positivist assumptions about or approaches to the data. It was not long before members of the team understood that these qualitative data could be helpful to LGBs who had been through the experience of the campaign and election and, perhaps, even to those who had not.

### Qualitative Data: How Do We Use Them?

Because we view and analyze data differently when we work outside a positivist framework, our considerations about their potential usefulness in other contexts are also different. Important information may be obtained from studies that are not tightly controlled in the fashion deemed essential for internal validity within the positivist framework; indeed, we expect lesbians, bisexuals, and gay men to directly convey useful information to us about their experience of anti-gay politics.

Similarly, we expect that what LGBs have told us about their reactions to anti-gay politics might be helpful in other situations. Our expectation is not based on the positivist search for general laws that describe how any group of gay people behaves when subjected to a hostile campaign and election. At the extreme, the generation of such laws would require far too many hostile campaigns and elections to be (even remotely) acceptable. Rather, we use the results of this study as a "sensitizing device," to use Gergen's term (1973:317). Specifically, the results of this study help us identify themes that might be relevant when gay people come under attack. Among the most obvious candidates for such themes are the major codes in this study and, from there, overarching understandings derived from the confluence of several codes.

The potential application of understandings drawn from this study's results to other anti-gay actions will vary in accordance with the nature, source, duration, and severity of anti-gay actions. For example, the results of this study might be of greater relevance when LGBs are subjected to anti-gay electoral campaigns than when an LGB individual faces discrimination in an employment situation. Research results from one time and situation, then, can be used not by extrapolating general laws but rather by being sensitive to the dominant themes of the research and deciding how those themes might be relevant to different times and situations.

In the service of such sensitivity and judgment, it is useful to view the current study as a paradigm case (or family resemblance; see Kuhn 1970) of a hostile action against LGBs. Some of the important characteristics of the paradigm case have been established by the nature of the action itself. Among these are: the action collectivized gay people but was experienced by many LGBs in very personal terms; the action was political in focus; it involved the impact of strangers—the voters as a whole—and, sometimes, of loved ones and acquaintances; and it put LGBs at the center of a hostile and often misleading discourse. The relevance of the current study to other anti-gay actions could be judged on the basis of their similarity to the paradigm case of Amendment 2.

Using the results of the Amendment 2 study in this way allows us to consider relevant themes for use in other circumstances where LGBs are targeted. Within a postmodern framework, this can be done without appeal to—and without the constraints of—the positivist demand for a traditionally well-controlled study and for severely restricted generalizability. In the remainder of this chapter, we look at several instances in which the results of this study have been put to use, both directly and quite circuitously.

## Direct Routes of Returning Research to the LGB Community

The first time I read the data from this study, I knew that they contained important information for gay men, bisexuals, and lesbians. I also knew that I would do everything I possibly could to return what I had learned from LGBs back to the community.[1] Some of my efforts to do so have been quite direct. Even before the coding and analysis of the data had been completed, I gave talks about our preliminary findings regarding the psychological effects of Amendment 2 all over the state, and in conferences of LGBs in other states as well. I spoke to community groups, classes, political gatherings, and informal groups of friends. Whenever I did so, I emphasized not only the stresses associated with the experience but the sources of resilience that were described in the data. In response to requests, I made a tape of one of these talks and made it available at cost. LGBs purchased it for themselves; friends bought it for friends; and parents bought it for their gay children. Clearly, some segment of the public was quite interested in hearing how research findings related to their lives.

This book can also be included among my efforts to return to LGBs what they told me about themselves. I have written it with the intention that readers with no interest in qualitative research could read the chapters on LGBs' experiences. Especially in those chapters (but throughout the book as well) I have avoided the use of psychological jargon as much as possible. Most importantly, I have used the voices of Colorado LGBs to illustrate the findings from the study. Their words have guided me every step of the way. I believe, with Banyard and Miller (1998) and others, that it is empowering for people to tell their own stories. (One need only recall the THANKS code to be reminded of that.) I also believe that it is empowering for people to read their own stories in print.

## Less Direct Routes: Working with Gatekeepers

Getting information to the community can often be accomplished by getting the information into the hands of key people who have broad access to the community—the so-called gatekeepers. Prior to and in anticipation of the Supreme Court's decision on Amendment 2, I provided consultation to a public university, a public college, several private schools, and a municipal government to help them plan appropriate responses to the Court decision. Not knowing what the outcome of the decision would be, we had to construct contingencies for positive, negative, and ambiguous judicial outcomes.

In providing these consultations,[2] I emphasized central themes from the research and how these might be addressed. Mindful of the importance of witnessing (especially SUPPORT), for example, Boulder's municipal team arranged to have a poster created for public display. The poster's background consisted of rainbow colors in a flowing pattern. At the top of the poster was a dictionary definition of "community," followed by the word "COMMUNITY" centered and in large print. Beneath that was written, "Following the Supreme Court decision on Amendment 2, please consider what the word community can mean" and then, in bold letters: "Boulder Values Diversity." At the bottom of the poster were the city seal and contact information for relevant municipal offices. In the weeks leading up to the decision, the posters appeared on municipal buses and were made available to businesses for display. The city also sponsored an unofficial march and an official rally on the day of the decision, with a follow-up public information meeting two days later.

In addition, Sean, Lou, and I met with members of a Boulder city program called "Valuing Diversity: Education on Homophobia and Heterosexism," to help them formulate support interventions for LGBs and heterosexual allies in the event of a negative judicial outcome. We described central themes from the study to Valuing Diversity trainers and worked with them to devise a plan to respond to the Supreme Court decision. Most of that plan, fortunately, never needed to be put into effect, as it had anticipated a pro-Amendment 2 decision by the Court. However, the Valuing Diversity project did hold public gatherings for LGBs to discuss their reactions over several days after the decision.

Since that time, I have consulted with campaign leaders and workers who are facing anti-gay initiatives in other parts of the country. I have tried to use our findings in Colorado to sensitize them to issues they may face as they work for equal rights for LGBs.

# Other Indirect Routes of Returning Research Results to the Community

A project as big and as rich as this one carries ongoing potential for returning the results to the LGB and ally communities over time. In many cases, the opportunities for doing so come unexpectedly.

## *Psychotherapy*

The lessons LGBs taught me through this research have had a striking impact on the way I think about and conduct psychotherapy. The IHE and IHI codes especially have greatly enhanced my understanding of how to work with issues related to internalized oppression in therapy. Those codes sensitized me to recognizing more subtle manifestations of internalized oppression and the need always to identify the (current or historical) homophobia/heterosexism in which these manifestations are rooted. The results of my expanded understanding have been put to use not only in my work with LGB clients but also in my work with heterosexuals, especially when clients are contending with forms of internalized oppression.

## *The Anniversary of the Supreme Court Decision*

One year after the Court had announced the outcome of its deliberations on Amendment 2, anniversary celebrations were held at various sites around the state. At one of these, I spoke of recovery from the ordeal of Amendment 2. I used findings from the follow-up quantitative study as the basis for emphasizing the need for LGBs to work on issues associated with the GRASP, MOVE, IHE and IHI, AG, SUPPORT, and COMM codes.

## *Anti-Gay Politics' Different Manifestations*

The following year, in the aftermath of Matthew Shepherd's murder in Wyoming, various community gatherings were held in Colorado. I reminded LGBs of what they had told me through the Amendment 2 study: of the need to feel and express pain and anger and to place all their reactions to this event into a MOVE context.

## *Transforming Research Results into Cultural Expressions*[3]

In addition to the more usual direct and indirect avenues for returning research to communities of interest, it is sometimes possible to work with others to transform research into art forms. Here, I describe two such projects, one a video and the other an oratorio.

### Video: "Inner Journeys, Public Stands"

After Amendment 2, I was interested in trying to understand the experiences of heterosexuals who had taken a public stand against the amendment. Many of these allies had encountered homophobia and heterosexism; some were treated with the hostility usually reserved for members of target groups but occasionally visited upon members of the dominant group who stand with and for the target group.

While I was in the process of undertaking an interview research project with heterosexual allies, a friend suggested that I videotape the interviews. Given what I had learned about the importance LGBs attached to positive witnessing and the distress associated with the failure to witness, I thought a video might itself be a witnessing device. The editing of the comments made by allies interviewed for the video was based on codes drawn from a qualitative analysis of the interviews. The video explores the motivations, costs, and rewards for this group of heterosexuals who publicly opposed Amendment 2.

Feedback has suggested that the video performs at least two functions: it imparts information about important dimensions of being an ally to heterosexual viewers, and it demonstrates positive witnessing by heterosexuals to LGB viewers. The sheer diversity of allies shown in the documentary challenges LGBs' biases about who is—and might become—an ally. Called "Inner Journeys, Public Stands,"[4] the documentary has been shown on PBS stations in many parts of the country and has become an example of research transformed into cultural expression.

### Oratorio: "Fire"

Sometimes the ideas for transforming research into other forms of cultural expression originate in unexpected places. The researcher's task in such cases is to be open to possibilities that no one ever discussed in graduate school. The idea for an oratorio based on the qualitative research described in this book came from the board of Harmony: A Colorado Chorale, a Denver-based community chorus whose membership is drawn from the LGB and ally communities. The board wanted to commission a work about the amendment to be sung at an international gathering of LGB choruses slated to be held in Tampa, Florida, in July 1996. Because I had been a singing member of Harmony for several years and had gathered some of the data for the research on the amendment during rehearsals, members of the board were familiar with my research. Then board president, James Herringer, approached me with the idea of making the research the basis for the oratorio.

I was enthusiastic, though I did consult with the Ethics Board of my state psychology association to help me define appropriate parameters for how the data would be used. Harmony commissioned Bob McDowell, an off-Broadway composer, to transform the research into an oratorio. After our initial conversations, Bob examined the data, viewed "Inner Journeys, Public Stands," read a number of papers about the campaign and election, and talked with other members of the chorus. He and I consulted at various points during his composing process, but nothing prepared me for the power of the oratorio he created. In "Fire," Bob captured many aspects of LGBs' experiences of Amendment 2.

Harmony's artistic director, Vicki Burrichter, asked that I give a talk to introduce "Fire" to the chorus. In that talk, I emphasized the importance of returning the findings from the research to LGBs because those findings represented our stories, our memory, and our culture. In addition, I wrote a synopsis of the oratorio to help the chorus understand the intricacies of "Fire." I explained that Bob intended the piece to take the chorus and listeners through the grief cycle—from denial and shock to regret, to sadness and anger and, finally to renewal and rejuvenation. The title of each movement was a quote drawn directly from the data. I then wrote an explanation of how each of the five movements in the oratorio related to our research findings.

I include that description of "Fire" below. It is in much the form that the chorus received it, except that I have inserted the relevant codes from the data analysis here.

*Part I—"I Was Really Naive . . ."* The first part of "Fire" opens with a kind of dialogue between denial of homophobia and heterosexism on the one hand (SHOCK), and their acknowledgment on the other (GRASP). It is a dialogue that, during the campaign, was played out on at least two levels: within the hearts and minds of virtually every LGB person, and between and among LGBs in both private and public settings. Acknowledging the intensity and pervasiveness of homophobia and heterosexism is a painful proposition. As with so many difficult realities, the individual often moves back and forth between denying their existence and acknowledging it. Sometimes, this dialogue—whether it occurs within oneself or between oneself and another—has an almost humorous quality to it. At other times, as reality emerges, the humor gives way to pathos, as in the refrain of "Kyrie eleison" ("Lord, have mercy"). It is in Part I that the first metaphorical use of "fire" occurs: "but one crucial phrase that no one said / is where there's smoke, there's fire." Despite the struggle to deny their presence and impact, homophobia and heterosexism really do exist, Amendment 2 really could pass, danger is afoot.

*Part Ia—". . . They Said . . ."* A new meaning of fire emerges in this brief section. The altos tell a story very similar to that offered by one of the LGB respondents in the survey, a story of being fired the week after Amendment 2 passed (DISC). Here, one message of the amendment becomes clear: it is acceptable to fire an LGB person. There may be some debate—again internal or external—as to how much the firing was related to sexual orientation or with Amendment 2, "But whether it was or whether it wasn't / I thought about it." The lyrics here remind us that one of the effects of anti-gay actions, including Amendment 2, is confusion about what precisely caused the negative events.

*Part II—"I Chose Not to Be Active . . ."* Based often on the denial of the likelihood of Amendment 2's passage, many LGBs decided not to work against it. In Part II, fire becomes a new metaphor—something that needs to be tended. When we fail to tend to our political worlds, fires indeed go out. While we revel in our plenty or look only in the eyes of our loves, the political landscape can change dramatically. And we are left with the poignant "What if?" (REGRET). Part II stands as a powerful, though certainly not hostile, reminder of our need to tend to the larger world.

*Part III—"On November 3 . . ."* The pain (SAD, LOSS, OVER) of Amendment 2 is highlighted in this section of the piece. It reads like the parable of the Good Samaritan but it's ". . . not quite the parable we'd hoped for." Part III is based on the story of one LGB respondent whose psychological pain about the election was translated directly and immediately into a physical injury, one for which she sought help and received none (TRAUMA, VWP). Every trauma—and, for many of us, Amendment 2 was a trauma—has three participants: the person victimized, the person who carries out the victimization, and witnesses who either respond or fail to respond. The person who has hurt her knee seeks assistance from witnesses—from a brother, from a sister (FAMR), from a stranger who passes by—but no one helps. This section is reminiscent of the many sad and angry comments about the failure to witness, on the part of so many Coloradans, including the voters (ASTATE), heterosexuals in general (AHET), Christians in general (ACHRIST), and the media (AMEDIA). It ends with the sounding of "Alarm!" (FEAR). The reality of homophobia and heterosexism is clearly revealed in the pain it causes.

*Part IV—". . . Wanted to Burn Down the Churches"* The "Alarm!" sounded at the end of the previous section becomes more insistent in Part IV. Pain has given way to fury (AG). The "threatening fires are burning," no longer to be ignored. The imagery in this section is of soldiers and war (WAR). So, too, was much of the imagery in the comments in our study. Many of the images in the score are almost stereotypical in nature: "Glory! Shout to Glory!"; "to keep the peace we'll go to war"; "Hold the standard high with pride." In the aftermath of a traumatic experience, especially one brought on by other people, anger is a frequent response, and a normal one. Anger is part of the process by which people who feel victimized make sense of their victimization and identify who was responsible for it. Anger also keeps the person or group who has been victimized bound to the person or group who has done the victimizing. The "No! No! No!" is a response; it is not an affirmation. We see the impulse toward self-affirmation at the very end of Part IV: "No!" becomes "No more!" becomes "No more hate!" A profound transformation is beginning.

*Part V—"Another Door Was Opened"* For many LGB Coloradans, Amendment 2 was the catalyst for thinking about ourselves and our community

(COMM) in a new way. This final section of "Fire" illustrates some of that change. It begins with the impulse to sing a different song, a simpler song—"One that everyone can sing together / One that you can hum along or open your heart and let soar." The request is for a song that reflects our ability to see the world, including its political realities (GRASP), without sacrificing the focus on ourselves as individuals who can find a position from which we are not reacting as oppressed victims bound to those who would oppress us: "One that reaches in while it reaches up to glory." It is not a song of capitulation or even of compromise. The lyrics are clear: we are not willing to "stay out of sight" (OUTM). To the contrary, "I'm here, I'm proud, I'm a person too." It is a song, finally, of self-definition and self-affirmation, of drawing closer to the fire—this time, a fire that warms and enlightens—with my brothers and sisters (COMM). It is the best possible outcome of the Amendment 2 experience: we, as lesbians, gay men, and bisexuals, transform our pain and anger to a greater sense of ourselves as a community and to a broad commitment to working against oppression of all kinds (ISMS, MOVE). That transformation directly changes our lives and the lives of others around us. It is the kind of change where true revolutions begin (PERSONAL).

"Fire"
Below are the lyrics to Bob McDowell's oratorio. They represent Colorado LGBs' reports of Amendment 2. The piece also represents data transformed into a musical act of witnessing both history and individual experience.

*Fire*
An Oratorio by Bob McDowell

Part I—I was really naive . . .

Ready, Aim, Fire.

Just remind yourself that when all is lost,

then you've everything to gain.
So let's drink a toast to our sinking ship
with a glass of cheap champagne.

Kyrie Eleison, Christe Eleison.

Everybody said, "I'm amazed, I'm astounded.
I can scarcely believe my ears."
Yes, everybody said that it never could happen
in a thousand, in a million years.

Everybody said, "It's a shame, it's a pity,
but of course I am on your side."
Well, if everybody said that,
fifty-three percent of them lied.

Yes, everybody said that the tide would turn
when it came down to the wire,
but one crucial phrase that no one said,
is where there's smoke, there's fire.

Kyrie

Everybody said, "Never fret, never worry."
Everybody said, "You'll be fine."
But, tell me, would you just let it go at that
were it *your* ass on the line?
I thought not.

Everybody said, "It will all blow over.
It's a tempest in a teapot, kid."
Huh? Everybody said, "This too, will pass."
Well, guess what, it did.

Still, everybody said that the tide would turn
when it came down to the wire.
But, one crucial phrase that no one said,
is where there's smoke, there's fire.
"Everybody said" which goes to show that
talk is cheap.
"Everybody said" but the price of freedom's steep.
Kyrie! Sing Kyrie! Kyrie Eleison.
Kyrie! Sing Kyrie! Queer today,
but maybe gone tomorrow.

I said not here, not now.
No, the right isn't quite that strong, I hope.
I said don't panic yet, but regretfully I was wrong.
Dead wrong.

Part Ia—. . . they said . . .

One week after the election, I lost my job.
"Downsizing," they said.
"Consolidating," they said.
But whatever they "said," however they said it,
I was fired. *Fire*
But whether it was or whether it wasn't,
I thought about it.

Part II—I chose not to be active . . .

When the sun was high,
I paid no heed to the dark.
When the breeze was warm,
I gave no thought to the winter's chill.
"What if?" I wonder, and I always will.
If only I'd tended the fire in time.
When the harvest was bountiful
I set nothing aside for seed.
How we reveled in our plenty!
We danced and we ate our fill.
"What if?" I wonder and I always will.
If only I'd tended the fire in time.
"What if?"

I sang my love a lullaby
that dulled the sound of the storm.
and the fire burned on.
We sang, "There is naught in the world but love,"
and believed because we wished it were so.
and the fire burned on.

We closed our eyes and dreamed,
convinced we were safe and warm.
But the fire burned fainter, and the fire grew dim,
then ember, then ash, then the cold.

When the sun was high. "What if!"

Part III—on November 3 . . .

I fell and hurt my knee and as I lay in misery,

my brother passed.
"Ho! Brother Ho!" called I.
"Do help me brother. Help." I cry,
but my brother passed me by that day
and cast his glance the other way
as if he never knew me.

Heigh! Hey it's a funny world.
Heigh! Hey down a diddle die dee.

Oh, I fell and hurt my knee and as I lay in misery,
my sister passed.
"Ho! Sister Ho!" called I.
"Do help me sister. Help," I cry,
but my sister passed me by that day
and cast her glance the other way
as if she never knew me.

Heigh! Hey it's a funny world.
Heigh! Hey down a diddle die dee.

Oh, I fell and hurt my knee and as I lay in misery,
a stranger passed.
"Ho! Stranger Ho!" called I.
"Do help me stranger. Help," I cry,
but the stranger passed me by that day
and cast her glance the other way
as if he'd never heard me.

Heigh! Hey not quite the parable we'd hoped for.
Heigh! Hey down a diddle die dee.

Alarm! Alarm!

Part IV—. . . wanted to burn down the churches

Quickened by the scent of war,
watchful eyes are turning.
Alarm! Alarm! Burn.
Heigh! Hey down a diddle die dee.
Now in numbers too great to ignore,
see threatening fires are burning.
Burn!

Soldiers, heed the call to arms
in your rival's camp it echoes clear.
Keep your weapons close at hand
it advances ever nearer.
Burn!

Cock your ear to the foe's alarm,
it awaits to rend the peaceful air.
Ever keep a watchful eye
for the battle ground's prepared.

Glory! Shout to glory!
Alleluia! Glory! Shout to glory!
Is that rosy warmth you feel
self-satisfied glow, or the fire?
Burn!
We seek no quarrel not our own,
but to keep the peace we'llgo to war.
See the lesson's never forgot
and be unaware no more. No more!
Hold the standard high with pride.
and prepare to make the sacrifice.

Glory! Glory! Glory!
Naught is gained where naught is lost.
Every freedom has its price.
Glory! Shout to glory! Alleluia.

See the lessons never forgot
and be unaware no more.
No! No! No!
Fight fire with fire!
No more! No more hate!
No more! No more hate!

*[In the section above, individual chorus members recite
statements akin to comments from the data.]*

Part V—Another door was opened

Can't we sing a simpler song?

One that everyone can sing together.
One that you can hum along,
or open your heart and let soar.
One that reaches in while it reaches up to glory.
A simpler song, something to inspire
as we draw closer to the fire.

In a world so very small,
we need songs that we can sing together.
Songs that celebrate us all and give us a reason.
No, it's simpler than that.
Take away the poetry,
take away the harmony,
take away rhyme.

It's as simple as this: no one's getting anywhere
standing nose to nose shouting, "No!"
Your hate. My hate. Same damn thing.
So we agree to disagree.
You stay over there and I stay out of sight.
"Don't ask, don't tell."
Now, could you live like that?
I thought not.

See, what you have to understand
is this is my life we're talking about.
I'm here. I'm proud. I'm a person, too.
And the more you say no,
the more my brothers and sisters and I
draw closer to the fire.
Closer to each other. Closer to the fire.

Funny how the fire that was our enemy
returns to comfort later on.
Funny.

No more No.
No more No.
No more. Yes.
No more. Yes.
Yes. Yes. Yes.

## Performances

"Fire" was performed by Harmony in a Denver concert in June 1996 and a month later at the Gay and Lesbian Choral Associations of America (GALA) gathering in Tampa. The responses from both audiences were enthusiastic. Two members of the coding team, Sean and Lou, were in attendance at the first concert. Both said they were able to code the oratorio spontaneously using the system we had developed in our work together. The richness of the data—the grief and rage, the pain and confusion, the resilience—had been returned to the community of lesbians, gay men, and bisexuals. A perfect circle of giving and receiving had been completed. It was a satisfying moment for me.

## Some Final Statements

Five of us analyzed the 496 comments from LGBs in Colorado. We worked as a team and listened with the greatest attentiveness and respect we could muster, individually and collectively. It is only fitting that this book close with all our voices represented. The following statements came from the narratives written by the members of the coding team about their experiences.

Sean wrote: *Having had only minimal exposure to the analysis of clinical material prior to this experience, I regard the project now, as I complete my third year of graduate school, to have been one of the most clinically rich experiences I've had. Not only did it teach me about LGB issues, trauma theory, and research, but it also greatly improved my clinical skills, contributed to my professional development, and showed me how psychologists could influence and help heal their communities in ways I hadn't imagined.*

Lou wrote: *I recall the difficult yet momentous personal growth that I experienced during the project. Looking inside oneself can always be a difficult process, but the project was a particularly intense experience. Coming out as a gay man during Amendment 2, and reading about all the pain participants of the survey shared with us in the project were both challenging. At the same time, I recall the sense of empowerment which I found in being a part of such an experience. I believe that the dichotomy just described is the most profound aspect of what we discovered in the project and within ourselves.*

Sylvie wrote: *I really don't have a favorite memory because I enjoyed it all, and the sessions run together into one great experience. The experience definitely opened me up to new ideas, new kinds of research, new understanding of difference and, then, what followed was a new understanding of myself.*

Rob wrote: *I guess I would have to say that I was surprised with the data at certain points. Granted, I have never been the target of hateful legislation. However, the force and emotion behind some of the comments was astounding. Given a voice, these respondents spilled their anger, frustration, and sadness onto the page. It was striking just how the presence of a questionnaire like this in one's hand could unleash such passion. Many (most) of our respondents were unaware of the effect that their voices would have through the research. But they still felt the need to make their voices known. I am tremendously impressed with our respondents and their passion and commitment for positive change. Thinking back, I can hear them, and I can picture their words on the printed page, and I can feel the desperation in their voices. I will forever have a lump in my throat when I think back to what Amendment 2 did to Colorado.*

I began this book by introducing two stories. The first was the story of the paradoxical consequences of Amendment 2 on gay men, lesbians, and bisexuals. It is the story of the courage of LGBs who responded to efforts to vote them *out* of the political process by choosing to *come out* instead. The second story chronicles a research team listening together to hear the paradoxes in the words of Colorado LGBs.

Both stories reached closure in this last chapter as we explored some of the many ways in which psychological research can find its way back to the communities from which it emerged. In the end, there was a dynamic and reciprocal relationship between those who spoke of their experiences and those who strove to understand them. A similar reciprocity enlivened the interactions among team members. Both are stories in which the distinction between giving and receiving disappears.

■ ■ ■ ■ ■ ■ ■ ■ ■

# Appendix A

Each symptom within the *major depression, post-traumatic stress disorder* (PTSD), and generalized anxiety diagnoses was associated with three separate 10-point Likert-style scales on which respondents could rate the degree to which they experienced the symptom (from "not at all" to "very often"). Because of the survey nature of the study, only symptoms and not rule-out criteria for major depressive episode were included. Therefore, all DSM-III-R symptoms under criterion A were included for major depressive episode. These symptoms constitute the "Major Depressive Syndrome," according to DSM-III-R (American Psychiatric Association 1987:222). Omitted from the DSM-III-R criteria for major depressive episode were Criterion B (ruling out the presence of an underlying organic factor or bereavement), Criterion C (ruling out the presence of psychotic symptomatology in the absence of mood symptoms for as long as two weeks), and Criterion D (ruling out other disorders with psychotic features). For the diagnostic category for post-traumatic stress disorder, Criterion A was omitted. Criterion A addresses the experience of a "markedly distressing" event "outside the range of usual human experience" (American Psychiatric Association 1987:250). For the purposes of this study, the campaign for and passage of Amendment 2 were considered to fulfill Criterion A for PTSD.

Table I. *Cronbach Alpha Reliability Estimates for Each of Three Symptom Scales at Two Time Periods*

| | Cronbach's Alpha | |
| --- | --- | --- |
| | before the Campaign | after the Election |
| Depression Scale (15 items) | .92 | .92 |
| PTSD Scale (14 items) | .84 | .88 |
| Anxiety Scale (18 items) | .90 | .92 |

The three Likert scales for each symptom allowed respondents to rate the degree to which they were troubled by the symptoms for each of three distinct time periods: before January 1, 1992 (i.e., before the campaign began); between January 1, 1992 and November 3, 1992 (during the campaign and up to election day); and between November 4, 1992 and January 14, 1993 (after the election but before a District Court judge granted a temporary injunction against Amendment 2). The use of the first time frame for each symptom was for purposes of retrospectively establishing a baseline for each symptom. I offered the second time frame for each symptom in an effort to provide respondents with a reference point for their symptoms before completing the symptom check list for the third time frame that assessed the effects of the election.

In calculating the data, I counted a symptom as present only when a respondent endorsed the intensity of that symptom at a level of 8 or above on the 10-point scale. This system was significantly more conservative for most symptoms than the criteria required by DSM-III-R guidelines.

For purposes of calculating the presence or absence of the three diagnoses, I used DSM-III-R specifications. The formula for each diagnosis corresponded to DSM-III-R requirements, with the exception of the aforementioned Criteria B, C, and D in major depressive episode and Criterion A in PTSD. For example, the diagnosis of PTSD was given only if the respondent indicated levels of 8 or greater on the following: at least one of the four symptoms in Criterion B; at least three of the seven symptoms in Criterion C; and at least two of the six symptoms in Criterion D.

*Diagnostic Scales.* For purposes of analysis, the criteria for each of the three DSM-III-R criteria were summed up to create a score for each diagnosis. The scale for major depressive episode was comprised of 15 criteria and ranged from 15 to 150. The PTSD scale included 14 items; this scale's range was 14 to 140. The generalized anxiety scale was based on 18 items and it ranged from 18 to 180. A total symptom scale ranging from 44 to 440 was constructed using the 44 nonoverlapping symptoms from the three diagnostic categories.

Reliabilities for each of the three symptom scales were computed by means of Cronbach's alpha and are available in Table I.

# Appendix B

*Frequencies, Means, and Standard Deviations for Open versus Closet Status Items for Baseline (before the Campaign Began) and after the Election*

| | Before the Campaign | | | | After the Election | | | |
|---|---|---|---|---|---|---|---|---|
| | "Yes" Response | "No" Response | Mean | S.D. | "Yes" Response | "No" Response | Mean | S.D. |
| I am generally pretty closeted; only very few people know that I'm gay, lesbian, or bisexual | 130 (19.6%) | 531 (80.1%) | 1.80 | .398 | 53 (8%) | 608 (91.7%) | 1.92 | .270 |
| Most of my friends know I'm gay, lesbian, or bisexual | 424 (64%) | 237 (35.7%) | 1.36 | .480 | 435 (65.6%) | 226 (34.1%) | 1.34 | .480 |
| I'm very open about being gay, lesbian, or bisexual at work | 215 (32.4%) | 445 (67.1%) | 1.67 | .469 | 284 (42.8%) | 376 (56.7%) | 1.57 | .495 |
| Most members of my biological family (i.e., family of origin) know I'm gay, lesbian, or bisexual | 386 (58.2%) | 274 (41.3%) | 1.42 | .493 | 395 (59.6%) | 265 (40.0%) | 1.40 | .491 |

■ ■ ■ ■ ■ ■ ■ ■ ■

# Appendix C

## Univariate Analyses

*Symptom Scales*

Table I shows the descriptive statistics for each of four symptom scales—for depression, PTSD, anxiety, and total symptoms—for each of two time periods, before the campaign began and after the election.

Table II offers descriptive statistics for the changes in each of the four symptom scales from the baseline, before the campaign began to after the election.

Table I. *Descriptive Statistics for Diagnostic Scales for Baseline (before the Campaign Began) and after the Election Time Frames*

| Scale | Before the Campaign | | | | After the Election | | | |
|---|---|---|---|---|---|---|---|---|
| | Min | Max | Mean | S.D. | Min | Max | Mean | S.D. |
| Depression Scale | 4 | 122 | 41.66 | 19.94 | 4 | 144 | 54.37 | 25.11 |
| PTSD Scale | 3 | 99 | 37.84 | 16.32 | 7 | 120 | 62.81 | 21.17 |
| Anxiety Scale | 5 | 141 | 45.16 | 21.57 | 5 | 172 | 65.63 | 28.09 |
| Total Symptom Scale | 44 | 312 | 116.31 | 47.64 | 52 | 387 | 169.98 | 61.29 |

Table II. *Descriptive Statistics for Changes in Symptom Scales from Baseline (before the Campaign Began) to after the Election*

| Scale | Change Scores | | | |
|---|---|---|---|---|
| | Minimum | Maximum | Mean | S.D. |
| Depression Scale | −86 | 95 | 12.70 | 21.36 |
| PTSD Scale | −33 | 81 | 24.89 | 18.92 |
| Anxiety Scale | −81 | 105 | 20.46 | 19.87 |
| Total Symptom Scale | −161 | 232 | 54.30 | 48.13 |

Table III. *Frequencies of Discrete DSM-III-R Diagnoses for Each Time Period (n = 663)*

| | Before Campaign | After Election |
|---|---|---|
| Depression only | 7 (1%) | 10 (1.5%) |
| PTSD only | 1 (.1%) | 30 (4.5%) |
| Anxiety only | 2 (.3%) | 25 (3.7%) |
| PTSD & Depression | 0 | 5 (.7%) |
| Anxiety & Depression | 0 | 12 (1.8%) |
| PTSD & Anxiety | 0 | 8 (1.2%) |
| Anxiety, Depression, and PTSD | 0 | 16 (2.4%) |
| Total Number of Diagnosed Respondents | 10 | 106 |

## DSM-III-R Diagnoses

DSM-III-R diagnostic criteria were used to assess the frequency of each of three diagnoses in the sample population for the baseline and postelection times. The criteria used for assigning diagnoses were identical to those offered in DSM-III-R, with the exception that a given criterion was met only if it were endorsed at a level of 8 or greater on the 10-point Likert scale. Table III describes the nonoverlapping frequencies of the diagnoses, singly and in combination, during the two time periods.

## Other Variables

Table IV summarizes descriptive data for each of 11 items designed to assess effects of the election not within the province of specific diagnostic changes.

Table IV. *Baseline (before the Campaign Began) and Post (after the Election) Means, Standard Deviations, and Change Scores for Miscellaneous Items*

| Item | Baseline | | Postelection | | Change: Baseline to Post | | | |
|---|---|---|---|---|---|---|---|---|
| | Mean | S.D. | Mean | S.D. | Minimum | Maximum | Mean | S.D. |
| Trouble in your primary relationship because of disagreement about how open/closeted to be | 2.446 | 2.058 | 2.963 | 2.640 | −7.00 | 9.00 | .540 | 2.411 |
| Fearful of being verbally assaulted because you are gay, lesbian, or bisexual | 3.973 | 2.333 | 6.521 | 2.699 | −5.00 | 9.00 | 2.529 | 2.544 |
| Fearful of being physically assaulted because you are gay, lesbian, or bisexual | 3.461 | 2.142 | 6.244 | 2.627 | −7.00 | 9.00 | 2.774 | 2.436 |
| Concerned you will lose something (be discriminated against) if you disclose your sexual orientation | 4.901 | 2.764 | 6.732 | 2.749 | −9.00 | 9.00 | 1.829 | 2.688 |
| Tired of being the object of discussion and debate | 4.163 | 2.801 | 6.839 | 3.149 | −9.00 | 9.00 | 2.664 | 3.078 |
| Feeling that heterosexual family members have a better sense of what homophobia is | 3.044 | 2.323 | 4.966 | 3.088 | −8.00 | 9.00 | 1.915 | 2.603 |
| Feeling that heterosexual friends and colleagues have a better sense of what homophobia is | 3.372 | 2.231 | 5.890 | 2.783 | −8.00 | 9.00 | 2.515 | 2.634 |
| Feeling a sense of community with other gays, lesbians, and bisexuals | 5.526 | 2.597 | 7.584 | 2.346 | −8.00 | 9.00 | 2.043 | 2.965 |
| Comfortable working on causes related to civil rights for gay, lesbian, or bisexual people | 5.359 | 2.962 | 6.901 | 2.726 | −9.00 | 9.00 | 1.524 | 2.822 |
| Feel comfortable being gay, lesbian, or bisexual | 7.614 | 2.574 | 8.031 | 2.258 | −8.00 | 9.00 | .391 | 2.674 |
| Discovering a sense of empowerment by virtue of working with other gays, lesbians, and bisexuals | 5.455 | 2.894 | 7.087 | 2.727 | −9.00 | 9.00 | 1.613 | 2.756 |

Table V. *Summaries of Regression Analyses Related to Symptom Changes from Baseline to Postelection*

| Scale | Change Score | Sex | Age | Race |
|---|---|---|---|---|
| Depression Scale | F = 5.86* | F = 4.72* | NS**** | NS**** |
| PTSD Scale | F = 999.** | F = 6.09* | NS**** | NS**** |
| Anxiety Scale | F = 606.** | F = 4.53* | NS**** | NS**** |
| Total Symptom Scale | F = 700.** | F = 8.00*** | NS**** | NS**** |

* p < .05
** p < .0001
*** p .01
**** nonsignificant F, deleted from model

## Multivariate Analyses

### Changes in Symptom Scales

Multiple regressions were conducted to test the significance of changes in depression, PTSD, anxiety, and total symptom scores and to test their relationships to demographic variables. Change scores were computed by subtracting baseline levels from post levels for each respondent so as to avoid capitalizing on the repeated measures design of the study. (Note: degrees of freedom may vary due to missing data.) Results of the regression analyses demonstrated that the pre-to-post differences were significant for the depression scale ($F[2, 642] = 5.86, p < .05$). Differences between baseline and postelection change scores for the PTSD scale were also significant ($F[1, 649] = 999, p < .0001$). Differences between baseline and postelection change scores for the generalized anxiety scale were significant (with ($F [1, 640 = 606, p < .001$). Finally, the pre-to-post change scores for the whole-symptom scale were also statistically significant ($F [1, 624] = 700, p < .0001$).

Sex, race, and age were entered simultaneously as predictors of each change score. Race and age had F statistics of less than 1 and were removed from the model. Sex, however, was a significant predictor of all four pre-to-post change scores, with women reporting greater changes in depression, PTSD, anxiety, and total symptoms than did men. The addition of sex to the regression equations, however, accounted for less than 1 percent of the variance of each of the four scales. Table V offers summaries of these regression analyses.

■ ■ ■ ■ ■ ■ ■ ■ ■

# Notes

*Notes to Chapter 1*

1. For descriptions of campaigns and nonelectoral conflicts related to equal rights for LGBs elsewhere, see Bradley 1992; Conrad 1983; Davies 1982; Douglass 1997; Eastland 1996a; Ehrlich 1992; Haider-Markel and Meier 1996; McCorkle and Most 1997a; Sarbin 1996; Smith 1997.

2. One other statewide anti-gay ballot issue, albeit with a different focus, had taken place. In 1977, Californians voted by a three-to-two margin to defeat the Briggs Initiative which would have prohibited openly gay people from teaching in the state's public schools (Miller 1995). In addition, on the same day as the Amendment 2 election in Colorado, Oregonians defeated a statewide anti-LGB ballot measure. This ballot issue, Measure 9, was more egregiously far-reaching than Amendment 2. The Oregon campaign relied on much of the same official campaign materials as did Colorado for Family Values (Chew 1993b; Douglass 1997). If anything, though, Oregon's campaign grew even more heated than did Colorado's (e.g., Bull and Gallagher 1996; Sullivan 1992). One reason for this difference may have been the nature of Measure 9 itself. The measure grouped LGB orientations with pedophilia, sadism, and masochism. According to Herek,

> Among its many expected effects, Oregon's Measure 9 could have done the following: required public libraries in Oregon to remove books presenting the view that homosexuality is not wrong or unnatural, required public schools to teach that homosexuality is perverse and wrong, barred programs that provide counseling for gay and lesbian young people in developing a healthy understanding of

their sexuality, and prevented state property or facilities from being used by any groups or individuals that oppose discrimination against gay people or that do not condemn homosexuality. (Herek 1994:97–98)

While Measure 9 was defeated at the polls in 1992, a series of efforts to reinstate anti-LGB laws at the state and local levels followed (Chew 1993a, b; J. Gallagher 1994; Gay-Rights Opponents 1993; Harris 1994; Steele 1995).

3. Epistemology refers to the issue of how knowledge is acquired. Salient questions within the epistemological domain are: what is knowledge, how is knowledge attained, and what standards do we use to consider something as knowledge?

4. For more extensive critiques of positivist epistemologies, see Gergen (1979), Harding (1986), Koch (1981), Leary (1979), Morawski (1988), Polkinghorne (1983), and Sampson (1978).

5. For discussions of the difficulty of obtaining representative samples of LGBs, see Badgett (1997); Harry (1986); and Herek (1998).

6. Many positivists would hold that self-reported data of any kind are suspect since people cannot be expected to know themselves with sufficient depth and accuracy to provide reliable data. According to the extremes of this view, it is science and not the individual that must be the final arbiter of the person's experience.

7. Psychologists typically speak of memory in a way that belies an unspoken assumption of realism—that is, the assumption that a real, extralinguistic, observable, measurable world exists. That reality, in turn, can be used to verify or challenge the goodness of an individual's memory. By acknowledging the elusiveness of memory, I do not wish to suggest that the "real world" is any less elusive. Memory, imperfect as it may be by positivist standards, seems to serve most of us well enough most of the time.

8. Within a positivist framework, the use of a standardized instrument(s) would have been preferable to using DSM-III-R criteria to explore the levels of symptomatology. DSM-III-R criteria were designed to be used for clinical interview and observation rather than as a paper-and-pencil measure. Even within the positivist framework, it is necessary to take several factors into account in order to consider the use of DSM-III-R criteria, as opposed to a standardized instrument, in its full perspective. First, the measure of reliability for each of the four scales was high enough to be acceptable for research purposes. In addition, a very high cutoff was required for any of the DSM-III-R symptoms to be considered to be present. Only symptoms endorsed at levels of 8, 9, or 10 ("often" or "very often") on the 10-point scale were considered to be present. This represents a far more stringent use of DSM-III-R criteria than is mandated by the DSM system or is customary. When instruments based on DSM criteria have been used to assess trauma-related symptoms, the form and content of the items have been quite similar to the items in standardized measures (Kilpatrick et al. 1989).

9. An extensive discussion of social constructionism is beyond the scope of this book. For further information, see Berger and Luckmann (1966), Bohan (1990),

Gergen (1985), Giorgi (1970), Hare-Mustin and Marecek (1988, 1990), and Sampson (1993a).

### Notes to Chapter 2

1. I do not mean to suggest that qualitative researchers are unique in affecting their studies and that more positivistly inclined researchers are exempt from exerting a personal influence on their studies. All researchers use themselves as tools to formulate questions and methods and to collect, analyze, and interpret results. Their personal characteristics can and do influence the empirical process every step of the way. Perhaps the two most significant differences between positivist and qualitative researchers are that the former typically downplay the effects of personal characteristics in their research while the latter more often explicitly consider these personal effects, and that the influence of personal effects on the research may often be more subtle in positivist studies than in qualitative ones.

2. The use of multiple researchers—what Adler and Adler (1987:21) have called a "multiperspectival view"—is not predicated on a positivist position that espouses the use of multiple observers to control for or to correct one another's subjective bias (e.g., Flick 1992). In fact, the use of this approach is designed "to counter the positivist presupposition of a uniform and objective social reality" (Sarbin and Kitsuse, 1994:8). It is useful precisely because we have no access to a uniform and objective social reality. It is because of that absence that we use multiple researchers who can identify one another's person and position vis-à-vis the data to be understood (Haraway 1988).

### Notes to Chapter 3

1. Somewhere early in the process, one of us referred to our coding team members as "coders." This term hardly did justice to the difficulty or the intensity of the work we did together. Nonetheless, we used it throughout the project and in our separate narratives about our experiences on the team. So I use it here.

2. To create this numbered format and for other manipulations of the data, we used a software package, Ethnograph (Seidel, Kjolseth, and Seymour 1988), available from Qualis Research Associates, P.O. Box 2070, Amherst, Mass. 01004.

3. In fact, some qualitative approaches—notably some forms of content analysis—use frequencies of terms as a major component of qualitative analysis.

4. Those familiar with the notion of the hermeneutic circle will see parallels between that concept and the macroscopic/microscopic analogy I have used here. For discussions of the hermeneutic circle, see Dilthey 1976; Giorgi 1970; Habermas 1971; Morgan 1989; Ricoeur 1981; Rubovits-Seitz 1986; Silvern 1988; Tappan 1997; and Way 1998.

### Notes to Chapter 4

1. While our team ultimately rejected the grief framework, it emerged later

when composer Bob McDowell used it as the structure for an oratorio based on this research. The oratorio is discussed in chapter 11.

2. It is interesting to note that I chose four comments to illustrate how mistrust can develop into hypervigilance, three of which were penned by men and three by people of color. My selections were based on the comments themselves and how well they conveyed the theme under discussion, not on the demographics of the respondents. I wonder if the demographic representation conveys something of importance about the mistrust-hypervigilance theme. Gay men may well be more attentive to the need to assess the potential for danger from heterosexuals, as they report more public harassment and violence based specifically on their sexual orientation than do lesbians (Berrill 1992). Similarly, LGBs of color report greater levels of victimization than do white LGBs (Berrill 1992). It seems plausible that gay and bisexual men (in contrast to lesbians and bisexual women) and LGBs of color (in contrast to white LGBs) needed to be especially alert to signs of possible danger posed by heterosexuals, particularly in the aftermath of Amendment 2's passage.

### Notes to Chapter 5

1. Our coding team's observation about linguistic differences between the ACFV and ACHRIST codes on the one hand, and the AHET, AMEDIA, APROC, and ASTATE codes on the other, illustrates one of the paradoxes about qualitative analysis that uses codes to delineate themes in the data. Each code has to stand alone and be understood on its own merits. However, a code can also be elucidated by its similarities to and differences from other codes. ACFV is like ACHRIST in one respect, but it differs from the other anger codes on this same dimension. Each code is understood alone and is simultaneously understood as part of the whole data set. Because codes have the reciprocal ability to elucidate one another it is important for coders to be thinking about the whole even as they are focused on the specific.

2. While Colorado for Family Values is not on record as a Christian organization and its spokespeople sometimes decry a religious link, in fact CFV has strong religious ties, both in Colorado and elsewhere in the country (Booth 1993b; Meyer and Woodward 1993).

3. As we saw examples of this being played out over and over in comments, we asked ourselves an unanswerable question: When our respondents' angry statements so clearly reflected (their construals of) the systems to which their anger was directed, were the respondents not demonstrating that they were in the throes of those very systems? Put another way: the respondent's use of the perpetrator's concepts suggested that the victim was held in the perpetrator's sway. One is reminded of Audre Lorde's dictum, "The master's tools will never dismantle the master's house (Lorde 1984:110).

4. The reader may have noticed that the angry comments cited are disproportionately from women. When we correlated the coded comments with the demo-

graphic data, we were all surprised to find our gender-role expectations significantly challenged: women were overrepresented in making angry comments.

5. In a couple of instances, respondents generalized from the limited class of Christians who had promoted the amendment not only to all Christians but to all religions. This generalization underscores the thoroughly Christian-centered nature of all the comments related specifically to religion. On the one hand, this generalization made sense, given CFV's ties to the Christian right. At the same time, the exclusive focus on Christianity was also consistent with the broader cultural tendency of Americans to ignore the presence and role in this country of religions other than Christianity.

6. In fact, a significant number of Christians took public stands in opposition to Amendment 2. Literature from EPOColorado, the campaign against the amendment, was endorsed by a number of religious groups, including parishes, interfaith groups, and conferences of various churches (EPOColorado 1992). In addition, other campaign materials carried the names of several hundred clergy opposed to the amendment.

7. Also called lateral hostility, horizontal oppression refers to the negative interactions between and among members of an oppressed group that are rooted in and express the oppressive attitudes to that group by society in general. The concept is addressed more thoroughly in chapter 6 in the context of codes explicating LGBs' relationships with one another and their communities. Popular expositions of horizontal oppression can be found in Hardy 1997; Lobel 1997; Osborn 1996; Stevens 1992; Vaid 1995. More academic discussions of internalized homophobia are available in Batts 1989; Bickelhaupt 1995; Brown 1986; Gonsiorek 1995; Kominars 1995; Malyon 1982; Margolies, Becker, and Jackson-Brewer 1987; Meyer and Dean 1998; Shidlo 1994; and Sophie 1987.

8. The prominence of verbal harassment in the reports of LGBs in the survey is consistent with its prominence in larger quantified samples of LGBs (e.g., Berrill 1992).

9. That gay people viewed the campaign and election as an aggressive act by CFV is not surprising. However, it is ironic, in view of CFV's claim throughout the campaign and afterward, including in its leaders' testimonies in district court, that Amendment 2 was designed to counter "militant gay aggression" in Colorado (Keen and Goldberg, 1998:178).

10. Many of the comments assumed that the media had the potential to be fundamentally "objective," an assertion that has been called into question by some media theorists and practitioners as well as by philosophers (for example, Alwood 1996; Dines and Humez 1995; McQuail 1994).

### Notes to Chapter 6

1. In reference to the qualitative data, we did not assume that we could conclusively identify the presence or absence of a PTSD symptom solely on the basis of a respondent's comment. Here we were looking for indications of traumatic

symptomatology within a phenomenological perspective rather than within a formal diagnostic framework. The diagnostic framework was the focus of the quantitative part of study, the results of which are given in Appendix C.

2. The truth of Sylvie's statement had been foreshadowed by a phone call I had received while the surveys were being distributed for this research. A gay man from Denver called and asked that I send a copy of the survey to his therapist. I agreed to do so and asked for the reason for his request. He explained that he had been in therapy with this person for some time and that he had "been doing better" until the fall. At that time, he had felt worse and neither he nor his therapist had been able to understand why. It was only when he was filling out the survey that he realized he had begun to feel worse just after the election. He had since spoken with his therapist about his new insight and she apparently agreed that the election had had a very negative impact on him.

3. At the time data were collected for this study, the diagnostic manual in general use was DSM-III-R (American Psychiatric Association 1987). All specific references to DSM post-traumatic stress disorder rely on that edition—rather than on any later edition—of the manual.

4. Because this research focused on the reactions of LGBs to Amendment 2, the perspective of the members of various groups—heterosexuals, the voters, and others—that might have occupied witness roles before and after the election have been omitted. Understanding the roles of witnesses from their own perspective is worthy of exploration, and has been the focus of other research (Russell 1996; Russell and Bohan 1999a). Of central importance to that perspective is the dehumanizing effect that the failure to act as a witness often has on the witnesses themselves (Staub 1993).

5. Our choice of the code name BARRIERS indicates that during the coding process the team shared respondents' assumption that divisions inevitably represented negative forces in the LGB community. The BARRIERS code originally referred to barriers to a (unified) community, as we agreed with many of the respondents that a unified LGB community response was necessary. Some of us on the coding team would question that assumption now, especially in the reflective aftermath of working on a project in which differences became strengths rather than barriers to the goal—whether that goal be defined as conducting research or community strength.

6. The assimilationist (or accommodationist) position emphasizes the sameness between LGBs and heterosexuals and argues for the full integration of LGBs into the larger society. This position stands in counterdistinction to the separatist or queer position, which emphasizes the differences between lesbian, gay, bisexual, and transgendered people (LGBT) and heterosexuals and argues that LGB people and politics challenge orthodox heterosexual ideologies in important ways. For more information, see Bohan and Russell (1999b), D'Emilio (1983), Epstein (1987), and Gamson (1998).

7. Team members had had experiences as members of marginalized groups or

by failing to conform to the expectations of high-power groups. Each of us contributed our personal expertise and efforts, and we all learned from one another. An important tone for the discussions of internalized oppression was borrowed from my participation in a variety of workshops conducted by VISIONS (68 Park Avenue, Cambridge, Mass. 02138; 617–876–9257). These workshops focused most particularly on undoing racism but inevitably gave some of their attention to other forms of social oppression, including homophobia and heterosexism. One of the strengths of the VISIONS format was the opportunity to work on internalized oppression in its various manifestations.

8. We used an overinclusive definition of internalized homophobia, preferring to make inaccurate inferences about the presence of IH rather than missing IH when it was present. Consider this summary by Bohan (1996:95) of the variety of manifestations of IH:

> Internalized homophobia takes many forms. At its most blatant, it is reflected in self-hatred specifically attached to one's LGB identity. The desire to renounce homophilia and somehow become acceptably heterosexual also reflects a condemnation of this identity. Internalized homophobia may also be expressed more indirectly—through low self-esteem, isolation, self-destructive behaviors, substance abuse, even suicide. Behavioral patterns that reaffirm one's inferiority may also be indicative—self-defeating behaviors, tolerance for prejudicial treatment, the sense that one deserves ill fortune. Remaining closeted may demonstrate internalized homonegativity in that it reveals feelings of shame at one's true identity.

9. Some writers on stigma theory use the term "normalization" rather than assimilation. Becker and Arnold, for example, refer to normalization as "the way in which stigmatized individuals adapt themselves to society by attempting to reduce their variance from cultural norms" (Becker and Arnold 1986:50–51).

10. This strategy of arguing that sexuality is private and no one else's business is akin to—or a variation on—efforts to conceal a stigmatized condition (Goffman 1963).

11. The language indicative of the internal and external aspects of human experience has undergone significant critiques. See especially Sampson (1993a). While its use here does not reflect those critiques, it is clear that my analysis in this section has been informed by them. In emphasizing the importance of a "balance between the internal and external" in matters of homonegativity, I effectively argue that the presumed boundary between the two dimensions is an artifact of that very language rather than something that exists "out there" and is inevitable.

### Notes to Chapter 7

1. In reality, there is a range of opinions about the relationship between qualitative and quantitative research in the abstract, some holding the position that the two methods are complementary and others contending that they are rooted in

such different epistemologies that no commerce between them is expected or desirable. See, for example, Rabinowitz and Weseen 1997.

### Notes to Chapter 8

1. In the PRIMARY code analysis, we have focused on relationships in which both members were women or both were men. In fact, a few statements with the PRIMARY code came from bisexual individuals who were involved in relationships with members of the other sex.

2. Roy Romer, Colorado's governor in 1992, was a vocal opponent of Amendment 2 before and after the election. Wellington Webb, then mayor of Denver, also opposed the amendment. At the time of the election, the cities of Aspen, Boulder, and Denver had equal rights ordinances that included protection against discrimination based on sexual orientation. Soon after the election, the cities of Telluride and Crested Butte enacted equal protection provisions covering sexual orientation, all clearly in defiance of Amendment 2 (Foes Applaud 1993).

3. The U.S. Supreme Court's decision, delivered by Justice Kennedy, retrospectively and explicitly validated the view of so many gay people who had experienced and characterized Amendment 2 as a hateful action. In using the word "animus," Justice Kennedy implicitly endorsed the validity of the slightly modified campaign slogan: "Animus is not a family value."

4. Most of the members of our coding team had not had the opportunity to interpret respondents' statements about ourselves and our work before. Nonetheless, the two of us with formal clinical training and experience had previously encountered a similar dynamic in working with clients' feelings toward us in psychotherapy.

5. This remark is meant as an observation about LGB communities in general. In Colorado Springs, the home of the author of this comment, there were a variety of nonpolitical (at least in the narrow sense of the word "political") and cultural events being organized during the campaign and after the election.

6. This example serves as an excellent reminder of how data that stand out as "discrepant" in a qualitative set can be very useful. In quantitative data sets, such "outliers" can be problematic and sometimes require extra statistical manipulation or are dropped from analyses. In qualitative data sets, however, the anomalous datum often alerts researchers to the presence of an undetected central theme, elucidates a central theme, or brings up a whole new understanding of the data. Far from being problematic, these unexpected data often promote new understandings of the data set as a whole.

7. Related peripherally to the ISOLATE code was the way some respondents seemed to use withdrawal from their world as one side of the intrusion-constriction cycle of traumatic reactions (Herman 1992). That issue is discussed more extensively in the RECOVER section later in this chapter.

8. Repeating quotations in the discussions of more than one code—beyond the limited number of times in the book thus far—may serve a pedagogical purpose. By quoting participants' comments to illustrate only one code, I have made an ef-

fort both to bring in as many participants' voices as possible and to keep the narrative interesting for readers. I may inadvertently have created a false impression in the process. Encountering statements that qualified for only one code was actually rare in this data set. Most lines of data had multiple codes, some many codes; a few outstripped the eight codes allowed by the software program we used. The fact that most statements were complex enough to warrant multiple codes was yet another reason why it was so helpful to have a team of coders. It would be easy for a single coder to identify one applicable code and miss others. Having several coders helped us to see the layered nature of respondents' statements.

9. The interplay of legal and psychological safety was very apparent in this comment. The gay man who wrote it did not live in a city that had an antidiscrimination ordinance. Legally, he was susceptible to being fired without recourse whether or not Amendment 2 took effect. It was not clear from his statement whether or not he or his employers were aware of the legal realities. Certainly, in my contacts with LGBs around the state before and after the election, I encountered many who did not know whether they were covered by existing ordinances. There was some anecdotal indication that many heterosexuals were also unaware of the legal situation. Among other issues, this man's statement spoke to a belief shared by many LGBs that if Amendment 2 had been in effect, it would have offered psychological permission to fire LGBs even when no legal "permission" was necessary.

10. See footnote 9. The same considerations apply here.

11. See footnote 9. The same considerations apply here.

12. Cain (1991) identified six motivations associated with the decision to come out. The first is therapeutic disclosure, in which individuals act to enhance their self-esteem and social support. Relationship-building disclosure, the second, occurs in the context of efforts to improve a relationship by removing the secrecy about sexual orientation from it. Third, problem-solving disclosures are designed to solve a particular problem created by a person's secrecy about his or her sexual orientation. Fourth, preventative disclosure is an LGB individual's effort to disclose sexual orientation in an effort to reduce the potential for a problem to surface later. Fifth, spontaneous disclosures occur without intention through, for example, slips of the tongue. Finally, political disclosure is intended to make LGB individuals and issues more visible at the social level.

13. Throughout the OUTM code, coming out and being out are used in the sense of their interpersonal meaning.

14. Many respondents' statements about coming out despite significant fears were an inspirational illustration to us that courage is not something one has but something one does.

### Notes to Chapter 11

1. As I have acknowledged before (Russell and Bohan 1999a), the language of "returning data to the community" is not altogether fitting, implying as it does

that there has been some break in the community's ownership of and access to the data. In fact, I have never left the community and, therefore, neither has this study. The language of returning data to the community is concise and conveys one aspect of the process—that is, the data certainly originated in the LGB community. It fails to convey another aspect: the data never really left.

2. It warrants noting that the city and educational institutions approached me for consultations only because they knew me through my social and political activism. This indicates that social scientists who want their research results to be useful must be visibly active in their communities. They must also be willing to expect no fees for their work.

3. Descriptions of these projects are also available in Russell and Bohan 1999a.

4. "Inner Journeys, Public Stands," Barbara Jabaily, Producer/Director and Glenda Russell, Co-Producer/Interviewer." Available from G. Russell.

# References

Adam, B. S. (1992). Sex and Caring among Men: Impact of AIDS on Gay People. In K. Plummer (ed.), *Modern Homosexualities: Fragments of Lesbian and Gay Experience* (pp. 175–83). London: Routledge.

Adler, P. A., and P. Adler (1987). *Membership Roles in Field Research*. Newbury Park, Calif.: Sage.

Ainlay, S. C., L. M. Coleman, and G. Becker (1986). Stigma Reconsidered. In S. C. Ainlay, G. Becker, and L. M. Coleman (eds.), *The Dilemma of Differences: A Multidisciplinary View of Stigma* (pp. 1–13). New York: Plenum.

Albee, G. W. (1981). Politics, Power, Prevention, and Social Change. In J. M. Jaffe and G. W. Albee (eds.), *Prevention through Political Action and Social Change* (pp. 3–24). Hanover, N.H.: University Press of New England.

———. (1990). The Futility of Psychotherapy. *Journal of Mind and Behavior, 11,* 369–84.

Altheide, D. L., and J. M. Johnson (1994). Criteria for Assessing Interpretive Validity in Qualitative Research. In N. K. Denzin and Y. S. Lincoln (eds.), *Handbook of Qualitative Research* (pp. 485–99). Thousand Oaks, Calif.: Sage.

Alwood, E. (1996). *Straight News: Gays, Lesbians, and the News Media*. Thousand Oaks, Calif.: Sage.

Amabile, T. M. (1983). The Social Psychology of Creativity. *Journal of Personality and Social Psychology, 45,* 357–76.

American Psychiatric Association (1987). *Diagnostic and Statistical Manual of Mental Disorders* (3d ed. revised). Washington, D.C.: Author.

Anti-Gay Adviser Stirs Controversy. (1985, August 19). *San Francisco Chronicle*, p. 7.

Badgett, M. V. L. (1997). Beyond Biased Samples: Challenging the Myths on the Economic Status of Lesbians and Gay Men. In A. Gluckman and B. Reed (eds.), *Homoeconomics: Capitalism, Community, and Lesbian and Gay Life* (pp. 65–71). New York: Routledge.

Bakan, D. (1977). Political Factors in the Development of American Psychology. *Annals of the New York Academy of Sciences, 291*, 222–32.

Ballot Wording. (1992, October 11). (Boulder) *Daily Camera*, p. 3A.

Bantel, K. A., and S. E. Jackson (1989). Top Management Innovations in Banking: Does the Composition of the Top Team Make a Difference? *Strategic Management Journal, 10*, 107–24.

Banyard, V. L., and K. E. Miller (1998). The Powerful Potential of Qualitative Research for Community Psychology. *American Journal of Community Psychology, 26*, 485–505.

Bard, M., and D. Sangrey (1979). *The Crime Victim's Book*. New York: Basic Books.

Bartunek, J. M., and M. R. Louis (1996). *Insider/Outsider Team Research*. Thousand Oaks, Calif.: Sage.

Batts, V. A. (1989). "Modern Racism: New Melody for the Same Old Tunes." Unpublished manuscript. Cambridge, Mass.: VISIONS.

Beardslee, W. R. (1989). The Role of Self-Understanding in Resilient Individuals: The Development of a Perspective. *American Journal of Orthopsychiatry, 59*, 266–79.

Becker, G., and R. Arnold (1986). Stigma as a Social and Cultural Construct. In S. C. Ainlay, G. Becker, and L. M. Coleman (eds.), *The Dilemma of Difference: A Multidisciplinary View of Stigma* (pp. 39–57). New York: Plenum.

Becker, H. S. (1986). *Writing for Social Scientists: How to Start and Finish Your Thesis, Book, or Article*. Chicago: University of Chicago Press.

Bennett, W. L., and M. Edelman (1985). Toward a New Political Narrative. *Journal of Communication, 35*, 156–71.

Berger, P., and T. Luckmann (1966). *The Social Construction of Reality*. New York: Anchor.

Berlet, C. (ed.). (1995). *Eyes Right! Challenging the Right Wing Backlash*. Boston: South End Press.

Berrill, K. T. (1992). Anti-Gay Violence and Victimization in the United States: An Overview. In G. M. Herek and K. T. Berrill (eds.), *Hate Crimes: Confronting Violence against Lesbians and Gay Men* (pp. 19–45). Newbury Park, Calif.: Sage.

Bickelhaupt, E. E. (1995). Alcoholism and Drug Abuse in Gay and Lesbian Persons: A Review of Incidence Studies. *Journal of Gay and Lesbian Social Services, 2*, 5–14.

Blumenfeld, W., and D. Raymond (1993). *Looking at Gay and Lesbian Life* (2d ed.). Boston: Beacon.

Bohan, J. S. (1990). Social Constructionism and Contextual History: An Expanded Approach to the History of Psychology. *Teaching of Psychology, 17*, 82–89.

———. (1992). Prologue: Re-Viewing Psychology, Re-Placing Women—An End Searching for a Means. In J. S. Bohan (ed.), *Seldom Seen, Rarely Heard: Women's Place in Psychology* (pp. 9–53). Boulder, Colo.: Westview.

———. (1993). Regarding Gender: Essentialism, Constructionism, and Feminist Psychology. *Psychology of Women Quarterly, 17*, 5–21.

———. (1996). *Psychology and Sexual Orientation: Coming to Terms.* New York: Routledge.

Bohan, J. S., and G. M. Russell (1999a). Conceptual frameworks. In J. S. Bohan and G. M. Russell, *Conversations about Psychology and Sexual Orientation* (pp. 11–30). New York: New York University Press.

———. (1999b). *Conversations about Psychology and Sexual Orientation.* New York: New York University Press.

Booth, M. (1992a, September 27). Controversial Researcher Focus of Rights Debate. *Denver Post*, p. 6A.

———. (1992b, November 5). Therapists Hear Gays Pour Out Their Anguish and Anger. *Denver Post*, p. 9A.

———. (1993a, January 7). Child Watches "Bashing" of Her Lesbian Mother. *Denver Post*, pp. 1B, 5B.

———. (1993b, March 23). The Man Who Sold Amendment 2. *Denver Post Magazine*, pp. 10–14.

Bradford, J., and C. Ryan (1987). *National Lesbian Health Care Survey. Mental Health Implications.* Washington, D.C.: National Lesbian and Gay Health Foundation.

Bradley, R. (1992). The Abnormal Affair of "*The Normal Heart.*" *Text and Performance Quarterly, 12*, 362–71.

Brewer, M. B. (1995). Managing Diversity: The Role of Social Identities. In S. E. Jackson and M. N. Ruderman (eds.), *Diversity in Work Teams: Research Paradigms for a Changing Workplace* (pp. 47–68). Washington, D.C.: American Psychological Association.

Brown, L. S. (1986). Confronting Internalized Oppression. *Journal of Homosexuality, 12*, 99–107.

Brydon-Miller, M., and D. L. Tolman (1997). Engaging the Process of Transformation. *Journal of Social Issues, 53*, 803–10.

Bull, C., and J. Gallagher (1996). *Perfect Enemies: The Religious Right, the Gay Movement, and the Politics of the 1990s.* New York: Crown.

Bullis, C., and B. W. Bach (1996). Feminism and Disenfranchisement: Listening Beyond the "Other." In E. B. Ray (ed.), *Communication and Disenfranchisement: Social Health Issues and Implications* (pp. 3–28). Mahwah, N.J.: Lawrence Erlbaum.

Burt, M. R., and B. L. Katz (1987). Dimensions of Recovery from Rape: Focus on Growth Outcomes. *Journal of Interpersonal Violence, 2*, 57–81.

Buss, A. R. (1975). The Emerging Field of the Sociology of Psychological Knowledge. *American Psychologist, 30*, 988–1002.

Cain, R. (1991). Stigma Management and Gay Identity Development. *Social Work, 36*, 67–73.

Callaway, H. (1992). Ethnography and Experience: Gender Implications in Fieldwork and Texts. In J. Okely and H. Callaway (eds.), *Anthropology and Autobiography* (pp. 29–40). New York: Routledge, Chapman and Hall.

Campbell, D. T., and J. C. Stanley (1963). *Experimental and Quasi-Experimental Designs for Research*. Chicago: Rand McNally.

Caplan, N., and S. D. Nelson (1973). On Being Useful: The Nature and Consequences of Psychological Research on Social Problems. *American Psychologist, 28*, 199–211.

Cecchin, G. (1992). Constructing Therapeutic Possibilities. In S. McNamee and K. J. Gergen (eds.), *Therapy as Social Construction* (pp. 86–95). Thousand Oaks, Calif.: Sage.

Charmaz, K., and R. C. Mitchell, Jr. (1997). The Myth of Silent Authorship: Self, Substance, and Style in Ethnographic Writing. In R. Hertz (ed.), *Reflexivity and Voice* (pp. 193–215). Thousand Oaks, Calif.: Sage.

Chew, S. (1993a, February/March). Ding, Dong, Mabon Calling. *Out*, 40–47.

———. (1993b, February/March). Rocky Mountain Low, *Out*, 44.

Cohen, S., and T. A. Wills (1985). Stress, Social Support, and the Buffering Hypothesis. *Psychological Bulletin, 98*, 310–57.

Coleman, L. M. (1986). Stigma: An Enigma Demystified. In S. C. Ainlay, G. Becker, and L. M. Coleman (eds.), *The Dilemma of Differences: A Multidisciplinary View of Stigma* (pp. 211–32). New York: Plenum.

Colker, D. (1993, June). Anti-Gay Video Highlights Church's Agenda. *The Equal Times*. Denver, Colo.: Equality Colorado, pp. 3–4. (Reprinted from *Los Angeles Times*, February 22, 1993).

Collins, P. H. (1991). *Black Feminist Thought: Knowledge, Consciousness, and the Politics of Empowerment*. New York: Routledge.

Colorado for Family Values (1992a). *Equal Rights—Not Special Rights!* Campaign tabloid. Colorado Springs: Author.

———. (1992b). *What's Wrong with "Gay Rights"?* You *Be the Judge!* Campaign brochure. Colorado Springs: Author.

Conrad, C. (1983). The Rhetoric of the Moral Majority: An Analysis of Romantic Form. *Quarterly Journal of Speech, 69*, 159–70.

Conrad, P. (1997). Public Eyes and Private Genes: Historical Frames, News Constructions, and Social Problems. *Social Problems, 44*, 139–54.

Cornett, L. (1992, October 11). Amendment 2 Controversy: Polls Show State Split Over Homosexual Rights. (Boulder) *Daily Camera*, 1A, 3A.

Cox, T., Jr. (1995). The Complexity of Diversity: Challenges and Directions for Future Research. In S. E. Jackson and M. N. Ruderman (eds.) *Diversity in Work*

*Teams: Research Paradigms for a Changing Workplace* (pp. 235–46). Washington, D.C.: American Psychological Association.

Crawford, M., and J. Marecek (1989). Psychology Reconstructs the Female, 1968–1988. *Psychology of Women Quarterly, 13,* 147–65.

Crocker, J., and N. Lutsky (1986). Stigma and the Dynamics of Social Cognition. In S. C. Ainlay, G. Becker, and L. M. Coleman (eds.), *The Dilemma of Difference: A Multidisciplinary View of Stigma* (pp. 95–121). New York: Plenum.

Crocker, J., and B. Major (1989). Social Stigma and Self-Esteem: The Self-Protective Properties of Stigma. *Psychological Review, 96,* 608–30.

D'Augelli, A. R. (1994). Lesbian and Gay Male Development: Steps Toward an Analysis of Lesbians' and Gay Men's Lives. In B. Greene and G. M. Herek (eds.), *Lesbian and Gay Psychology: Theory, Research, and Clinical Applications* (pp. 118–32). Thousand Oaks, Calif.: Sage.

D'Augelli, A. R., and L. D. Garnets (1995). Lesbian, Gay, and Bisexual Communities. In A. R. D'Augelli and C. J. Patterson (eds.), *Lesbian, Gay, and Bisexual Identities over the Lifespan: Psychological Perspectives* (pp. 293–320). New York: Oxford University Press.

Davies, C. (1982). Sexual Taboos and Social Boundaries. *American Journal of Sociology, 87,* 1032–63.

D'Emilio, J. (1983). *Sexual Politics, Sexual Communities: The Making of a Homosexual Minority in the United States, 1940–1970.* Chicago: University of Chicago Press.

de Monteflores, C. (1986). Notes on the Management of Difference. In T. Stein and C. Cohen (eds.), *Contemporary Perspectives on Psychotherapy with Lesbians and Gay Men* (pp. 73–101). New York: Plenum.

Denzin, N. K. (1994). The Art and Politics of Interpretation. In N. K. Denzin and Y. S. Lincoln (eds.), *Handbook of Qualitative Research* (pp. 500–515). Thousand Oaks, Calif.: Sage.

Denzin, N. K., and Y. S. Lincoln (eds.). (1994a). *Handbook of Qualitative Research.* Thousand Oaks, Calif.: Sage.

———. (1994b). Introduction: Entering the Field of Qualitative Research. In N. K. Denzin and Y. S. Lincoln (eds.), *Handbook of Qualitative Research* (pp. 1–17). Thousand Oaks, Calif.: Sage.

———. (1994c). Strategies of Inquiry. In N. K. Denzin and Y. S. Lincoln (eds.), *Handbook of Qualitative Research* (pp. 199–208). Thousand Oaks, Calif.: Sage.

de Raismes, J. (1993). Homosexual Rights: Constructive Responses to Colorado's Amendment 2. Working Paper 93–27. Conflict Research Consortium, University of Colorado, Boulder.

DeVault, M. L. (1997). Personal Writing in Social Research: Issues of Production and Interpretation. In R. Hertz (ed.), *Reflexivity and Voice* (pp. 216–28). Thousand Oaks, Calif.: Sage.

Dilthey, W. L. (1976). *Selected Writings*. Cambridge, UK: Cambridge University Press. (Originally published in 1900).

Dines, G., and J. M. Humez (eds.). (1995). *Gender, Race and Class in Media*. Thousand Oaks, Calif.: Sage.

DiPlacido, J. (1998). Minority Stress among Lesbians, Gay Men, and Bisexuals: A Consequence of Heterosexism, Homophobia, and Stigmatization. In G. M. Herek (ed.), *Stigma and Sexual Orientation: Understanding Prejudice against Lesbians, Gay Men, and Bisexuals* (pp. 138–59). Thousand Oaks, Calif.: Sage.

Donovan, T., and S. Bowler (1997). Direct Democracy and Minority Rights: Opinions on Anti-Gay and Lesbian Ballot Initiatives. In S. L. Witt and S. McCorkle (eds.), *Anti-Gay Rights: Assessing Voter Initiatives* (pp. 107–25). Westport, Conn.: Praeger.

Douglass, D. (1997). Taking the Initiative: Anti-Homosexual Propaganda of the Oregon Citizens' Alliance. In S. L. Witt and S. McCorkle (eds.), *Anti-Gay Rights: Assessing Voter Initiatives* (pp. 17–32). Westport, Conn.: Praeger.

Dworkin, J., and D. Kaufer (1995). Social Services and Bereavement in the Lesbian and Gay Community. *Journal of Gay and Lesbian Social Services, 2*, 41–60.

Eastland, L. S. (1996a). Defending Identity: Courage and Compromise in Radical Right Contexts. In E. B. Ray (ed.), *Case Studies in Communication and Disenfranchisement: Applications to Social Health Issues* (pp. 3–14). Mahwah, N.J.: Lawrence Erlbaum.

———. (1996b). The Reconstruction of Identity: Strategies of the Oregon Citizens' Alliance. In E. B. Ray (ed.), *Communication and Disenfranchisement: Social Health Issues and Implications* (pp. 59–75). Mahwah, N.J.: Lawrence Erlbaum.

Ehrlich, H. J. (1992). The Ecology of Anti-Gay Violence. In G. M. Herek and K. T. Berrill (eds.), *Hate Crimes: Confronting Violence against Lesbians and Gay Men* (pp. 105–12). Newbury Park, Calif.: Sage.

Ehrlich, H. J., B. E. K. Larcom, and R. D. Purvis (1995). The Traumatic Impact of Ethnoviolence. In L. Lederer and K. Delgado (eds.), *The Price We Pay: The Case against Racist Speech, Hate Propaganda, and Pornography* (pp. 62–79). New York: Hill and Wang.

Ellis, C., C. E. Kiesinger, and L. M. Tillmann-Healy (1997). Interactive Interviewing: Talking about Emotional Experience. In R. Hertz (ed.), *Reflexivity and Voice* (pp. 119–40). Thousand Oaks, Calif.: Sage.

Ely, R. J. (1995). The Role of Dominant Identity and Experience in Organizational Work on Diversity. In S. E. Jackson and M. N. Ruderman (eds.), *Diversity in Work Teams: Research Paradigms for a Changing Workplace* (pp. 161–86). Washington, D.C.: American Psychological Association.

EPOColorado. (1992, August 21). *Voting No! These Organizations Have Resolved to Oppose Amendment 2*. Campaign brochure. Denver: Author.

Epstein, S. (1987). Gay Politics, Ethnic Identity: The Limits of Social Constructionism. *Socialist Review, 93,* 9–54.

Erickson, F. (1986). *Qualitative Methods.* In M. C. Wittrock (ed.). *Handbook of
Research on Teaching* (pp. 119–61). New York: Macmillan.

Erickson, K., and D. Stull (1998). *Doing Team Ethnography: Warnings and Advice.* Thousand Oaks, Calif.: Sage.

Family Research Institute (1992). *Medical Consequences of What Homosexuals Do.*
Brochure. Washington, D.C.: Author.

Fejes, F., and K. Petrich (1993). Invisibility, Homophobia, and Heterosexism: Lesbians, Gays, and the Media. *Critical Studies in Mass Communication, 10,*
396–422.

Feldman, M. S. (1995). *Strategies for Interpreting Qualitative Data.* Thousand
Oaks, Calif.: Sage.

Fernald, J. L. (1995). Interpersonal Heterosexism. In B. Lott and D. Maluso
(eds.), *The Social Psychology of Interpersonal Discrimination* (pp. 80–117). New
York: Guilford.

Fettner, A. G. (1985, September 23–29). The Evil That Men Do. *New York Native,* pp. 23–24.

Fine, M. (1994). Working the Hyphens: Reinventing Self and Other in Qualitative
Research. In N. K. Denzin and Y. S. Lincoln (eds.), *Handbook of Qualitative
Research* (pp. 70–82). Thousand Oaks, Calif.: Sage.

Finley, B. (1992, August 16). Poll Shows Anti-Gay Rights Measure Losing. *Denver Post,* pp. 1C, 6C.

Flanders, L. (1995). Hate on Tape: The Video Strategy of the Fundamentalist
Right. In C. Berlet (ed.), *Eyes Right! Challenging the Right Wing Backlash* (pp.
105–8). Boston: South End Press.

Flick, U. (1992). Triangulation Revisited: Strategy of Validation or Alternative?
*Journal for the Theory of Social Behavior, 22,* 175–97.

Foes Applaud; Backers Determined (1993, July 20). (Boulder) *Daily Camera,* pp.
1A, 3A.

Frank, J. (1993, September 26). Tracking Hate Crimes against Homosexuals.
(Boulder) *Daily Camera,* p. 3C.

Gadlin, H., and G. Ingle (1975). Through the One-Way Mirror: The Limits of Experimental Self-Reflection. *American Psychologist, 30,* 1003–9.

Gallagher, J. (1994, November 15). Anti-Gay Initiatives. *Advocate,* pp. 34–36, 38.

Gallagher, M. J. (1994). Amendment 2. *Law and Sexuality, 4,* 123–94.

Gamson, J. (1998). Must Identity Movements Self-Destruct? A Queer Dilemma.
In P. M. Nardi and B. E. Schneider (eds.), *Social Perspectives in Lesbian and Gay
Studies: A Reader* (pp. 589–604). New York: Routledge.

Ganellen, R. J., and P. H. Blaney (1984). Hardiness and Social Support as Moder-
ators of the Effects of Life Stress. *Journal of Personality and Social Psychology,
47,* 156–63.

Garnets, L., G. M. Herek, and B. Levy (1992). Violence and Victimization of Lesbians and Gay Men: Mental Health Consequences. In G. M. Herek and K. T. Berrill (eds.), *Hate Crimes: Confronting Violence against Lesbians and Gay Men* (pp. 207–26). Newbury Park, Calif.: Sage.

Garnets, L., and D. Kimmel (1991). Lesbian and Gay Male Dimensions in the Psychological Study of Human Diversity. In J. Goodchilds (ed.), *Psychological Perspectives on Human Diversity in America* (pp. 143–92). Washington, D.C.: American Psychological Association.

Gavin, J. (1992, July 14). Tactics of Gay Rights Foes Criticized. *Denver Post*, pp. 1B, 5B.

Gay-Rights Opponents Follow Colorado's Lead. (1993, April 3). *Rocky Mountain News*, p. 40A.

Gergen, K. J. (1973). Social Psychology as History. *Journal of Personality and Social Psychology, 26*, 309–20.

———. (1979). The Positivist Image in Social Psychological Theory. In A. Buss (ed.), *Psychology in Social Context* (pp. 193–212). New York: Irvington.

———. (1985). The Social Constructionist Movement in Modern Psychology. *American Psychologist, 40*, 266–75.

Gibbons, F. X. (1986). Stigma and Interpersonal Relationships. In S. C. Ainlay, G. Becker, and L. M. Coleman (eds.), *The Dilemma of Difference: A Multidisciplinary View of Stigma* (pp. 123–44). New York: Plenum.

Gibney, J. (1992, November 14). Suicide Prompts Funeral March. *Denver Post*, p. 3B.

Gibson, J. L., and K. L. Tedin (1988). The Etiology of Intolerance of Homosexual Politics. *Social Science Quarterly, 69*, 587–604.

Giorgi, A. (1970). *Psychology as Human Science*. New York: Harper and Row.

Godard, R. W. (1985). Bringing New Ideas to Light. *Management World, 14*, 8–11.

Goffman, E. (1963). *Stigma: Notes on the Management of Spoiled Identity*. Englewood Cliffs, N.J.: Prentice-Hall.

Gonsiorek, J. (1993, May). Testimony in Colorado: Treading the Fine Line between Scientific Rigor, Passion, and Social Justice. *American Psychological Association Division 44 Newsletter, 9* (1), 2.

Gonsiorek, J. C. (1995). Gay Male Identities: Concepts and Issues. In A. R. D'Augelli and C. J. Patterson (eds.), *Lesbian, Gay, and Bisexual Identities over the Lifespan* (pp. 24–47). New York: Oxford University Press.

Gottlieb, A., and V. Culver (1992, November 15). A House Divided? Influx of Religious Groups Rattles Springs. *Denver Post*, pp. 1C, 7C.

Gow, D. D. (1991). Collaboration in Development Consulting: Stooges, Hired Guns, or Musketeers. *Human Organization, 50*, 1–15.

Gross, L. (1991). Out of the Mainstream: Sexual Minorities and the Mass Media. *Journal of Homosexuality, 21*, 19–46.

Habermas, J. (1971). *Knowledge and Human Interest* (J. J. Shapiro, trans.). Boston: Beacon. (Originally published in 1968).

Haider-Markel, D. P., and K. J. Meier (1996). The Politics of Gay and Lesbian Rights: Expanding the Scope of the Conflict. *Journal of Politics, 58,* 332–49.

Hamilton, D. (1994). Traditions, Preferences, and Postures in Applied Qualitative Research. In N. K. Denzin and Y. S. Lincoln (eds.), *Handbook of Qualitative Research* (pp. 60–69). Thousand Oaks, Calif.: Sage.

Haraway, D. (1988). Situated Knowledges: The Science Question in Feminism and the Privilege of Partial Perspective. *Feminist Studies, 14,* 575–99.

Harding, S. (1986). *The Science Question in Feminism.* Ithaca, N.Y.: Cornell University Press.

Hardy, K. V. (1997, January). Not Quite Home: The Psychological Effects of Oppression. *In the Family,* pp. 6–8, 26.

Hare-Mustin, R., and J. Marecek (1988). The Meaning of Difference: Gender Theory, Postmodernism, and Psychology. *American Psychologist, 43,* 455–64.

———. (1990). *Making a Difference: Psychology and the Construction of Gender.* New Haven, Conn.: Yale University Press.

Harkavy, W. (1996, October 3–9). Slay It with a Smile. *Westword,* pp. 20–24, 26.

Harris, E. (1994, November). Seizing the Initiative. *Out,* pp. 102–6, 146, 148, 152.

Harry, J. (1986). Sampling Gay Men. *Journal of Sex Research, 22,* 21–34.

Herek, G. M. (1992a). Psychological Heterosexism, and Anti-Gay Violence: The Social Psychology of Bigotry and Bashing. In G. M. Herek and K. T. Berrill (eds.), *Hate Crimes: Confronting Violence against Lesbians and Gay Men* (pp. 149–69). Newbury Park, Calif.: Sage.

———. (1992b). The Social Context of Hate Crimes: Notes on Cultural Heterosexism. In G. M. Herek and K. T. Berrill (eds.), *Hate Crimes: Confronting Violence against Lesbians and Gay Men* (pp. 89–104). Newbury Park, Calif.: Sage.

———. (1994). Heterosexism, Hate Crimes, and the Law. In M.Costanzo and S. Oskamp (eds.), *Violence and the Law* (pp. 89–112). Thousand Oaks, Calif.: Sage.

———. (1995). Psychological Heterosexism in the United States. In A. R. D'Augelli and C. J. Patterson (eds.), *Lesbian, Gay, and Bisexual Identities over the Life Span* (pp. 320–46). New York: Oxford University Press.

———. (1996). Why Tell If You're Not Asked? Self-Disclosure, Intergroup Contact, and Heterosexuals' Attitudes toward Lesbians and Gay Men. In G. M. Herek, J. B. Jobe, and R. M. Carney (eds.), *Out in Force: Sexual Orientation and the Military* (pp. 197–225). Chicago: University of Chicago Press.

———. (1998). Bad Science in the Service of Stigma: A Critique of the Cameron Group's Survey Studies. In G. M. Herek (ed.), *Stigma and Sexual Orientation: Understanding Prejudice against Lesbians, Gay Men, and Bisexuals* (pp. 223–55). Thousand Oaks, Calif.: Sage.

Herman, D. (1997). *The Antigay Agenda; Orthodox Vision and the Christian Right.* Chicago: University of Chicago Press.

Herman, J. L. (1992). *Trauma and Recovery.* New York: Basic Books.

Hertz, R. (1997). Introduction: Reflexivity and Voice. In R. Hertz (ed.), *Reflexivity and Voice* (pp. vii–xviii). Thousand Oaks, Calif.: Sage.

Hobfoll, S. E., and J. R. Freedy (1990). The Availability and Effective Use of Social Support. *Journal of Social and Clinical Psychology, 9,* 91–103.

Hoffman, L. (1992). A Reflexive Stance for Family Therapy. In S. McNamee and K. J. Gergen (eds.), *Therapy as Social Construction* (pp. 7–24). Thousand Oaks, Calif.: Sage.

Holstein, J. A., and J. F. Gubrium (1994). Phenomenology, Ethnomethodology, and Interpretive Practice. In N. K. Denzin and Y. S. Lincoln (eds.), *Handbook of Qualitative Research* (pp. 262–72). Thousand Oaks, Calif.: Sage.

Jackson, S. E., and M. N. Ruderman (1995). Introduction: Perspectives for Understanding Diverse Work Teams. In S. E. Jackson and M. N. Ruderman (eds.), *Diversity in Work Teams: Research Paradigms for a Changing Workplace* (pp. 1–13). Washington, D.C.: American Psychological Association.

Janis, I. L. (1978). Groupthink. In W. E. Natemeyer (ed.), *Classics of Organizational Behavior* (pp. 156–64). Oak Park, Ill.: Moore Publishing.

Janoff-Bulman, R. (1992). *Shattered Assumptions: Towards a New Psychology of Trauma.* New York: Free Press.

Johnson, D. (1992, November 8). Colorado Homosexuals Feel Betrayed. *New York Times,* p. 19.

Jones, A. C. (1993). *Wade in the Water: The Wisdom of the Spirituals.* New York: Orbis.

Joseph, S., R. Williams, and W. Yule (1993). Changes in Outlook Following Disaster: The Preliminary Development of a Measure to Assess Positive and Negative Responses. *Journal of Traumatic Stress, 6,* 271–79.

Kast, V. (1994). *Joy, Inspiration, and Hope.* New York: Fromm.

Keen, L., and S. B. Goldberg (1998). *Strangers to the Law: Gay People on Trial.* Ann Arbor: University of Michigan Press.

Kilpatrick, D. G., and H. S. Resnick (1993). Post Traumatic Stress Disorder Associated with Exposure to Criminal Victimization in Clinical and Community Populations. In J. R. T. Davidson and E. B. Foa (eds.), *PTSD: DSM-IV and Beyond* (pp. 113–43). Washington, D.C.: American Psychiatric Association.

Kilpatrick, D. G., B. E. Saunders, A. Amick-McMullan, C. L. Best, L. J. Vernonen, and H. S. Resnick (1989). Victim and Crime Factors Associated with the Development of Crime-Related Post-Traumatic Stress Disorder. *Behavior Therapy, 20,* 199–214.

Kimmel, D. C. (1978). Adult Development and Aging: A Gay Perspective. *Journal of Social Issues, 34,* 113–30.

Kite, M. E. (1994). When Perceptions Meet Reality: Individual Differences in Reactions to Lesbians and Gay Men. In B. Greene and G. M. Herek (eds.), *Les-*

*bian and Gay Psychology: Theory, Research and Clinical Applications* (pp. 25–53). London: Sage.

Kitzinger, C., and S. Wilkinson (1996). Theorizing Representing the Other. In S. Wilkinson and C. Kitzinger (eds.), *Representing the Other: A* Feminism and Psychology *Reader* (pp. 1–32). London: Sage.

Koch, S. (1981). The Nature and Limits of Psychological Knowledge: Lesson of a Century *qua* "Science." *American Psychologist, 36,* 257–69.

Kominars, S. B. (1995). Homophobia: The Heart of Darkness. *Journal of Gay and Lesbian Social Services, 2,* 29–39.

Kuhn, T. S. (1970). *The Structure of Scientific Revolutions* (2d ed.). Chicago: University of Chicago Press.

Kurdek, L. A. (1988). Perceived Social Support in Lesbians and Gays in Cohabiting Relationships. *Journal of Personality and Social Psychology, 54,* 504–9.

Larson, C. E., and F. M. LaFasto (1989). *Teamwork: What Must Go Right/What Can Go Wrong.* Newbury Park, Calif.: Sage.

Lather, P. (1988). Feminist Perspectives on Empowering Research Methodologies. *Women's Studies International Forum, 11,* 569–81.

Leary, D. C. (1979). Wundt and After: Psychology's Shifting Relations with the Natural Sciences, Social Sciences, and Philosophy. *Journal of the History of the Behavioral Sciences, 15,* 231–41.

Lerner, M. J. (1980). *The Belief in a "Just" World.* New York: Plenum.

Lerner, M. J., and G. Matthews (1967). Reactions to Suffering of Others under Conditions of Indirect Responsibility. *Journal of Personality and Social Psychology, 5,* 319–25.

Lerner, M. J., and C. Simmons (1966). Observer's Reaction to the "Innocent Victims": Compassion or Rejection? *Journal of Personality and Social Psychology, 4,* 203–10.

Levin, D. (1997). The Constitution as Rhetorical Symbol in Western Anti-Gay Rights Initiatives: The Case of Idaho. In S. L. Witt and S. McCorkle (eds.), *Anti-Gay Rights: Assessing Voter Initiatives* (pp. 33–49). Westport, Conn.: Praeger.

Lifton, R. J. (1980). The Concept of the Survivor. In J. E. Dimsdale (ed.), *Survivors, Victims, and Perpetrators: Essays on the Nazi Holocaust* (pp. 113–26). New York: Hemisphere.

Linde, H. A. (1993). When Initiative Lawmaking Is Not "Republican" Government: The Campaign against Homosexuality. *Oregon Law Review, 72,* 19–45.

Lindy, J. D. (1985). The Trauma Membrane and Other Clinical Concepts Derived from Psychotherapy Work with Survivors of Natural Disasters. *Psychiatric Annals, 15,* 153–60.

Lobel, K. (1997, April 1). Take Me to Your Leaver. *Advocate,* p. 11.

Lorde, A. (1984). *Sister/Outsider.* Freedom, Calif.: Crossing.

Lowe, P. (1992, November 15). Ideas Clash in Focus on Family Values: Colorado Springs at Storm's Center. (Boulder) *Daily Camera,* pp. 1A, 6A.

Lyons, J. A. (1991). Strategies for Assessing the Potential for Positive Adjustment Following Trauma. *Journal of Traumatic Stress, 4,* 93–111.

Maines, D. R. (1989). Herbert Blumer on the Possibility of Science in the Practice of Sociology: Further Thoughts. *Journal of Contemporary Ethnography, 18,* 160–77.

———. (1993). Narrative's Moment and Sociology's Phenomena: Toward a Narrative Sociology. *Sociological Quarterly, 34,* 17–38.

Malyon, A. K. (1982). Psychotherapeutic Implications of Internalized Homophobia in Gay Men. In J. C. Gonsiorek (ed.), *Homosexuality and Psychotherapy: A Practitioner's Handbook of Affirmative Methods* (pp. 59–69). New York: Haworth.

March, J. S. (1993). What Constitutes a Stressor? The "Criterion A" Issue. In J. R. T. Davidson and E. B. Foa (eds.), *PTSD: DSM-IV and Beyond* (pp. 37–54). Washington, D.C.: American Psychiatric Association.

Marecek, J., M. Fine, and L. Kidder (1997). Working between Worlds: Qualitative Methods and Social Psychology. *Journal of Social Issues, 53,* 631–44.

Margolies, L., M. Becker, and K. Jackson-Brewer (1987). Internalized Homophobia: Identifying and Treating the Oppressor Within. In Boston Lesbian Psychologies Collective (eds.), *Lesbian Psychologies* (pp. 229–41). Urbana: University of Illinois Press.

Marmar, C. R. (1991). Brief Dynamic Psychotherapy of Post-Traumatic Stress Disorder. *Psychiatric Annals, 21,* 405–14.

Marmar, C. R., D. Foy, B. Kagan, and R. S. Pynoos (1993). An Integrated Approach for Treating Posttraumatic Stress. In J. M. Oldham, M. B. Riba, and A. Tasman (eds.), *Review of Psychiatry* (vol. 12), (pp. 239–72). Washington, D.C.: American Psychiatric Press.

McCorkle, S., and M. G. Most (1997a). Fear and Loathing on the Editorial Page: An Analysis of Idaho's Anti-Gay Initiative. In S. C. Witt and S. McCorkle (eds.), *Anti-Gay Rights: Assessing Voter Initiatives* (pp. 63–76). Westport, Conn.: Praeger.

———. (1997b). The Idaho Anti-Gay Initiative: A Chronology of Events. In S. L. Witt and S. McCorkle (eds.), *Anti-Gay Rights: Assessing Voter Initiatives* (pp. 51–61). Westport, Conn.: Praeger.

McFarlane, A. C. (1986). Posttraumatic Morbidity of a Disaster: A Study of Cases Presenting for Psychiatric Treatment. *Journal of Nervous and Mental Disease, 174,* 4–14.

McGrath, J. E., J. L. Berdahl, and H. Arrow (1995). Traits, Expectations, Culture, and Clout: The Dynamics of Diversity in Work Groups. In S. E. Jackson and M. N. Ruderman (eds.), *Diversity in Workteams: Research Paradigms for a Changing Workplace* (pp. 17–45). Washington, D.C.: American Psychological Association.

McQuail, D. (1994). *Mass Communication Theory.* Thousand Oaks, Calif.: Sage.

Meyer, I. H., and L. Dean (1998). Internalized Homophobia, Intimacy, and Sexual Behavior among Gay and Bisexual Men. In G. M. Herek (ed.), *Stigma and Sexual Orientation: Understanding Prejudice against Lesbians, Gay Men, and Bisexuals* (pp. 160–86). Thousand Oaks, Calif.: Sage.

Meyer, M., and K. L. Woodward (1993, March 1). Onward Muscular Christians! *Newsweek*, p. 68.

Miller, N. (1995). *Out of the Past: Gay and Lesbian History from 1869 to the Present.* New York: Vintage.

Mishler, E. G. (1979). Meaning in Context: Is There Any Other Kind? *Harvard Educational Review, 49*, 1–19.

Moos, R. H., and J. A. Schaefer (1986). Life Transitions and Crises: A Conceptual Overview. In R. H. Moos (ed.), *Coping with Life Crises: An Integrated Approach* (pp. 3–28). New York: Plenum.

Morawski, J. G. (1985). Contextual Discipline: The Making and Unmaking of Sociality. In R. L. Rosnow and M. Georgoudi (eds.), *Contextualism and Understanding in Behavioral Science* (pp. 47–67). New York: Praeger.

———. (1988). Impossible Experiments and Practical Constructions: The Social Bases of Psychologists' Work. In J. G. Morawski (ed.), *The Rise of Experimentalism in American Psychology* (pp. 72–93). New Haven, Conn.: Yale University Press.

Morgan, E. (1989). Toward the Development of a Superordinate Epistemology for Clinical Psychology: A Critique and a Proposal. Unpublished doctoral dissertation, University of Colorado, Boulder.

Moritz, M. J. (1992). How U.S. media Represent Sexual Minorities. In P. Dalgren and C. Sparks (eds.), *Journalism and Popular Culture* (pp. 154–70). London: Sage.

———. (1995). "The Gay Agenda": Marketing Hate Speech to Mainstream Media. In R. K. Whillock and D. Slayden (eds.), *Hate Speech* (pp. 55–79). Thousand Oaks, Calif.: Sage.

Moses-Zirkes, S. (1993, April). Gay Issues Move to Center of Attention. *APA Monitor*, pp. 28–29.

Murray, A. I. (1989). Top Management Group Heterogeneity and Firm Performance. *Strategic Management Journal, 10*, 125–41.

Mykhalovskiy, E. (1997). Reconsidering "Table Talk": Critical Thoughts on the Relationship between Sociology, Autobiography, and Self-Indulgence. In R. Hertz (ed.), *Reflexivity and Voice* (pp. 229–51). Thousand Oaks, Calif.: Sage.

Myrdal, G. (1969). Biases in Social Research. In A. Tiselius and S. Nillson (eds.), *The Place of Values in a World of Facts* (pp. 155–61). New York: Wiley.

Naples, N. A. (1997). A Feminist Revisiting of the Insider/Outsider Debate: The "Outsider" Phenomenon in Rural Iowa. In R. Hertz (ed.), *Reflexivity and Voice* (pp. 70–94). Thousand Oaks, Calif.: Sage.

Nash, C. (1999). Colorado's Amendment Two: The Effects on the Lesbian and Gay Community. Unpublished manuscript, University of Colorado at Boulder.

Nash, P. (1992, November 21). Victory of Amendment 2 Is Driving Colorado Gays Out of the Closet. *Denver Post*, p. 7B.

Newberger, C. M., and E. De Vos (1988). Abuse and Victimization: A Life-Span Developmental Perspective. *American Journal of Orthopsychiatry, 58*, 505–11.

'92 Election Results. (1992, November 5). (Boulder) *Daily Camera*, p. 4A.

Nkomo, S. M. (1995). Identities and the Complexity of Diversity. In S. E. Jackson and M. N. Ruderman (eds.), *Diversity in Work Teams: Research Paradigms for a Changing Workplace* (pp. 247–53). Washington, D.C.: American Psychological Association.

Northcraft, G. B., and M. A. Neale (1993). Negotiating Successful Research Collaboration. In J. K. Murninghan (ed.), *Social Psychology in Organizations* (pp. 204–24). Englewood Cliffs, N.J.: Prentice Hall.

Northcraft, G. B., J. T. Polzer, M. A. Neale, and R. M. Kramer (1995). Diversity, Social Identity, and Performance: Emergent Social Dynamics in Cross-Functional Teams. In S. E. Jackson and M. N. Ruderman (eds.), *Diversity in Work Teams: Research Paradigms for a Changing Workplace* (pp. 69–96). Washington, D.C.: American Psychological Association.

O'Rourke, S. P., and L. K. L. Dellinger (1997). *Romer v. Evans:* The Centerpiece of the American Gay-Rights Debate. In S. L. Witt and S. McCorkle (eds.), *Anti-Gay Rights: Assessing Voter Initiatives* (pp. 133–39). Westport, Conn.: Praeger.

Osborn, T. (1996). *Coming Home to America: A Roadmap to Gay and Lesbian Empowerment*. New York: St. Martin's.

Ostrow, J. (1992, November 5). Sardella Got to Heart of Amendment 2. *Denver Post*, pp. 1E, 4E.

Paul, J. P., R. P. Hays, and T. J. Coates (1995). The Impact of the HIV Epidemic on U.S. Gay Male Communities. In A. R. D'Augelli and C. J. Patterson (eds.), *Lesbian, Gay, and Bisexual Identities over the Lifespan* (pp. 347–97). New York: Oxford University Press.

Pearlin, L. I., and C. Schooler (1978). The Structure of Coping. *Journal of Health and Social Behavior, 19*, 2–21.

Perlman, M. L. (1973). The Comparative Method: The Single Investigator and the Team Approach. In R. Naroll and R. Cohen (eds.), *A Handbook of Method in Cultural Anthropology* (pp. 353–65). New York: Columbia University Press.

Pharr, S. (1992, July/August). Divisions That Kill: The Enemy Without and Within. *Transformation, 7*, 1–4, 9.

———. (1993, January/February). The Oregon Campaign. *Transformation, 8*, 1–3, 8.

———. (1996). *In the Time of the Right: Reflections on Liberation*. Berkeley: Chardon Press.

Pheterson, G. (1986). Alliances between Women: Overcoming Internalized Domination. *Signs, 12*, 146–60.

Pitman, H. (1997). In Their Own Words: Conversations with Campaign Leaders. In S. L. Witt and S. McCorkle (eds.), *Anti-Gay Rights: Assessing Voter Initiatives* (pp. 77–93). Westport, Conn.: Praeger.

Polkinghorne, D. (1983). *Methodology for the Human Sciences: Systems of Inquiry.* Albany: State University of New York Press.

Prilleltensky, I. (1989). Psychology and the Status Quo. *American Psychologist, 44,* 795–802.

———. (1994). *The Morals and Politics of Psychology: Psychological Discourse and the Status Quo.* Albany: State University of New York Press.

Rabinowitz, V. C., and S. Weseen (1997). Elu(ci)d(at)ing Epistemological Impasses: Re-viewing the Qualitative/Quantitative Debates in Psychology. *Journal of Social Issues, 53,* 605–30.

Ricoeur, P. (1981). *Hermeneutics and the Human Sciences* (J. B. Thompson, trans.). Cambridge: Cambridge University Press.

Robbins, L. (1993, March 12). Study: Hate Crimes Rise 129 Percent. (Boulder) *Daily Camera,* p. 3C.

Rohrbaugh, J. (1979). Improving the Quality of Group Judgment: Social Judgment Analysis and the Delphi Technique. *Organizational Behavior and Human Performance, 24,* 73–92.

Root, M. P. P. (1992). Reconstructing the Impact of Trauma on Personality. In L. S. Brown and M. Ballou (eds.), *Personality and Psychopathology: Feminist Reappraisals* (pp. 229–65). New York: Guilford.

———. (1996). Women of Color and Traumatic Stress in "Domestic Captivity": Gender and Race as Disempowering Statuses. In A. J. Marsella, M. J. Friedman, E. T. Gerrity, and R. M. Scurfield (eds.), *Ethnocultural Aspects of Posttraumatic Stress Disorder: Issues, Research, and Clinical Applications* (pp. 363–87). Washington, D.C.: American Psychological Association.

Rubovits-Seitz, P. (1986). Clinical Interpretation, Hermeneutics, and the Problem of Validation. *Psychoanalysis and Contemporary Thought, 9,* 3–42.

Russell, G. M. (1996, August). Qualitative Research Is the Message: Film Is the Medium. In G. M. Russell (Chair), *Research for Public Viewing: A Documentary on Heterosexual Allies.* Symposium conducted at the meeting of the American Psychological Association, Toronto, Ontario, Canada.

Russell, G. M., and J. S. Bohan (1999a). Hearing Voices: The Uses of Research and the Politics of Change. *Psychology of Women Quarterly, 23,* 405–20.

———. (1999b). Implications for Public Policy. In J. S. Bohan and G. M. Russell, *Conversations about Psychology and Sexual Orientation* (pp. 139–64). New York: New York University Press.

Russell, G. M., J. S. Bohan, and D. Lilly (in press). Queer Youth: Old Stories, New Stories. In S. L. Jones (ed.), *A Sea of Stories: The Shaping Power of Narrative in Gay and Lesbian Cultures.* New York: Haworth.

Russell, G. M., and E. M. Greenhouse (1995). Homophobia in the Supervisory Relationship: An Invisible Intruder. In J. M. Glassgold and S. Iasenza (eds.),

*Lesbians and Psychoanalysis: Revolutions in Theory and Practice* (pp. 173–90). New York: Free Press.

Sampson, E. E. (1978). Scientific Paradigms and Social Values: Wanted: A Scientific Revolution. *Journal of Personality and Social Psychology, 36,* 1332–43.

———. (1983). Deconstructing Psychology's Subject. *Journal of Mind and Behavior, 4,* 135–64.

———. (1993a). *Celebrating the Other: A Dialogic Account of Human Nature.* Boulder: Westview.

———. (1993b). Identity Politics: Challenges to Psychology's Understandings. *American Psychologist, 48,* 1219–30.

Sanderson, W. C., P. A. DiNardo, R. M. Rapee, and D. H. Barlow (1990). Syndrome Comorbidity in Patients Diagnosed with a DSM-III-R Anxiety Disorder. *Journal of Abnormal Psychology, 99,* 308–12.

Sarason, S. B. (1981). *Psychology Misdirected.* New York: Free Press.

Sarbin, T. R. (1996). The Deconstruction of Stereotypes: Homosexuals and Military Policy. In G. M. Herek, J. B. Jobe, and R. M. Carney (eds.), *Out in Force: Sexual Orientation and the Military* (pp. 177–96). Chicago: University of Chicago Press.

Sarbin, T. R., and J. I. Kitsuse (1994). A Prologue to Constructing the Social. In T. R. Sarbin and J. I. Kitsuse (eds.), *Constructing the Social* (pp. 1–18). Thousand Oaks, Calif.: Sage.

Schneider, W., and J. A. Lewis (1984). The Straight Story on Homosexuality and Gay Rights. *Public Opinion, 7,* 16–20, 59–60.

Schwandt, T. A. (1994). Constructivist, Interpretist Approaches to Human Inquiry. In N. K. Denzin and Y. S. Lincoln (eds.), *Handbook of Qualitative Research* (pp. 118–37). Thousand Oaks, Calif.: Sage.

Scott, J. (1985). *Weapons of the Weak: Everyday Forms of Peasant Resistance.* New Haven, Conn.: Yale University Press.

———. (1990). *Domination and the Arts of Resistance: Hidden Transcripts.* New Haven, Conn.: Yale University Press.

Seidel, J. V., R. Kjolseth, and E. Seymour (1988). *The Ethnograph: A User's Guide.* Amherst, Mass.: Qualis Research Associates.

Shatan, C. (1973). The Grief of Soldiers: Vietnam Combat Veterans' Self-Help Movement. *American Journal of Orthopsychiatry, 43,* 640–53.

Shaw, S. (1997). No Longer a Sleeping Giant: The Re-Awakening of Religious Conservatives in American Politics. In S. L. Witt and S. McCorkle (eds.), *Anti-Gay Rights: Assessing Voter Initiatives* (pp. 7–16). Westport, Conn.: Praeger.

Shidlo, A. (1994). Internalized Homophobia: Conceptual and Empirical Issues in Measurement. In B. Greene and G. M. Herek (eds.), *Lesbian and Gay Psychology: Theory, Research, and Clinical Applications* (pp. 176–205). Thousand Oaks, Calif.: Sage.

Shinn, M., S. Lehmann, and N. W. Wong (1984). Social Interaction and Social Support. *Journal of Social Issues, 40,* 55–76.

Silvern, L. E. (1988). Is Clinical Psychology a Science? Yes, but within Limits. Unpublished manuscript. University of Colorado, Boulder.

Smith, C. L. (1993). Undo Two: An Essay Regarding Colorado's Anti-Lesbian and Gay Amendment 2. *Washburn Law Journal, 367,* 367–78.

Smith, R. R. (1997). Secular Anti-Gay Advocacy in the Springfield, Missouri, Bias Crime Ordinance Debate. In S. L. Witt and S. McCorkle (eds.), *Anti-Gay Rights: Assessing Voter Initiatives* (pp. 95–106). Westport, Conn.: Praeger.

Snyder, C. R. (1994). *The Psychology of Hope.* New York: Free Press.

Solomon, A., A. Bleich, M. Koslowsky, S. Kron, B. Lerer, and M. Waysman (1991). Post-Traumatic Stress Disorder: Issues of Co-Morbidity. *Journal of Psychiatric Research, 25,* 89–94.

Solomon, S. D., E. M. Smith, L. N. Robins, and R. L. Fischbach (1987). Social Involvement as a Mediator of Disaster-Induced Stress. *Journal of Applied Social Psychology, 17,* 1092–1112.

Sophie, J. (1987). Internalized Homophobia and Lesbian Identity Development. *Journal of Homosexuality, 14,* 53–66.

Spears, L. (1992, July 20). Concord Anti-Gay Video Showing in Other States. *Contra Costa* (Calif.) *Times,* pp. 1A, Back.

Spring, T. (1992a, December 14). Gays Gird for Amendment 2 Results. *Colorado Daily,* pp. 1, 3.

———. (1992b, December 14). Hate Crimes on Rise. *Colorado Daily,* pp. 1, 3.

Stafford, J. (1993, June 28). At Least 50,000 March. (Boulder) *Daily Camera,* pp. 1A–2A.

Staub, E. (1993). The Psychology of Bystanders, Perpetrators, and Heroic Helpers. *International Journal of Intercultural Relations, 17,* 315–41.

Steele, C. (1995, spring). Oregon Faces Eight Anti-Gay Initiatives. *PFLAGpole,* p. 14.

Stepanek, M. (1992, December 23). Gay-Bashing on Rise in Colorado. *San Francisco Examiner,* p. A9.

Stevens, M., and J. Gibney (1993, June 21). 2,500 March in Gay Parade. *Denver Post,* pp. 1B, 6B.

Stevens, R. (1992, August 13). Eating Our Own. *Advocate,* pp. 33–41.

Sullivan, R. (1992, November 9). Postcard from Oregon: Resolution Number 9. *New Yorker,* pp. 67, 69–70, 79.

Tappan, M. B. (1997). Interpretive Psychology: Stories, Circles, and Understanding Lived Experience. *Journal of Social Issues, 53,* 645–56.

Taylor, S. E. (1983). Adjustment to Threatening Events: A Theory of Cognitive Adaptation. *American Psychologist, 38,* 1161–73.

Tedeschi, R. G., and L. G. Calhoun (1995). *Trauma and Transformation: Growing in the Aftermath of Suffering.* Thousand Oaks, Calif.: Sage.

Tedeschi, R. G., C. L. Park, and L. G. Calhoun (eds.) (1998). *Posttraumatic Growth: Positive Changes in the Aftermath of Crisis.* Mahwah, N.J.: Lawrence Erlbaum.

Unger, R. K. (1992). Through the Looking Glass: No Wonderland Yet! (The Reciprocal Relationship between Methods and Models of Reality). *Psychology of Women Quarterly, 8*, 9–32.

U.S. Department of Commerce. (1992). 1990 Census of Population: General Population Characteristics—Colorado (USDC Publication No. 1990 CP-1-7). Washington, D.C.: U.S. Government Printing Office.

Vaid, U. (1995). *Virtual Equality: The Mainstreaming of Gay and Lesbian Liberation*. New York: Anchor.

van der Kolk, B. A. (1987). The Psychological Consequences of Overwhelming Life Experiences. In B. A. van der Kolk (ed.), *Psychological Trauma* (pp. 1–30). Washington, D.C.: American Psychiatric Press.

———. (1996). The Complexity of Adaptation to Trauma: Self-Regulation, Stimulus Discrimination and Characterological Development. In B. A. van der Kolk, A. C. McFarlane, and L. Weisaeth (eds.), *Traumatic Stress: The Effects of Overwhelming Experience on Mind, Body, and Society* (pp. 182–213). New York: Guilford.

van der Kolk, B. A., and M. S. Greenberg (1987). The Psychobiology of the Trauma Response: Hyperarousal, Constriction, and Addiction to Traumatic Reexposure. In B. A. van der Kolk (ed.), *Psychological Trauma* (pp. 63–87). Washington, D.C.: American Psychiatric Press.

van der Kolk, B. A., and W. Kadish (1987). Amnesia, Dissociation, and the Return of the Repressed. In B. van der Kolk (ed.), *Psychological Trauma* (pp. 173–90). Washington, D.C.: American Psychiatric Press.

van der Kolk, B. A., and A. C. McFarlane (1996). The Black Hole of Trauma. In B. A. van der Kolk, A. C. McFarlane, and L. Weisaeth (eds.), *Traumatic Stress: The Effects of Overwhelming Experience on Mind, Body, and Society* (pp. 3–23). New York: Guilford.

Walsh, R. T. (1989). Do Research Reports in Mainstream Feminist Psychology Journals Reflect Feminist Values? *Psychology of Women Quarterly, 13*, 433–44.

Walter, D. (1985, October 20). Paul Cameron. *Advocate*, pp. 28–30, 32.

Way, N. (1998). *Everyday Courage: The Lives and Stories of Urban Teenagers*. New York: New York University Press.

Whillock, R. K. (1995). The Use of Hate as a Stratagem for Achieving Political and Social Goals. In R. K. Whillock and D. Slayden (eds.), *Hate Speech* (pp. 28–54). Thousand Oaks, Calif.: Sage.

Wolcott, H. F. (1988). Ethnographic Research in Education. In R. M. Jaeger (ed.), *Complementary Methods for Research in Education* (pp. 187–249). Washington, D.C.: American Educational Research Association.

———. (1992). Posturing in Qualitative Inquiry. In M. D. LeCompte, W. L. Milbray, and J. Preissle (eds.), *The Handbook of Qualitative Research in Education* (pp. 3–52). New York: Academic Press.

Wortman, C. B. (1983). Coping with Victimization: Conclusions and Implications for Future Research. *Journal of Social Issues, 39*, 195–221.

Zeman, N., and M. Meyer (1992, November 23). No "Special Rights" for Gays. *Newsweek*, p. 32.

Zimmerman, M. A. (1995). Psychological Empowerment: Issues and Illustrations. *American Journal of Community Psychology, 23*, 581–99.

# Index

■ ■ ■ ■ ■ ■ ■ ■ ■

# About the Author

GLENDA M. RUSSELL, Ph.D., is a member of the core faculty in the department of clinical psychology at Antioch New England Graduate School in Keene, New Hampshire, where she also maintains a private practice. Previously, she practiced in Boulder, where she was also a research associate in women studies and clinical instructor in psychology at the University of Colorado, Boulder. She maintains a private practice in Boulder as well. Dr. Russell's work as an activist predates her career as a psychologist and spans political spheres as varied as guerrilla theater, participation in Boulder's Human Relations Commission, and active involvement in the campaign to defeat Colorado's anti-gay Amendment 2. In this book she pursues her fascination with the intersection of the personal and the political, invoking both her interest in psychological research and her experience in clinical practice. She is coauthor with Janis S. Bohan of *Conversations about Psychology and Sexual Orientation* (New York University Press, 1999).